JOHN LITTLE spent 25 years working as a reporter and producer in television current affairs, before becoming a full-time author. His previous non-fiction books are: *Inside 60 minutes*, *The Hospital by the River* (with Dr Catherine Hamlin), *The Man Who Saw Too Much*, *Down to the Sea* and *Jem, a Father's Story*. He has also written a political thriller, *Letters from the President*.

jdlittle@bigpond.com

Also by John Little

Inside 60 minutes
Letters from the President
The Hospital by the River
(with Dr Catherine Hamlin)
The Man Who Saw Too Much
Down to the Sea
Jem, a Father's Story

Christine's Ark

The extraordinary story of Christine Townend
and an Indian animal shelter

John Little

MACMILLAN
Pan Macmillan Australia

This one's for Kristin

First published 2006 in Macmillan by Macmillan Australia Pty Limited
1 Market Street, Sydney

National Library of Australia
Cataloguing-in-Publication data:

Little, John, 1942–.
Christine's ark.

ISBN-13: 978 1 4050 3729 7.

ISBN-10: 1 4050 3729 6.

1. Townend, Christine. 2. Help in Suffering (Organization)
– History. 3. Animal rights activists – India – Jaipur –
Biography. 4. Animal shelters – India – Jaipur – History.
5. Jaipur (India) – Biography. I. Title.

636.0832

Typeset in 12/14 pt FairfieldLH Light by Midland Typesetters, Australia
Printed in Australia by McPherson's Printing Group

PROLOGUE

It's morning in Jaipur. A weak sun slowly lifts the lingering chill from the bitter desert night. Christine Townend is in her chilly little office at the Help in Suffering compound, wrapped in a parka, a scarf and woollen gloves. Her breath condenses in the air; there is a glass of *chai* at hand as she contemplates the day's work ahead. Glancing out the window she sees a thin man with the swarthy, high-cheekboned, dark-eyed, moustached face of a typical Rajasthani. He's wearing a white turban, white *kurta* and *dhoti*. A threadbare woollen shawl is wrapped around his shoulders; the bones show through his skin.

The man is leading a large camel. The beast pads majestically down the driveway, its powerful thigh muscles like pistons, long legs balancing on feet like bags of jelly. Christine admires the camel for a moment before noticing that its lower jaw is twisted and hanging limply. As she rises to her feet, two of the shelter's veterinarians, Dr Devi and Dr Sunil, go to greet the man. He falls at their feet, touching their toes with his forehead, and implores them to help. Although she has witnessed scenes like this countless times, Christine's heart goes out to both man and animal. Respectfully, observing the proper forms of greeting, she approaches and listens while he recounts his story.

His name is Roduram. He comes from a village called Choru, about 50 kilometres from Jaipur. A landless labourer, until recently he had worked other people's fields with the goal of one day earning enough money to buy his own camel. He tells Christine that his wife is always ill. He doesn't know the exact ages of his children. One is a boy, about twelve, and there are four girls aged about eight, six, four and two. The last three monsoons have failed so, despite his hard labour, the crops of *bajra* (millet) have not yielded well. Roduram had already been in debt, he says. So desperate was he to feed his family that he decided to borrow the money for a camel. The money-lender demanded an interest rate of 48 per cent.

With his stake Roduram went to the annual Luniawas fair not far from his village, where animals are traded. Although he had never owned a camel himself, he knew a great deal about them, because many people in his village had camels, and he had grown up in their presence. Walking among the rows of tethered animals, bargaining and negotiating, he eventually purchased the fine, strong beast called Moti, together with a traditional cart with wooden platform and pneumatic tyres, for 27,000 rupees (about 800 Australian dollars). At the fair he also noticed the Help in Suffering mobile clinic where the vets were giving treatment, and he learned about this free service run by an unusual white woman back in Jaipur.

After the purchase, Roduram drove the camel to his village. The camel cart rolled smoothly, and the camel pulled obediently. When they arrived home, the family performed a *puja* (prayer service) in which they made offerings to the protecting god, Bhairuji.

Proudly, Roduram began work at the brick kilns. They were situated in another village, Dabach, about forty kilometres from Choru, so his whole family relocated to live in one of the small mud huts on site. It was hot, uncomfortable and crowded; his wife kept the earth floor neatly swept, despite the dust outside, and did her best to make it a home. At night they unrolled their bedding, which was stored on a bench, and slept outside on the ground with the stars above.

Now Roduram was his own boss. No longer did he need to labour from dawn to dusk, sweating under the sun on another person's land, waiting anxiously for the monsoon which did not come for season after season. With his great, powerful beast and the smoothly rolling cart he could load the raw mud bricks and move them across the fields to the kiln, where he would unload them for firing.

Then, only three days after starting his new life, while Moti was lying down resting, another camel crossed closely in front of him. Moti felt affronted. He rose to his feet and fixed his teeth in the back of the passing camel's neck, who quickly twisted, and in the process Moti's jaw was broken. It hung limply. Unable to eat, he would certainly die. Faced with utter ruin, Roduram had driven his suffering camel for fifty kilometres to the shelter. Now he stood before Christine, Sunil and Devi, and wept.

Christine noticed that the camel had an oily black substance oozing from behind his ears, indicating that he was in rut. The

Help in Suffering veterinarians saw many broken jaws during this season when the male camels fought one another in competition for females. Dr Devi, who was in charge of the camel project, gave Moti an anaesthetic and wired his jaw together. It would take a month convalescing at the shelter, eating soft food such as *gur* (raw sugar cane) and lucerne, before the camel could go back to work.

It was a simple tale of hope rising from despair, like so many Christine has seen. But the story did not end there. She offered to drive Roduram back to his village. After travelling through semi-desert country for about an hour they turned off the main thoroughfare and bumped along increasingly pot-holed roads, to a devastated, empty landscape bereft of trees, with just a few thorny weeds poking up through the parched earth. Here in the middle of nowhere was a village of about ten mud and dung houses, each one proudly painted with coloured designs around the doorway. There was no water, no electricity, no vegetable patch, no animals . . . nothing at all to make life bearable. The people were thin, the children all had colds and running noses. Roduram's father showed Christine a worn bit of rag which passed as a blanket. The family had nothing with which to keep themselves warm at night.

Even though Christine had lived in India for fifteen years she was shocked. She arranged to give Roduram 100 rupees a day while his camel was recuperating. The next day HIS (Help in Suffering) staff returned with two blankets for each family and a supply of milk, green vegetables and fruit. Christine promised to find a way to get a bore sunk so that the women would not have to walk for kilometres to fetch water.

Christine is often asked why she goes to the trouble of looking after animals in India when there are so many people in need. The simple tale of this one man and his camel answers the question. The fact is, millions of families depend entirely on an animal for their livelihood. That scrawny little pony carting vegetables to the market may support a family of ten. If the pony is injured and cannot work or, worse still, dies, they will starve – it is as straightforward and as pitiless as that.

This story is about one woman's extraordinary devotion to the world's suffering creatures. Furthermore, it is also about self-belief, determination, spiritual search, hope, optimism and love. One could argue that such an epic tale deserves a grand beginning – there is much to say, for instance, about the magnificent working elephants which she also cares for – but perhaps it would be better to start with more insignificant creatures, in a place and a culture far removed from India.

WHAT ISSA HEARD

Two hundred years ago Issa heard the morning birds
singing sutras to this suffering world.
I heard them too, this morning
which must mean
since we will always have a suffering world
we must always have a song.

[David Budbill]

BOOK ONE
AUSTRALIA

CHAPTER 1

A colony of ants bustles to and from a nest, each homeward-bound ant carrying a load far bigger than itself. They climb the ramparts urgently, then scrabble down shifting scree to the entrance. Entering ants bump into exiting ants, pause for half a second, wag their feelers politely then continue on their way.

This little cameo of ant life is being enacted at the Melbourne Cricket Ground in the year 1947. Christine is three. Her mother and father have taken her to watch a test match. Or, rather, they have taken her with them while they watch. Although Christine's father is an unabashed cricket tragic he has little hope that his daughter will share his passion. He fully expects her to be bored, so he is both surprised and pleased to see that she sits quietly during the entire day's play.

As they are leaving, Christine's parents remark on what a good girl she has been. 'You must love cricket, do you, darling?' says her mother. 'You were so quiet and good.'

Christine sweetly demurs. 'I wasn't watching the cricket, Mummy, I was watching all the little ants.'

Why is this scene remarkable? It seems so commonplace, does it not? Who has not idled away a few moments on a warm summer day observing ants, perhaps carelessly stomping on a few, or breaking up the nest with a twig to see how they react? Yet these little insects hurrying backwards and forwards along the parapet at the MCG are Christine's earliest memory, every detail as sharp now as it was six decades ago. For those given to portents, as the adult Christine certainly is, the scene has weight. Here are some of the most insignificant of God's creatures going about their business, and on that day the only person in the entire cricket ground who cares about them is one little girl. In the decades to come, this devotion to all creatures great and small will dominate Christine's life, although, unlike the pleased reaction of her parents that day, her single-minded passion will often be the despair of those dear to her.

Flash forward a year. Christine is four. Her mother and her mother's sister, Diana, are visiting Christine's grandparents at Cheltenham in Victoria. Her grandfather is the medical director of a nursing home. The large house with its cellar, the wards where the patients live, the dispensary, are magical places to a child. In the grounds there are a dairy, a piggery and a pond with ducks and geese. And, most exciting of all, there are horses.

Aunt Diana's horse is called Ginger Meggs. She suggests that Christine might like to sit on his back. Christine's mother, Suzanne, has never felt comfortable with horses. 'Oh, Diana, is it safe? Do think you should be putting her up there?'

'Of course it's safe. Ginger Meggs is so quiet.'

The sisters bicker a little until Aunt Diana prevails. The child is lifted up, and: 'I had this wonderful feeling of sitting on this creature who absolutely understood that I was some little tiny helpless thing, and he was absolutely radiating his energy of horseness that says we have always been here to carry you and transport you, and we have suffered long to fulfil this purpose.'

Can a child have such profound thoughts? Even at the age of four, Christine says, she was aware that 'animals are terribly connected with human life; that without them we can do nothing.' Perhaps even then her vocation was sealed. But despite these glimmerings of the passion to come, she was, after all, still a child. There were fish and frogs in that pond. Little Christine, curious about what might be inside the tadpoles, took a stone and squashed one. To her horror it kept on swimming with its innards hanging out. The other tadpoles started to eat it. She realised her crime and was devastated, thinking it the most terrible thing she had ever done.

Christine Woolcott, as she was then, was a wartime baby. Her mother, Suzanne Carlile, had been a girl of sixteen when she went with her Aunt Gwenda to Spencer Street Railway Station in Melbourne to farewell Gwenda's son Guy, who had been home on leave from his unit in the Middle East. Accompanying Guy was a slender, shy young man, Harold Woolcott. In the few minutes they had together, Harold told Suzanne a little about his life. He had been 22 and living in Germany when the war had broken out. His father, an importer of printing machinery, sent him to live with a family in Leipzig, where he studied printing and lithography. Kurt Keller, his wife Liselotte, and their two daughters, Gisela and Zigrid, treated Harold as one of the family. He told Suzanne how he had learned to play the flute; he rhapsodised over his love of the German language and the German people. However, when hostilities were declared his duty had been clear: he had immediately gone home to Australia and joined up. It hurt him terribly to be fighting against the country that he loved almost as much as his own.

After chatting for a while, the two soldiers boarded their train to begin the long journey back to Syria. Suzanne and Gwenda caught the tram home, discussing the young men who were going heroically into harm's way. Suzanne was short with her mother that day. 'I've met the man I love,' she declared. 'I'm going to love him always, and I'll never see him again because he's going to war.'

'Don't worry, dear,' said her mother. 'He'll probably come home one day.'

About a month later Suzanne received a letter from Harold. 'Permit me to introduce myself,' it began. 'I have prevailed upon Guy to give me your address . . .' The letter went on in precise, formal language to remind her of their meeting, and to venture the hope that he might be honoured with a reply. A regular correspondence began. Four years later, when Harold was again home on leave, they married. Suzanne was twenty and Harold was 26.

The attraction, they soon discovered, was an attraction of opposites. Suzanne was vibrant and outgoing, intelligent, eager to learn about life, an enthusiastic hostess, and an inveterate traveller. Harold was quiet, sensitive, gentlemanly, and honourable to a fault. Christine was born a year after they married. Three years later they had another daughter, Anne.

The Woolcotts' modest East Malvern home was shared with a kitten and two bantam hens. Christine loved the birds dearly, and used to constantly carry them around with her, cuddling and talking to them.

When Christine was eight, the family moved from Melbourne to Manly in Sydney. They lived in a top-floor flat situated at the back of a rising block of land flanked by lawns and gardens. The flats and another house on the block were owned by her father's two sisters, Aunt Nest and Aunt Muriel.

One day a family friend, Sylvia Eaton, came with two of her children to spend the day. Kere and Brian were the same ages as Christine and Anne. While the mothers chatted, the four children went for a walk down to the Manly shops where Christine wanted to show them four rabbits on display in a pet shop. They concocted a plan to steal money from their mothers' purses, which were lying on a bed in the flat, and to buy the rabbits. Christine clearly recalls that she had an overwhelming desire to 'rescue' the rabbits from the tiny cage in which they had been held for a couple of weeks. The children assumed that because the rabbits were so cute their mothers could not possibly be annoyed.

The theft went off without discovery and the pet-shop owner, rather irresponsibly, handed over four baby rabbits in a shoe box, two white ones and two grey. After their initial shock the mothers looked upon the whole episode with warm understanding. Anne kept a white one, naming it Snowflake, while Christine took the prettier of the two greys. She called it Cuthbert. Neither of them lived very long. It was an early example of Christine's attempts to give a small creature a better life.

The incident of the rabbits is not the only memory Christine has of animals being significant in her life.

Underneath the Woolcotts' flat there lived a Collie dog. Every time it saw Anne it would rush at her aggressively; and

5

the more fear Anne showed the more vicious the dog became. By contrast, Christine remembers having a sense of communication with the dog. It was completely compliant with her, so when they had to walk up the path she would hold it until Anne was safely out of the way.

Christine was keen to do anything that involved animals. At the beach on the ocean side of Manly a man hired out Shetland ponies, charging a shilling to ride to a rope fence about half a kilometre up the sand and back again. A few lucky children earned pocket money by leading the horses. Christine longed to be one of them, and with great determination inveigled herself into a job. Joyfully she seized the bridle and led the prancing little pony up the beach and back again. She had noticed that some of the young wranglers would sometimes slip onto a pony's back for a ride, and so she decided to do likewise. The feisty little beast behaved itself until they turned towards home, whereupon it bolted and Christine fell off. The owner told her not to come back.

Christine's childhood memories are brimming full of pets. There was a succession of cats, budgerigars, silkworms, rabbits and dogs. One, a poodle named Ko Ko, had gorgeous reddish-brown hair. Christine's was fiery red. At the local dog show they won the prize for the pet most resembling its owner. Another much-loved pet was a bantam called Alfred. 'I absolutely adored this bantam. He would sit on my shoulder and kiss my ear, and he loved me as much as I loved him.'

One day when Anne was taking Ko Ko for a walk he saw a dog on the other side of the road, tore the lead out of Anne's hand and ran across the traffic flow. A car hit him and he was killed instantly. Christine grieved for weeks and forbade anyone to mention Ko Ko's name again.

Christine's father was the managing director of a company that imported printing machinery. As Harold grew more and more successful the family moved from Manly to Mosman, and then to a gracious home in Pymble on Sydney's north shore. Harold travelled frequently to Germany, and he and Suzanne entertained German business acquaintances often.

Harold's greatest joy was music. He played the flute well, and sang in a beautiful baritone voice. Some thought he could have had a professional career, but that was something he never contemplated. He told Suzanne he loved music too much to make money out of it.

Harold and Suzanne regularly attended concerts at the Sydney Town Hall. Even if he had arrived from the office grey and drawn, after the performance Harold would practically skip from the hall, chattering away about the marvellous arpeggio in the third movement, or the haunting cello passage leading to the coda, or some other delight. Suzanne would try to contribute but, sadly, she was tone deaf. The visiting virtuosi who so enriched Harold's life might as well have been playing to a stone where she was concerned. Nevertheless, she dutifully attended concerts with Harold, and took pleasure in his pleasure.

Christine inherited her father's musical talent, and began to show ability at the piano. Once, she proudly played for her mother a tune she had just mastered.

'That's nice, darling,' said Suzanne. 'I think I've heard it before.'

'Mum,' came the reply, 'it's the National Anthem.'

Suzanne's parents belonged to the Catholic Apostolic Church, a strict High Anglican order which has virtually disappeared today. Harold was a Christian Scientist, believing that reality is the mind, and the physical world is just an expression of what we are thinking. When Harold had petitioned Suzanne's father for her hand in marriage, Dr Carlile had naturally asked him which church he belonged to. The answer had not impressed. 'That's neither Christian, nor is it scientific,' huffed the doctor. 'I want you to give me your word that you won't try and tell Suzanne about this strange religion.'

Remarkably, Harold promised. In the years to come Suzanne would occasionally ask him to explain his religion, but he always refused, saying that he had given her father his word.

Harold was just as honourable where the children were concerned. His father-in-law had also extracted an assurance from him that he would not discuss Christian Science with either of the girls until they were eighteen. As a result, Christine and Anne spent each Sunday at the Catholic Apostolic church in Redfern learning 'great slabs of wretched catechism' under the strict tutelage of doddering church elders.

Although Harold played down his beliefs within the family he was, nevertheless, a serious Christian Scientist. He did not hold with medical intervention in case of illness. He believed that being sick was merely an appearance, and if you thought the right way the sickness would go. Once, when he was in Heidelberg on business, he rang Suzanne with a terrible cold. He asked her to get in touch with a friend who was a 'practitioner' to ask her to meditate for him. Interestingly, the cold quickly went away.

Christine remembers her parents as being very much in love. It was her father who earned the salary which kept them in a high degree of comfort during her teenage years; which afforded the girls a private-school education; and which allowed Suzanne to travel frequently to exotic parts of the world, usually without Harold, as he never cared much for travel except to Germany.

Yes, Harold was the breadwinner – yet, as Christine tells it, her mother was the stronger partner. 'My father loved my mother so much he basically did whatever she wanted. She ruled absolutely, and when she was, from my point of view, unjust, and I tried to explain to my father that she did this or that which I thought was wrong, he would say, "No dear, your mother is always right." So we didn't get far with that.'

Christine's sister Anne says of Harold, 'He was a total pacifist. He used to say, "Anything for a quiet life." It was his mantra.'

An addiction to adventure and travel ran in Suzanne's family. In 1951 her sister Diana had traversed Africa from north to south aged 25 – a distance of more than 4,000 miles, mostly alone and on foot. With a small rucksack containing a couple of spare shirts, pyjamas, a camera, and little else, she had hitchhiked in trucks through Eritrea and Ethiopia. She visited Lake Tana, the source of the Blue Nile, and wandered with local tribes until she reached the Ethiopian capital, Addis Ababa, where she met the emperor, Haile Selassie, and dined at the British Embassy.

From Addis Ababa Diana had hiked north into Danakil territory, where temperatures soared to 50 degrees Celsius and the people had a reputation for murdering strangers. Emerging unscathed she travelled in an Arab *dhow*, the only woman in a crew of fourteen men, to Aden. Then she joined a cargo ship to Djibouti in French Somaliland. She wandered south along the coast to British Somaliland, usually alone, before returning to Ethiopia and wild Ogaden country, where she hobnobbed with warring tribes and slept in the open in areas known to be infested with lions. In Kenya she hitchhiked and camped her way through Kikuyu country, where the Mau Mau Uprising was taking place, then on through Tanganyika, Northern and Southern Rhodesia, Transvaal, the Orange Free State and Natal. In Durban she caught a ship home.

Christine considers that she was probably more like her Aunt Diana than her own mother, who loved material possessions and was interested in her social life. 'My mother had attributes which I lacked. She was very funny, told great stories, was successful at parties, very gregarious and so on. I had none of these talents. They were passed on to Anne if anyone. I was more like my aunt, who loved animals, had horses and dogs and also loved walking in the bush.'

Diana was fond of her two nieces. She called Christine 'Chrissie Crumb' or 'Grog Blossom', because she was small and had a red mark on her cheek. When Diana came to stay with them in Sydney, Christine took her walking for the day down to her favourite place, Silver Lake in St Ives. They had a marvellous time together. Suzanne, who did not enjoy walking, stayed home.

Although markedly different from her sister, Suzanne seemed to have inherited the same traveller's genes. When Christine was fourteen and Anne was eleven the whole family went off on a tour of Asia. In Bangkok, Anne was bitten by a monkey. As a precaution against rabies, which results in inevitable death, she had to undergo a series of injections into the stomach every day for fourteen days. Those rabies shots were notoriously painful. Each day Anne would go to the Louis Pasteur Institute, where, coaxed by her mother, she reluctantly lifted her shirt and screamed with pain as the serum was pumped in. Her reward for submitting to this was to be allowed to watch the snakes being milked for antivenene. Barefoot Thai handlers would tread among the reptiles, now and then seizing one behind the head. Anne would watch with awe as the snake bit the rim of a glass container, which caught the venom.

Eventually time ran out for Harold and he had to go home. Christine missed him terribly when he left, not least because with Suzanne in charge the travel arrangements were much more disorganised. Suzanne and the two girls continued on to Cambodia. From the capital, Phnom Penh, they travelled north to Angkor Wat. On the morning they were due to visit the famous temples Christine developed an agonising pain in her abdomen. 'There's nothing we can do about it, dear,' said Suzanne. 'You'll just have to make the best of it.' So, off they went in a Jeep, bumping over terrible roads with Christine doubled up in the back seat in agony.

After two days the pain subsided. A year later in Australia it came back again and she was rushed to hospital for an emergency appendectomy. The doctor told her afterwards that the appendix must have been close to rupturing some time previously as it was twisted around behind the spleen. There was scar tissue where it had started to split.

After visiting Angkor Wat their adventures were not quite over. It was now Suzanne's turn to be bitten by a monkey, in the garden of their hotel. She, too, had to submit to a course of anti-rabies injections. The doctor gave her fourteen vials of serum and enough syringes for the complete course. They flew to Singapore and booked into a hotel. Every time Suzanne had the injection she was violently ill, but despite this severe reaction she kept up the daily dose, as the alternative was to die a painful death. For the next week or so the two girls nursed their mother in their hotel room, wondering all the time if she was going to die. After a fortnight the crisis had passed and they were all grateful to return home to Harold.

Christine spent her early primary-school years at Lauriston Private Girls' School in Melbourne. She was a shy, dreamy student, living for much of the time in her own internal world. 'I couldn't figure out what everyone was doing, walking around, drifting around. Everything looked like a dazzle, or shining. The question which really puzzled me all the time was, What were all these people doing? Why were we all here?'

As early as kindergarten Christine had put into words the first of a lifetime of questions concerning the human condition. Her interlocutor was her teacher, Miss Fraser – an unfortunate choice. 'I gathered up the courage to ask her, "How did all the humans get here? What are people here for?" Something like that, and she got in a panic. She must have thought I was asking a question about sex or something. It was in the playground at lunchtime; she was with other little children, holding their hands, and she didn't answer. She just turned and walked off, and at the end of that I was so acutely embarrassed by the fact that she didn't answer, I didn't ask the question again.'

Suzanne was a conscientious mother. She made sure that the family ate their meals together as often as Harold's work allowed. When Christine showed an interest in art at the age of ten Suzanne encouraged her, buying her a set of paints and books on art. Her talent for music was likewise nurtured: Christine won the music prize in second class and continued taking lessons until well into high school. She had the privilege of a warm and loving family life – however, the problem was that even as a child she felt instinctively that her mother's values were not her own.

Both Christine and Suzanne were extremely stubborn. When they disagreed about something it often erupted into a major argument. For instance, Christine hated it when her mother insisted she dress up and pass around the savouries at dinner parties. 'I was forced to go in and make conversation with the guests, and I probably had tantrums about that, and arguments with my mother, but my father wouldn't intervene. She said I had to do it, and that was that.'

If Christine had done something wrong and flung herself crying into bed, it was Harold who would come in, stroke her forehead and sing her to sleep. And it was Harold who sometimes played his records for her and told her about the great composers. Because of Harold she developed a deep love of classical music, especially Mozart. Christine's abiding memory of her father was that 'he was a very lovely, gentle person'.

Anne was popular with everyone, and never short of boyfriends. She agrees that she was less complicated than her older sister. 'I was terribly boring and mainstream. All I wanted to do was ride horses and live in the country.' Anne's room was pink, with lots of frills and lace and china horses, while Christine's had brown carpet and a little white desk where she would spend hours daydreaming, composing poetry and writing short stories.

Despite their different temperaments the two sisters got on very well. 'My sister and I adored each other from the moment I can remember,' says Christine. 'Of course we had a couple of fights, but I don't think we ever had many.'

The siblings invented their own language, called 'Up-language'. By putting 'up' in front of every vowel they were able to converse without being understood by others. For example, the sentence: 'If I talk to you it comes out like this,' would translate to: 'Upif upI tupalk tupo yupou upit cupomes upout lupike thupis.' Christine and Anne could converse in Up-language as effortlessly as in normal English (still can, in fact), much to the annoyance and frustration of their parents.

Christine went to high school at Abbotsleigh Girls' School in Wahroonga. Outwardly she seemed to fit in well with her peers. Her close friend, Kristin Parsons, remembers her as being a little bit shy and obviously extremely intelligent, but she was not bullied or ostracised as some others were. She joined in the gossip about boys, took part in group toenail-painting sessions, listened with others to Elvis Presley records, and played in the school hockey team where she was a creditable goalie.

Yet Christine had quite a different view of herself. Pale, with thick, wavy red hair, she was convinced that she was somehow freakish. 'I hated myself. I wanted to be like other girls. I sat with the other girls at lunchtime and had them as friends but I always thought that I wasn't one of them because I wasn't maybe good enough for them or something. I always felt I was a stranger, a witness, a watcher and not a participant. But I did value the friendship of those girls at school, and I would have hated to sit alone at lunchtime. I was very grateful they accepted me into their circle.'

She experienced occasional migraine headaches. They would start with a blinding light where the whole world went completely white. Knowing what was to come she would be filled with dread, then: 'This absolutely pounding, agonising headache would start, which would last for 24 hours or more, the worst of it for maybe eight hours. I'd just have to go to bed, I couldn't move.'

Mrs Elva Julien taught English to Christine at Abbotsleigh. If her contemporaries saw nothing particularly unusual in her, Mrs Julien, with the wisdom of experience, certainly did. A teacher doesn't have many students who stand out after four decades, yet even now Mrs Julien can remember the qualities that made Christine different. 'She was quiet and self-contained . . . she was one of the people in the class who you wanted to get to know straight away. She always had an interested, quizzical look when you were explaining texts and prose. She was interested in writing, and she had a way with words.'

At the age of fifteen Christine wrote a short novel. When it was finished she proudly showed it to her mother. 'I don't think it's very good, dear,' Suzanne commented. Shattered, Christine fled to her room with a migraine.

When she was sixteen she wrote a poem for the school magazine, *The Weaver*, which laid bare her feelings of inadequacy.

DESPERATION

Must my life fade as every other life,
gone flitting shadow passing over the earth?
Must I wear a little deeper the polished groove
ground down by so many bodies? Must I live
and die, and leave my only imprint in the graveyard?
Must I be as helpless, as weak, as lost as every other
    life?
Must I grow old? Must I be trapped in the choking grasp
    of a city?

Never will I stand alone on a mountain.
I will be trampled underfoot, and the world

will go on and on like a crazy clock,
whose face does not change, even when acknowledged.

And I, and my friends, my home, my life will pass away.
My experiences of painful years
will vaporise in the dust.
I will be forgotten,
like a briefly living note of singing music.

Christine spent long hours alone in her room writing and painting. Her mother worried about her being by herself so much. They once had a big row when Suzanne forced her to go and spend a weekend with a friend. 'I don't want to go,' Christine protested. 'It's a waste of a weekend.' But on this occasion her mother prevailed.

Curiously, Christine never thought at that stage of turning her writing talent into a career, although she fantasised often about what she might do with her life. She was fascinated by Papua New Guinea. In her early teens she decided she would like to be a patrol officer. She abandoned the idea when she learned that only men were acceptable.

When Christine was thirteen, she and Anne were lent an old pony by family friends who were going away on holiday. Merrylegs, a pretty, dappled pony with an Arab face, big brown eyes and a cream mane and tail, was kept on a block of land about a kilometre from their home. Christine's job was to brush her, comb her mane and tail, ensure the water trough was full and make sure she received her rations of dried food every day. She tried to coax Merrylegs into a gallop along the nature strip of the main road near her place, but the most she could manage was a slow canter. Although Christine loved looking after the gentle old horse, the thought of working with animals never occurred to her.

Shortly after publishing her *cri de coeur* in the school magazine, she remembers going into the garden. A weeping cherry tree had been shedding white blossoms onto the ground like dandruff. Her mind was in a turmoil about who she was and why she was here. Through the mental mists an idea emerged with startling clarity. 'I thought, there's much more to life than just eating to exist. I don't want to waste my life like everyone wastes their life. I want to do something useful.'

But what? For an unworldly teenager the answer to that question seemed unattainable. Although the signs had been there since she was a small child, it would be more than a decade before she realised where they pointed.

CHAPTER 2

Suzanne believed it was important to have social graces, a standing in society, to know the correct conduct at a dinner party and so on – all of which Christine regarded as a waste of time. She was, by her own admission, a trying child, but probably no more so than many. She did not run away from home, or take drugs, or fall shamefully pregnant. It was just that there was a wilful stubbornness about her that could be exasperating, especially when she thought she was the victim of injustice.

In her final year of high school Suzanne took Christine to a vocational guidance counsellor, who pronounced that she had exceptional literary ability. Her mathematical skills, on the other hand, didn't bear speaking about. The counsellor advised her to seek a career in journalism.

If she had done so one can speculate that her strong sense of justice might have led her to become a crusading journalist.

Instead, she accepted a scholarship to study teaching at Sydney University. Suzanne thought it would be good to have an arts degree, and, without giving it much thought, Christine went along.

Part of her confusion during early adolescence had been due to a hunger for spiritual knowledge. 'I searched everywhere for spiritual answers. The only thing I knew for sure was that there was this God, whatever God might have been. I wanted to know what was this God and what was my relationship to it.'

Conventional Christianity had been drummed into her from childhood. In her early teens she had sung in the choir at St Swithun's Church near her home. For a time in her early teens she had nurtured a fantasy about becoming a missionary. As she grew older, Christianity had gradually come to seem implausible. 'I could not understand about Father, Son and Holy Ghost. I could not understand that a loving God would give you only one chance at life and afterwards damn you to heaven or hell forever.'

When she reached the age of eighteen she was at last able to ask her father to explain Christian Science to her. After he did they had many deep discussions about religion, which brought them closer to one another. Christine attended meetings at the Christian Science churches at Chatswood or Hornsby with Harold, but she eventually found that this belief system did not seem to add up either. She was too hungry for knowledge to tread either of her parents' narrow religious paths for long. She was curious about such things as reincarnation, and was still constantly tormented by questions about why she was here. For one so young she took an inordinate interest in everything to do with spirituality.

She found what seemed to be a plausible answer to her

search when an anthropology lecturer at university put forward the theory that every tribe throughout history had invented gods as a way to comfort them and to bond the tribe together. He asserted that in fact there was no such thing as God. Of course it was easier to die if you believed in God, but atheists were more rational. 'That was a terrible thing to teach,' she says. 'I decided there wasn't a God, and that's when my life became very unhappy.'

Her studies gave her little solace. The course required her to spend a week teaching at St Ives Primary School. 'The little children were very gorgeous but I felt extremely embarrassed standing in front of a whole class of children having to pretend to know everything about geography. If I could have been playing with them it might have been OK, but to be up the front and delivering a lesson seemed terribly presumptuous when I knew nothing about what I was teaching.'

This first face-to-face experience made her wonder if she was really suited to a teaching career.

While some of her contemporaries at university seemed to think of nothing but boys, Christine had yet to experience the raptures and disappointments of love. A friend who worked for a French shipping company took her to meet some French sailors one night. There was one to whom she was attracted, but they were only in port for two days. Her only other vaguely romantic experience was a handful of dates with the son of a well-known writer, but it was hardly what you would call love.

She met her future husband at a 21st birthday party. Jeremy Townend was a handsome lad of 21, easy-going, with an open face, straight brown hair and a generous gap between his two front teeth. It was the day of a federal election. Jeremy had been helping some of his friends, who were young liberals, with absentee voting at the Sydney Town Hall. After voting closed they had all adjourned to the Newport Arms, a popular Northern Beaches watering hole. Jeremy remembers 'being well primed' by the time he got to the party, but this did not entirely overcome his natural reticence. Anne, taking a fancy to him, nicknamed him Chuckie, and spent some time pinching his cheek and teasing him for his shyness.

After Anne's attention wandered elsewhere, Jeremy and Christine gravitated together. Christine recalls: 'As soon as I saw Jeremy I was attracted to him. He was good-looking and he was slightly drunk and very cute, and laughing a lot, and I had that perplexing emotion of wanting to see this person again, and to be with him.'

Jeremy recalls that Christine was, in the vernacular of the times, 'a good sort'. They spent the rest of the evening talking. They discovered that they lived quite close to one another; Christine and Jeremy's brother, John, were both members of the St Ives Dramateurs and their parents moved in the same north-shore social circles. Christine had also spent part of the day duti-fully handing out Liberal how-to-vote leaflets with her parents, who were members of the Liberal party, although she had only the vaguest understanding of politics. Christine and Jeremy enjoyed one another's company so much that neither of them wanted to go home. After most of the party-goers had left they went upstairs to a large attic where a few of the remaining guests were dancing to LPs. Jeremy held her in his arms closely, but that was as far as it went. They left in the early hours of the morning.

Christine had a job in the university holidays at a gift shop in the city. Jeremy formed a plan to visit her there the following

week, but first he asked a friend to drive him on a recon-
naissance mission past her home. As they cruised down the
street they saw Christine walking home. Stricken with embar-
rassment, Jeremy hid under the dashboard. However, attraction
made him bold: the following day he called at the gift shop and
asked her out.

Jeremy was working as an articled clerk at a firm of solicitors
in the city while he studied for his law degree. By her second
year of university Christine had lost interest entirely in
teaching. She failed her exams and dropped out. She had for
some time been hinting to Jeremy that she would like to get
married. One night at another 21st birthday party, after they
had been seeing one another for about eight months, they went
outside to escape the noise. Jeremy was never one for extra-
vagant demonstrations of affection, but sitting on the steps in
the dark he murmured to her, 'Ich liebe dich,' which in German
means, 'I love you'. A strange way of putting it, but, then, he was
too shy to say the words in English. A few days later he asked
her to marry him, this time in his native tongue. Christine,
without hesitation, said yes.

As liberated as they were in some respects, the Sixties was
still the era of formal engagements, which were expected to run
for a respectable duration – in their case thirteen months.
Shortly before the wedding Suzanne organised an open day at
her home for guests to view the wedding presents – much to
Christine's horror. 'All the presents were laid out on the table.
It was excruciatingly embarrassing for me. The worst part of it
was that she absolutely forced me to hang up in my bedroom
all the nighties and negligees which she had bought at some
posh shop, with their ribbons, lace and embroidery. It was
totally mortifying.'

When they walked down the aisle for their white wedding, Christine was 21 and Jeremy 23. Even for those days this was rather young, but Christine had decided what she wanted, and Jeremy bent to her will. 'Jeremy didn't want to get married so young, but I really wanted to get married. I really wanted to have my own life. I wanted to be independent. We were very much in love. It seemed miraculous to be married. I was very proud of being called "Mrs".'

They had many friends in common, of similar ages and from the same background. They went to each other's places for dinner and on picnics; they occasionally stayed with old school friends in the country; their parents socialised together. On the face of it the marriage seemed like the natural pairing of two young people from conservative north-shore families, whose futures would surely follow a predictable and unremarkable path. Yet Christine very soon began to feel moments of unhappiness. 'It was quite disappointing, because I was still very immature. The thing about being married is you don't have to say to your parents any more, I'm going here or there or doing this or that. Suddenly you are your own master. But parents are very important in one's life; you still feel you want to share things with them, even when you become 60.'

Nor did marriage alleviate the strange mental turmoil which had troubled her since childhood. If anything it became worse. 'After I was married I had this feeling all the time, if I don't hold on to this chair I'm going to lift away – that feeling that you don't really belong at all. I was wondering if there was some mental problem; it was such a feeling of detachment and removal from the world. It was so powerful that, thinking back on it now, I think it was my real self saying, "Excuse me, I'm here and you must listen."'

At the time of their wedding Jeremy had still been four years off achieving his law degree. His salary was sixteen pounds a week. Their parents jointly loaned them almost two-thirds of the money for a tiny flat in Cremorne that cost 5,800 pounds. Christine got a job proofreading at the Law Book Company, then worked for the travel department of a shipping company. Neither job interested her. She could not escape the niggling sense that she was wasting her life.

From the beginning of her marriage Christine longed to have children. In 1966, thirteen months after their wedding, she gave birth to a healthy son, Miles. He weighed six pounds four ounces. In those days fathers were not encouraged to attend the birth of their children. Jeremy was told to leave the hospital and he would be phoned after the baby had been delivered.

Christine's first feeling on being a mother was overwhelming wonder. 'Miles looked like a small rosebud with fat cheeks and a tiny pink mouth and dark, golden hair. He seemed very beautiful.' However, the impersonal nature of the hospital system took away some of the joy. While she was giving birth the doctor called in a group of students and lectured them, pointing out various parts of her exposed anatomy as if she were not there. 'The beauty and sacredness of the birth was damaged by the institutionalised system which separated me and Jeremy. We should have been rejoicing together. Instead of treating it as a great miracle there was this mechanical ghastliness about the whole situation. None of this could, however, detract from this burning obsessiveness which must fill every mother, a sense of a baby being part of oneself and at the same time a separate being, and that profound aching when something is too precious, too dear, too unimaginably miraculous to believe in fully.'

The baby was kept behind glass and only produced at feeding times. When Jeremy came to collect them, and the three drove home together, Christine had a feeling of elation, as though she were escaping with a stolen child.

Miles was a beautiful boy – plump, with smooth white skin and little red cheeks. He loved being cuddled. Three years after Miles was born Cameron arrived. At six pounds two ounces he was even smaller than his brother though, in Christine's eyes, just as precious. 'He was this tiny, miraculous creature with perfect little fingers, a little life that could be folded in a blanket like a little toy doll, an adaptable, easy-going, fat little baby who laughed at everything. In fact one of his teachers in primary school told us that Cameron's major problem was that he would make everyone in the class laugh so loudly at his jokes that she couldn't control the class.'

In that same year, 1969, Jeremy became a junior partner at Gray and Perkins, the same firm where he had clerked, and they moved into and renovated their first proper house in Lindfield. With its substantial dwellings, big backyards and pockets of bushland, Lindfield was the epitome of middle-class suburbia.

Meanwhile, Anne had married a farmer in Coonamble in outback New South Wales, and by this time had had a daughter, Vanessa. When the boys were young Christine visited her sister frequently. They delighted in the three toddlers playing together. It was, Christine recalls, a happy, carefree time. Not for long though – far from growing easily into her role of conventional wife and mother, Christine began to feel strangely unsettled. The niggling feeling that she was wasting her life returned. 'The thing that was totally anathema to me was to be a housewife – one of those people who sat round playing bridge, or sunning by the pool or having luncheons with the high-heeled shoes and stockings. I never ever wanted to do that. I loathed it.'

She begged Jeremy to go and live in a commune. When he vetoed that idea she suggested that they buy a little house in the outback and he could work in a country town. Or else they could travel as backpackers with the two boys across Asia. But Jeremy had their future firmly mapped out. He had determined that it was his duty to become a partner in an established law firm in Sydney, send the children to a decent school and pay off the house.

Eventually, Christine realised that being at home with small children was the ideal circumstance in which to use her talent for writing. She wrote poetry at first, some of which was published in literary magazines, then a slim novel, *The Beginning of Everything and the End of Everything Else*. She sent the manuscript to an agent who advised her that while it had merit, it was too short.

However, writing did not still the restlessness in her, the feeling that she had yet to find her purpose in life. In the school holidays in early 1973 she announced that she wanted to leave Lindfield to live for a while in Redfern, a notorious slum, part of which contained an aboriginal ghetto. She cannot now remember if it was to research more material for her novel, if she had a sudden desire to support aboriginal rights, or if it was simply because she could not bear any longer what seemed to her a stifling, bourgeois existence. It was probably a combination of all those things.

Although this dramatic decision had been building for a couple of years it caught Jeremy by surprise. What with the renovations in their new home, being father to two young children, and a heavy workload at Gray and Perkins, he had not at first realised that Christine was dissatisfied, although he was well aware that she was not like most of their friends' wives. 'Chris was not interested in the more usual pursuits of a young married woman with young children. She began learning about the environment, writing articles, poetry, and then novels. I fully supported what she was doing, [but] I felt [her decision to go to Redfern] was ridiculous.'

Christine agonised over leaving her children to be cared for by her husband and her mother. 'I was torn about everything, irresolute about everything, and probably repulsively difficult. I think at the time I believed that Jeremy and I were not well-matched because I was interested in a different sort of life than was he. I had started reading books about environmental destruction – I think it was Charles Birch's *Confronting the Future* that came out at that time, and Paul Ehrlich's books on the terrible future of world overpopulation. I developed radical politics that were not at all in accord with Jeremy's thinking. Secondly, I had begun to meditate seriously for hours while the boys were at school. I had a sense of being removed from life as if some great power were unfolding within me which I had no idea how to direct. Everything was confused and I did all these stupid things. I can only liken it to the first time a young male elephant goes into *musth* and he doesn't know how to handle this huge power that awakens in him. He bangs his head against a tree and rolls his head in the water to try to cool it, and fights with everyone he sees.'

And so to Redfern she went. She rented a room in a rundown apartment building and worked as a volunteer at a church in Cleveland Street, helping aborigines who had come into the city from the bush. She hung out with aboriginal people in the Empress Hotel, listened to their stories and smarted over the injustices she heard. For a while she was fired with the idea of championing aboriginal rights, but that did not last long. 'It was really dumb. I knew absolutely nothing about their situation and was completely unqualified to do anything about it. It was all part of trying to find the reason for existence.'

Two weeks after leaving, she returned home to finish her book. With a new ending based on her experiences in Redfern, *The Beginning of Everything and the End of Everything Else* was published in 1974. The protagonist is a young girl, Persia, who falls in love with and marries a conventional man, Adrian, whom she comes to despise. One day Persia announces that she's going to go and live in Redfern.

Christine's descriptions of the squalor and hopelessness in Redfern reveal an already accomplished literary talent.

> They went to the Empress one night. It was the pub where whites did not drink, except in scattered exceptions. There were broken bottles and glasses over the floor. There was thinned vomit, and black grime on woodwork. And there were people, of wood, of bark, of trees and plains, of the desert past, now invaded with drink, and split open, lolling against wall benches, sinking into filthy corners, their heads falling on their chests, degraded, their hair tangled with booze.
>
> They had come to drink away their past and their future, and live in a few hours of pleasure, which would last only as long as their money. And although to others they were decayed perhaps, this was their only moment of power in a place which had deprived them, and ground them and pushed them in gutters and sod.

Persia, just like Christine in real life, does not last long in Redfern. The last line of the book articulates nicely the dilemma of those who seek to escape their heritage.

> And she went from the poor streets and the packed living and the packed lives and knew that it was not her privilege ever to be able to do anything about it.

The Beginning of Everything and the End of Everything Else was reviewed kindly, although not by all. The aboriginal activist, Bobby Sykes, took exception to intimations that there was room for reform from within, branding the author a racist.

'There are two sides to the story,' Christine responds. 'Because it is now recognised by the aboriginal community and their leaders and elders that there needs to be reform from within while at the same time white Australians need to address injustices which still remain.'

Christine had every reason to be happy with her life. Jeremy was advancing steadily in his law firm, and with the publication of her first book she seemed to have a promising literary career ahead of her. She began working an another novel, but at the same time she was becoming more and more discontented. 'Having rushed into the marriage, that's when I went through my rebellious period. Most people, I suppose, would have had one of those periods before they got married, so poor old Jeremy had to put up with me instead of the mother. That was one of the times I had to hold on to the table not to float away. You haven't had a proper night's sleep and you feel all dizzy, and you feel sort of removed, and you're looking from a distance at the world. That's how I felt – not every moment, it would come and go – this great compulsive *something* breathing beside you that was demanding to be heard or recognised.'

If she had tried to analyse her feelings she might well have concluded that her life was out of control. But, 'There was really no self-analysis. If I thought about it rationally I would have thought, What the hell do you think you're doing?'

Jeremy readily agrees that they had married far too young. 'For the first several years I had no reason to think that we weren't similar. The divergence of interests didn't begin to show until several years after. A lot of our development happened after we were married. We were still children.'

Through her research into spiritual matters Christine had begun to develop a fascination with India. One day in December 1974 she announced to Jeremy that she did not wish to be married any more. She wanted to take the children to India. When Jeremy refused to give his consent she declared that she would move into a friend's flat in Balmain. The friend had a room under his house which he was letting out.

Again she agonised over the effect this would have on the children, but she was convinced that she was not leading the right kind of life. After endless thought she had concluded that leaving temporarily to try to discover herself would be better for all concerned than remaining at home in her present state. Suzanne agreed to mind the boys while Jeremy was at work, and so Christine forsook Lindfield for the scruffy terraces and working-class cottages of Balmain. The suburb had not yet become gentrified, although it had been well and truly discovered by writers and artists and hippies. These creative types mingled together in the pubs and cafes with wharfies and council workers, giving the place an unpretentious, Bohemian ambience. It was a long way from the north shore and the ladies who lunched.

Yet just as marriage had failed to fulfil Christine's expectations of liberation, neither did the change of location automatically bring bliss into her life. 'I was unhappy,' she recalls. 'I didn't understand the world, and I didn't understand myself. I thought the world was in a mess. I'd read all these books about pollution and the destruction of the environment. I was feeling guilty about breathing, there wasn't enough air for everyone. I thought I was so useless. I wanted to do something, but didn't know what, and there was this strange driving force and this feeling that I shouldn't be where I was.'

Her flirtation with aetheism had lasted only briefly. She was now convinced that there was some sort of divine being ordering the world. She read books about spiritualism, yoga, Buddhism. One in particular, *The Thunder of Silence* by Joel Goldsmith, impressed her greatly. She spent hours at a time meditating, following the advice laid out by Goldsmith. She was floundering, desperately seeking something that would make sense of her life.

She had been living in Balmain for a fortnight when, in a state of agitation, she telephoned a friend, Gillian Coote, who lived in Hunter's Hill – an odd choice, as she did not know Gillian all that well. Gillian, sensing her distress, invited her to lunch the next day.

'I don't know why I rang Gillian,' Christine says now. 'I would have to say it was destiny.'

It was certainly a life-changing lunch. Gillian's husband Tony was an architect. Gillian was studying meditation and was keenly interested in spiritual practice. A crowd of their friends had spent the early part of the weekend painting a mural on one of the interior walls of their house. During the course of a long celebratory Sunday lunch Christine learned that her hosts were planning to go to India in ten days' time. They intended to study architecture and spend some time at an ashram. Their three-year-old son Gully was going with them.

Christine blurted out, 'Can I come too?'

Seeing no particular reason to say no, the Cootes replied, 'Sure, why not?'

Through her interest in the environment Christine had become aware of the lobby group called the Total Environment Centre. Before leaving Australia she visited their headquarters to ask if they knew of any similar organisations in India that she could contact. The centre had offices in an old wool store at The Rocks in Sydney. She climbed the stairs to the third floor and asked if there was anyone she could talk to. Milo Dunphy, the director, took her for a coffee at a next-door café. Christine described to him the pristine bushland on the north shore which she had known as a girl, and how upset she had been when it was cleared for a housing development. She told Milo that once, while walking through this bushland she had come upon an abandoned litter of kittens. Her mother told her to just leave them there. Instead she had carried them from door to door until she found homes for all of them.

Milo told her that he knew nothing about environmental groups in India. He was impressed by her passion, though. Before she left he suggested that she might like to join the Total Environment Centre. While Christine promised to consider it, as she was about to leave the country she thought it unlikely she would ever follow it up.

Christine could well afford the trip to India as she had recently received a $2,000 research grant from the Literary Board, and another $2,000 was due in a few months' time. After her initial shock, her mother was grudgingly supportive. 'Well if you've decided to go,' she grumbled, 'at least let me take you to Grace Brothers and get you something to wear.'

Christine declined. She told her mother she wanted to travel with the minimum of baggage. Suzanne once again agreed to look after the children while she was away. Jeremy, too, was surprisingly understanding. He bought her a camera and told her, 'Here, take some photographs and go and sort yourself out.'

He recalls: 'By this time it was obvious we had problems. Chris had moved to Balmain, and the boys were to-ing and fro-ing between myself, my mother and Chris's mother and Chris. She was going with friends. I thought it would be good for her. Maybe a chance to see things in balance. That not all was bad with her life here, and an enforced separation would give each of us a chance to work things out.'

A couple of days later Christine boarded an aeroplane carrying two changes of clothing in a little plastic rucksack – destination Madras.

CHAPTER 3

The moment Christine's feet touched the soil of India she felt that she had come home. 'It was a feeling of relief, that's the only word to describe it. I fell in love with India instantly, and lay awake the whole night in the hotel, I was so excited.'

The hotel was the Broadlands, a decrepit, romantic old building with colonnades and faintly Moorish features, situated in the Muslim quarter next door to a mosque. Woken before dawn by the muezzin calling for prayer, she got up and went for a walk, treading over bodies still sleeping in blankets on the footpaths, watching the shopkeepers pull up their shutters, the early morning workers taking *dosa* and *chai*, the jam-packed buses with their drivers honking bulb horns, shoals of rick-shaws and bicycles, farting auto-rickshaws, teeming pedestri-ans, mutilated, crippled, leprous beggars, the smell of curry and sewage and incense – India, in all its crowded, exotic beauty and squalor. She loved it all.

After touring around for a few days the Australians took a bus to the former French colony, Pondicherry. They were planning to visit Auroville, an international experimental township which had been the vision of the yogi, Sri Aurobindo, founder of the renowned Sri Aurobindo Ashram. Auroville had been inaugurated eight years previously in a ceremony attended by representatives of 124 nations and all states of India. In a gesture of symbolic unity a boy and girl from each nation had each poured a handful of sand from their homeland into a lotus-shaped marble urn. The Australians planned to visit an architect friend of the Cootes, John Allen, who was living in the township with his wife Jan.

Auroville today is set in the midst of beautiful forests, mostly planted by supporters from Europe. Back then it was a ruined landscape of bare, eroded hills and gullies, through which wound a nightmarish road where lumbering trucks, belching black fumes, bullied smaller vehicles off to the side. The trio, pedalling along on bicycles, had no idea where to find John and Jan Allen. They stopped to ask directions of a saffron-robed *saddhu* (priest), who was sitting in the street.

'I not knowing but I will call someone who will be knowing,' he said with a wag of his head. He disappeared behind a low wall into the grounds of a temple.

A few minutes later a European woman with a completely shaved head and enormous brown eyes appeared. Gillian Coote remembers 'a slight, brown woman in her late sixties, with an angular face, firm, strong legs and wearing sandals'. She remembers that her eyes were 'strong and penetrating'.

Christine was awestruck. 'She was the most totally beautiful, serene, loving person I'd ever seen in my entire life. The minute I saw her all my hairs stood on end. I thought that this person knows the answer to every question I'd ever have to ask her.'

The woman introduced herself as Diana, a French citizen who was living and studying at the temple. She stopped a man on a bicycle. He knew John and Jan; speaking in Tamil he gave directions for them. When that was sorted out Diana asked if there was anything more they needed. Gathering all of her courage Christine blurted out, 'I need to ask you a whole lot of questions.'

It was an extraordinary overture to someone she had just met. 'I was attracted to her by the light and radiance which emanated from her being. I knew that because of this light, she was a realised person. I could see this light and I was surprised that Tony and Gilly could not see it. This is why, even though hardly knowing her, I knew she had the answers.'

'I don't know if I can answer your questions,' Diana replied.

'But you seem to be so far ahead and to know so much.'

'We don't know where we are,' she said enigmatically.

'But, but, but . . .'

Gillian, who now teaches Zen Buddhism, has a theory about why Christine should have been so instantly smitten. 'In Zen we work with *koans*, which is a Chinese word meaning "public case". You live the question until it breaks open and you realise it, and it becomes resolved, and there's no question any more. Christine's whole being was holding this question: What am I to do with my life? Diana was able to be the person Christine reached out to and chose to be her spiritual teacher.'

Bowing before Christine's blandishments, Diana agreed that she could come back and see her. Christine bade the Cootes goodbye and moved into a room in the Sri Aurobindo Ashram.

Diana lived very simply in two small rooms in a hut in the

temple grounds. She had been studying the yogic path to self-realisation for many years. She was not one of those pop gurus of whom westerners were so enamoured in the Sixties and Seventies, and she had no wish to become one. She taught a select few students, but she had probably never come up against someone quite so avid for knowledge as Christine Townend. 'I don't think she wanted some bumbling, confused, harassed westerner, who was very stressed, troubling her, because she was really doing something.'

At first Diana attempted to introduce Christine to other spiritual teachers. But only Diana would do. Over the following weeks Christine visited her often. She quizzed her about spiritual philosophy, the soul, the purpose of the universe.

Diana taught that there is one Energy or God, or Absolute, from which matter, the phenomenal world, emanates. This material world is actually structured from the very Energy of that Source, hence we are ourselves little Gods. One of her first lessons was, 'Know that you are God'.

Secondly, Christ was the teacher of teachers, and was still an overseeing presence in the world. Therefore, 'Lay your head at his feet'.

Thirdly, within each one of us is a spark of that Energy, that God, which can be felt in the heart as Love, not the possessive, conditioned love, which selects one object of affection and excludes another, but an all-inclusive, all-pervading, infinite Energy of Love. Hence she taught, 'Always feel your Heart'.

In one of their meetings Christine mentioned that she suffered from terrible migraines. Diana looked into her eyes intently for a few moments. 'It's an imbalance,' she pronounced. From that day on Christine never had another headache. 'I don't know if she did something, but that was the end of my migraines.'

She missed Jeremy and the boys terribly. Phone calls were difficult and expensive. She did phone now and then, but for the most part they corresponded regularly via mail. At the ashram there was an office with pigeonholes where letters for residents were placed. Her first order of business each morning was to anxiously scan the pigeonhole under T-U-V for word from home.

Even as she yearned for her husband and sons she toyed with the idea of going into retreat in an ashram, forsaking family as some of the great sages, including the Buddha, had done. Diana advised her against it, saying, 'Right where you are is where you can do some good. You have to accept the place where you are and go from there.'

Looking back on that time Christine comments: 'Through my conversations with Diana I came to understand that everyone is born with a commitment, a *dharma*, a life duty of some order; that that *dharma* will reveal itself and it is then up to the individual whether they accept their commitment and work conscientiously for it, or whether they try to fight it.

'My spiritual duty, according to Diana, was to return to my family and find this *dharma*, which would manifest "right where you are". I began to understand that what I had to do was something of significance related to building (I still did not know it had anything to do with animals), that at last that uncontrolled drive would be directed and that I would find a way to contribute, and in finding that way great joy would come to me also.

'Diana saved my life, really. I would have no doubt gone crazy if I hadn't met her, and I can't believe that it was a coincidence – ringing up Gillian when I hardly knew her, and it was marvellous that they took me with them.'

Two and half months after leaving Australia Christine boarded a plane to return. Jeremy and the boys had spent the Easter break with Jeremy's parents at Mollymook on the NSW south coast. At the end of the holiday he was due to drop Miles and Cameron off with their other grandparents, as he had to go to work the next day. As he approached Sydney he felt a growing feeling of anticipation, coupled with anxiety, at the thought that Christine might be there.

She was. It was a warm and affectionate homecoming, although Jeremy's delight at having her back was tempered with caution. 'We had to re-establish our relationship and I didn't know how it would work out, and I think we were both apprehensive about how the other would react.'

Christine's mother and mother-in-law were decidedly frosty. While she had been away Suzanne had decided that she couldn't cope with the children, and had offloaded them onto Jeremy's mother Marjorie. Not having planned on looking after two small children for weeks on end, Marjorie was quite put out, and when she saw Christine she made sure that she knew it. Like Suzanne, Marjorie had been brought up in a world where men went out to work and their women took part in social activities. She neither understood nor approved of Christine's behaviour. For her part Christine was upset with her mother, regarding her action as high-handed and disloyal.

It didn't help when a few days later Christine asked a barber to shave off all her hair. 'Silly girl,' Suzanne huffed when she saw it for the first time. 'Why did you do that? You've got lovely thick hair. I feel embarrassed showing you to my friends.'

Jeremy told her she looked like a Hare Krishna. Miles and Cameron were mortified when she called to pick them up from school, and insisted that she remain in the car with a scarf hiding her baldness.

In retrospect Christine admits that it wasn't such a good idea. 'It was as if I was leaving the past behind and starting again. But it wasn't a successful experiment. It met with a lot of outrage.'

Christine had already written half of her second novel before she had gone away. Now, with her Indian experience to draw upon, she sat down at the typewriter to finish it. *Travels with Myself* was published in 1976. The cover notes described it thus:

> Black and white, body, spirit, sex, race, religion – revelations and returns.
>
> Christine Townend's second novel *Travels with Myself* is a new experience of love, enlightenment and growth. Leaving a bourgeois marriage, her husband and children, Jo sets out to meet and know the differences of the world. First to sexual adventure with black Aboriginal activists, then to retreat to – or pursue – spiritual peace in the ashrams of India.

It is a bleak book. The main character, Jo, is again a young middle-class housewife. Christine writes scathingly of the shallowness of Jo's bourgeois life. As with the first novel, the female character leaves her husband to live in Redfern, where she is sexually used and discarded by an aboriginal man, Matthew. The affair reveals the impossible gap between her and her embittered lover.

In the second half of the book Jo leaves Sydney and travels to India where she visits an ashram and meets a guru named

Penelope. They have intense philosophical discussions, and Jo travels for a while with some other Europeans. The novel ends, as did the previous one, with Jo coming to terms with her own heritage. She returns home to her husband, Weslyn:

> She loved him. It was as corny as chocolate cakes, but she was prepared to be corny for the sake of enjoyment. Everything was sure and strong now, and would never be sharp, or drop. It was the most of everything that Weslyn should be there, and Jo should be in the same place. Areas had only been hoaxes that they had made. Her heart was new and given back like children are given back at dawn. She did not mind being middle-class, milk-bottle, dressing-gown, Sunday-morning-in-bed. She was quite prepared to be unfashionable for the sake of happiness.

Travels with Myself was published in 1976 to good reviews. A literary career was there to be grasped if that had been the author's wish. But unlike the heroines of her novels, Christine was not yet resigned to the apparently obvious future which lay ahead.

CHAPTER 4

M ilo Dunphy from the Total Environment Centre, hearing
that Christine Townend was back from her travels, had
one of his staff call her with an invitation to come in for a
coffee. Milo is dead and gone now so we cannot be certain why
he courted Christine so avidly. Perhaps, as she talked of her
early interest in the environment, her love of the bush near
her home, the doom-laden writings which had influenced her,
he sensed the smouldering spark of activism waiting to be
fanned into flame. Canny campaigner that he was, he invited
her to join the Colong Committee, a powerful wilderness lobby
group of experienced environmental activists of which he was
a member.

Christine sat in on the fortnightly meetings and watched
avidly as they planned campaigns against such things as
uranium mining and threatened forests. She learned how to
organise demonstrations, how to lobby politicians and business

groups and how to use the media to advantage. She was soon editing the *Colong Bulletin* and writing articles for the media. Milo took a continuing interest in the progress of his new recruit. Often, while waiting for meetings to begin, or when the day's work was over, they had coffee or a drink together. They went bushwalking, and once or twice shared a tent. Despite what people might have thought, the relationship was purely platonic, although Milo made it clear on several occasions that he would have liked it to be otherwise.

Just before going to India Christine had heard the author Richard Ryder speaking on radio about his ground-breaking book on animal rights, *Victims of Science.* She had become a vegetarian there and then. 'It seemed to me the most obscene and disgusting part of human behaviour to eat animals. Not because of the cruelty, but because we're so close to the animals; as human beings we share our lives with them. We can't have a peaceful and harmonious world unless there's harmony and love at all levels, in all parts of the environment. Therefore to eat animals is to violate that most sacred relation-ship; you'd rather die than eat a friend.'

She had also read, with great excitement, *Animal Liberation,* by the philosopher Peter Singer. When the book had been published in 1976 it caused a sensation around the world. In its updated edition it is still enormously influential. *Newsweek* magazine credits the book for initiating the animal liberation movement. When Christine heard in 1976 that Peter Singer was going to take part in the popular ABC television program *Monday Conference,* she and Jeremy went along to hear what he had to say.

Under the *Monday Conference* formula the guest fielded questions from the audience while a moderator kept things moving along. The program was taped in the Great Hall at Sydney University. The room was so packed that people were standing around the sides. Singer's message was that human beings were practising 'speciesism' – that is, they unjustly treated their own species with greater respect than others. Just because animals are not human, he argued, we think we can do what we like to them. It was the same thinking that had caused white people to exercise tyranny over black slaves in the past. We must extend the circle of compassion, he said, to include all living things.

Christine recalls that evening in great detail. 'Many of the questions were hostile. Someone asked about ants and cockroaches – all those pathetic arguments. Peter Singer had an answer to everything. He said animals with a developed nervous system are the ones we have to think about first. He was not averse to eating an oyster but he drew the line at a prawn, because a prawn's nervous system feels something. Animals with nervous systems can feel suffering, and until there's no cruelty in the meat industry we shouldn't be eating meat, as a matter of principle. Suffering was the issue; if there was pain and suffering it was a moral issue and we had to do something about it.'

The logic and moral certainty of Singer's argument had a powerful effect on Christine. The next time she saw Milo she could talk of nothing but animal rights. 'Do you realise there's not a single group fighting for factory-farm animals?' she thundered. 'The RSPCA isn't interested. There's no group prepared to stand up for the rights of animals.'

'Well start one,' said Milo.

'How would I do that?'

'I'll show you. Use the Centre's facilities, call a meeting and get some of your friends to come along, and go from there.'

Christine had discovered the great cause she had been seeking all her life.

The first meeting of Animal Liberation was held on 7 December 1976. There were only six people present. Milo was there with two friends who helped advise them on strategic plans; Christine had invited a neighbour and a friend who worked for another animal welfare group; and Jeremy was there too. He, like most people, was fond of animals, but he was hardly passionate about them. 'I can distinctly remember the RSPCA had Labradors or golden retrievers sitting on the pavement with a collection box and I thought, I don't want to give money to animals when there are so many problems with humans.' He went to the meeting more as a show of support for his wife than a desire to change the world.

It was hardly a promising beginning. Years later Christine's friend told her how, as she had sat through the first meetings, she believed Animal Liberation would never survive, for those in attendance were so few.

The meeting resolved to have a letterhead designed, to print a leaflet with information about the new organisation and to write to Peter Singer asking him to be their patron. Their aims and objectives were based on the philosophy expressed in Singer's book – that is, to 'abolish speciesism'. As one of the most obvious examples of speciesism was the slaughter of animals, a major philosophy was vegetarianism which, of course, immediately alienated agribusiness, the farm lobby and conservative animal welfare organisations such as the RSPCA.

Christine plunged into a busy round of research and writing. Animal Liberation's first major foray into the world of activism was to prepare a ten-page submission to the Premier of New South Wales, Neville Wran, pointing out the evils of factory farming and cruel livestock practices. They received a polite note of thanks, and that was the last they heard.

Christine wrote articles which she submitted to the media. They were ignored by the mainstream outlets but one or two were accepted by small left-wing journals and magazines. Their first breakthrough came in September 1977 when the *Sydney Morning Herald* published a piece she wrote entitled, 'Animal Farm's Darker Side'. It stated in part:

> Last year in NSW almost 100,000 pigs were reared intensively, most of these living in sheds which are artificially ventilated, artificially illuminated, and cement-floored. Their tails were cut off and their tusks were removed to prevent them chewing each other in boredom.
>
> The situation is similar in the egg-laying industry. In 1976 almost seven million hens in NSW were confined to cages, each with approximately 450 square centimetres of space. Under these conditions the hen is unable fully to stretch her wings, she must stand on a sloping wire floor . . . The dead and dying can be seen lying on the floor on Monday morning after the post-weekend inspection.

After the article came out, Christine was invited to appear on the ABC radio program *City Extra*. She was 'absolutely terrified beyond words'. The program had a very large audience, Christine knew it was live, and she was ill with the flu. Nevertheless, when the time came she decided to soldier on.

The host, Caroline Jones, asked a question. Christine managed to mumble a few words then froze. She later recorded her mortification in her book, *A Voice for the Animals*: 'My mind wasn't functioning. I simply couldn't hear the questions that Caroline was asking me. She smiled very gently, said she hoped I would be able to return when I was feeling better, and put on a record while I was hastened out of the studio by a disgusted producer.'

Ashamed and embarrassed, she asked if she could come back when she felt well again. To her surprise the producer agreed. A week later, sick with terror and fear, she rang to say she was ready. The next day she was ushered into the glass-walled studio with its intimidating technical equipment to be interviewed by Caroline Jones's colleague, Steve Cosser. As the On-Air light went on a blanket of calm descended upon her. She spoke well.

Other radio interviews followed, and there was some lively correspondence in the letters pages of the *Herald* in response to her article. As a result, Animal Liberation had a spate of new memberships.

In 1977 Christine had begun to investigate conditions for factory-farmed animals in New South Wales. At that time the producers had received no public criticism of the way they kept their animals, so she was able to visit piggeries and poultry producers using the excuse that she wanted to buy a hen or a piglet. Once she took Miles with her to inspect a chicken processing plant where they killed 13,500 birds every day. In regimented rows upside-down, flapping birds slid one after the other through a machine that cut their necks as they passed. A girl in a neat white uniform and cap sat on a chair checking that the automatic killer did not miss any throat. Sometimes she jumped up and sliced a neck with a knife, then sat down again, her hands resting demurely in her lap.

With increasing horror Miles and Christine followed the foreman as he explained the process – the automatic decapitating machine; the plucking machine which tore the feathers out and washed them away in eddies of watery blood; the feet being cut away to be used for gelatine; the auto-evisceration process . . .

Miles, who was fond of fried chicken and the occasional hamburger, pulled on Christine's hand and said, 'I'm never going to eat meat again.' He was nine years old; and since that day he never has.

In one corner of the unloading bay about ten chickens were clustered together, pink and squawking. The foreman told them they were the ones who were lowest in the pecking order, and never got enough food and water and never got to sleep, so they didn't grow properly.

'We'll kill them later,' he said.

'Can I take one home?' Miles asked.

The foreman picked one up and thrust it into Christine's hand. It was so stiff with terror it did not move. The top half of its beak was clipped so that it could not peck its fellow chickens.

They went back to the foreman's office and stood holding the redeemed chicken. 'I'm afraid it'll soil your carpet,' Christine said tentatively.

He laughed. 'None of them have been fed or watered for forty-eight hours so you needn't worry about that.'

They thanked him and went home. When the chicken realised it was not going to die it sat on Miles's shoulder and clucked. They put it in a chicken run, and it dipped its head deep into water again and again. It walked in amazement clucking and pecking with its useless beak. They had saved one chicken out of 13,500 from one factory in one day in one State of one country.

A couple of weeks later the chicken's legs broke and it had to be euthanased. It had been bred to grow so fast that its legs could not support the weight of its body.

The visit to the chicken plant raised a question that would confront Christine on countless occasions throughout her life: how to balance the responsibilities of family and parenthood against her devotion to the cause?

'I didn't expect the slaughtering process to be as terrible as it was. Even so, I don't believe in hiding the reality of the world from a nine-year-old who should be old enough to understand that not everything is hunky-dory. I longed for my children to understand that it was important for every person to contribute something to the larger world, that there was great and terrible suffering that needed to be addressed, that it was a responsibility of life to help wherever possible, not just your own narrow family, but unknown people, unknown beings. There was something illogical, it seemed to me, in favouring one's own kith and kin over and above others who had far greater needs. School did not teach then (and perhaps does not now either) that beyond the nuclear family, with all its limited and enclosed relationships, lies a world groaning with need.

'It seemed to me then, as now, that it's not enough to say "There's nothing I can do to help." If there's one lesson which every child needs to learn, it's that there is something you can do to help. I believe in the ancient idea of the church of tithing, of giving a certain percentage of one's income to good works.

But there's another, greater tithing, which is giving one's time. This is more difficult, requires more determination, some sacrifices and discomforts, but it's a human duty.'

Christine bought hens from battery farms in order to study their behaviour. Removing the Animal Liberation sticker from the window of her car, she would drive to the outskirts of Sydney where the farms were located. On one trip on a hot, dusty summer's day, she came to a complex of long corrugated-iron sheds set in a bare paddock. Each shed was crammed with tier upon tier of cages. Unable to stand properly because of the wire, the hens jostled and fought each other for food and water. Many of them had rubbed raw patches, pecked flesh, ragged combs, callused feet and long, curling toenails hanging through the wire.

She asked the woman in charge if she could buy some. 'I love them, I want to give them a good life.'

The woman laughed. 'We've got 86,000 here, you can't save all of them.'

She went home with three hens. She named the most emaciated one Miss Chook. Miss Chook seemed to have forgotten that she was mobile, and that her legs were for walking. Christine placed her on the table and photographed her as evidence of her appalling condition.

After she put Miss Chook on the earth again the hen lifted one leg cautiously, extended one yellow foot then placed it carefully on the soil. She repeated the process with the other leg. Her toes spread out over the leaf litter in the garden. An ancient, innate instinct which could not be suppressed welled inside her, and she began frantically to scratch and peck with her mutilated beak, which could not lift the pecks from the soil. For the next few hours her compulsive behavioural needs, which had never before been satisfied, drove her ceaselessly to scratch and peck at the soil until she was exhausted.

Although she had never had the opportunity to make a nest Miss Chook found a warm, dry corner behind a rubbish bin which she claimed for her own. Scratching and fluffing her feathers, she settled herself into an indented hole as if she had done it every day of her life.

Miss Chook performed her first public duty the next day. Christine took her in a box to the television studios where she was to be interviewed for a morning program. They sat under lights behind a desk while the cameras rolled and Miss Chook rested serenely in Christine's lap, clucking slightly and extending her head. As Christine scratched with her fingernails around her neck Miss Chook's eyes glazed with ecstasy. Occasionally Christine had to shake her gently so that people knew she was there. She would squawk indignantly as her rest was disturbed.

That afternoon they went to a radio studio where, apart from a few noisy protests, Miss Chook behaved with great aplomb. Her wasted little body made it quite clear, without the need for words, that something was terribly wrong with the intensive production of eggs.

It soon became obvious that a year in a cage had slightly warped Miss Chook's mind. While the youngest bird, Miss Lay, who had only been in the cage a month, was well-adjusted, friendly and content, Miss Chook skulked in corners and had the mad, beady stare of someone who had known a life of suffering. One day Christine found her floating dead in the swimming pool. She had not understood the danger of water.

Miss Lay was a proud and beautiful bird, with a certain cunning. She always appeared if Christine had a plate in her hand. She ignored the dogs, and if the cats tried to stare her out she would rush at them screaming angrily until they fled.

Miss Lay was very affectionate. Her way of expressing love was to come up and peck people's toes – not too comfortable when they were barefoot. Often at night, when the doors were open, she would come strutting in and nest on the sofa, staring fixedly at the flickering television screen.

'Hens are often dismissed as being stupid,' Christine says. 'But I believe this to be a gross underestimation. Animals are dismissed as stupid because people can't be bothered observing them and learning to understand their language. If you label an animal a robot which does nothing but react to the prod of instinct, then you'll never find its personality, individuality and intelligence because you won't call it forth.'

In 1970, at the age of only 53, Christine's father Harold had been diagnosed with early onset Alzheimer's disease. As he had deteriorated, Suzanne thought of putting him into a nursing home, but when she looked at a few and saw the elderly patients sitting around in wheelchairs staring vacantly into space she couldn't bring herself to do it.

Looking after Harold at home was a heartbreaking, wearing business. One evening Suzanne wanted to go into the city to hear Christine give a talk. She prepared Harold's dinner for him, carefully locked him in the house and left at about five p.m. When she came home a few hours later he seemed quite happy. While she was telling him about the talk she noticed that the dog's food bowl was empty. 'I see you fed Nada,' she remarked. 'That's good.'

'Oh no,' said Harold. 'That was my dinner.'

Their dog, Nada, ate canned pet food. Shocked, Suzanne asked Harold how it had tasted.

'It was very nice, thank you.'

In his final year Harold went downhill very quickly. When he became incontinent it was clear that he would finally have to go to a nursing home. He had been there only a few days when he caught pneumonia. His body was unable to fight the disease and he died in October 1979. He was just short of his 63rd birthday.

By the time Christine had become involved with Animal Liberation, Harold's disease had been too far advanced for him to realise what she was doing. She feels sure he would have supported her. 'He was always gentle and supportive. He would just have said, "Well, if you're sure it's the right thing."'

Christine had loved Harold – loved his decency and his fairness. She had cherished the intimate times they had spent together when she was growing up at home, listening to music, discussing painting and literature. His loss affected her for a long time. 'I locked it away for many years; the whole thing had been so painful I didn't want to think about him or what had happened. It's only in the last ten years that I've been able to think about him without getting upset.'

CHAPTER 5

In July 1980 Christine was invited to Adelaide to attend the annual conference of the Agricultural Women's Bureau. When it had been founded four years previously, Animal Liberation had been viewed by the farming lobby as just a bunch of city-based ratbags. The organisation was now active in three states: NSW, Victoria and Queensland. They had campaigned against battery-chicken farming, intensive piggeries, and cruel farming practices such as de-horning, castrating and mulesing, where the flaps of skin around a sheep's anus are cut away without anaesthetic. As a result, some State governments had begun formulating codes of practice for farm animals; in NSW free-range eggs were available in shops, and the Victorian government was considering following suit. Animal Liberation had also brought about tighter veterinary supervision of the live-sheep trade to the Middle East. The organisation was now regarded by some as a serious threat to the agricultural industry. Christine had become used to being savagely vilified when she addressed farmers' gatherings. Therefore she was not surprised when one of the organisers told her on the way into town from Adelaide airport that there was a great deal of opposition to her being there.

'I don't mind,' she answered blithely, 'I'm used to that.'

The conference was already in progress when they arrived. They quietly took their seats just in time to hear a speech by the South Australian Minister for Agriculture. After talking about the achievements of his department, particularly in selling meat to the Middle East, he went on, 'Before I conclude, I note you have someone from Animal Liberation talking this afternoon. I don't pretend to understand these people, but if all we've heard in the press is true, then I think it's safe to say they're misinformed, and could destroy our livestock industry. The world needs good quality food, with its growing population to feed.'

The minister's talk received robust applause. Christine's hands grew sweaty. She sensed that this was not going to be an easy day. Next at the podium came a representative from the Agricultural Bureau of NSW. He also castigated the name of Animal Liberation, saying that they were already active in NSW, and were highly dangerous.

Sitting in her chair, still incognito, Christine thought, not for the first time, how she wished that people did not have to fight. It was against all that she believed in to be so divisive, and yet that was how it always seemed to end up.

It was time for her to speak. As she stepped up to the microphone a hush filled the room. The president stumbled nervously over her words as she read out her introduction. Two hundred or so unfriendly faces stared up from the auditorium. When Christine recalls that day it is the hostility she remembers most. 'Some I saw had such hatred in their eyes that they listened to nothing I said. An impenetrable barrier had been formed in their minds by their own prejudices, which forbade them to listen to anything which did not correspond to their own limited ideas.

'I'd carefully chosen my talk to emphasise our unity, and I spoke of how much graziers cared about their animals, and that a farmer would go out at night to untangle a sheep from the fence. "So please," I appealed, "let's not consider ourselves as coming from opposite sides. My sister lives in the country, and I understand the problems of the people who live on the land."

'The atmosphere grew increasingly tense. The more I spoke of love and compassion, the more that I appealed for a questioning of the things that were done, and for objective assessment of age-old accepted practices, the colder and harder and more hateful the faces grew. But the more they hated me, the more peace I began to feel within myself so that everything became removed from reality.'

When questions were invited a woman leapt to her feet and began to harangue Christine.

'What right have you got to interfere with country people and their way of life?' she shouted from the back of the room. 'How dare you tell us what to do with our cattle, and how dare you criticise us for being cruel to animals.'

'I don't believe farmers are cruel to animals,' Christine said. 'Only that some traditional practices need to be questioned.'

Another questioner asked her if she was a vegetarian. She replied that she was, but that this did not necessarily imply that she wanted to convert the whole of Australia to vegetarianism. She mentioned St Francis, who had reputedly said,

'The animals are my brothers, and I do not eat my brothers.'

That was the catalyst. A woman jumped up and yelled, 'I move that the Agricultural Women's Bureau disclaims the aims and objects of Animal Liberation, which are totally contrary to those of our bureau, and that the Women's Agricultural Bureau should not have invited Mrs Townend here to speak to us today. She would be better off worrying about the starving millions in Asia than poking her nose into our business.'

While everyone stared open-mouthed and slightly embarrassed, a second woman jumped up and shouted, 'I second the motion.'

The president seemed not to know what to do. Christine returned to her chair. The organiser of the conference, who had been one of those responsible for inviting her, jumped up and said that the motion had to be put, because it had been proposed and seconded. The president therefore asked for a vote, and the motion was passed by a show of hands, by about two-thirds of those present.

The ordeal was not quite over, for somebody else had an even more difficult task to perform. A trembling, nervous woman from one of the country branches had to take the microphone and thank Christine for giving her talk. She read a prepared statement, which had to do with the need for listening to all points of view, and taking account of both sides of the argument. There was a feeble clapping, and she presented Christine with a small gift, which was accepted.

The afternoon session had finished, and the meeting adjourned for tea. As Christine sat a little shocked, a few country women came up to tell her that they were extremely sorry for the events which had transpired, and that they supported and believed in the aims of Animal Liberation.

At last she was able to leave. She was waiting for the lift when she was joined by, of all people, the woman who had moved the motion against her. Her accuser pursed her lips and they stood in silence. The lift arrived and they stepped inside. As they began their descent, for want of anything useful to say, Christine remarked, 'I don't think you like me very much.'

The woman looked at the floor. 'It's not that I don't like you. I just don't think you should have been invited to import Animal Liberation into our State.'

'Don't you think it was good that you people were open-minded?'

'They encourage us to participate in meetings,' she snapped. 'Well I did. I said what I thought.'

The lift reached the ground floor. As they stepped out the woman said bitterly, 'You're a very clever lady, a very clever lady.'

'I'm sorry. I didn't mean to be like that. I don't understand what you mean.'

'Every time we asked a question you never answered us. You never told us what your movement really believes.'

'I didn't understand that was what you wanted. It's a philosophy. You can't reduce a philosophy to a list of dos and don'ts.'

But the woman did not hear her. As she went out the door her final words hung in the air. 'My husband and I have just invested $50,000 in an intensive piggery.'

The Age newspaper had described Christine as 'one of the most hated women in Australia'. One rural newspaper ran a cartoon that said, 'Mules Christine Townend'. Another depicted a demented woman with hair awry holding a placard saying, 'BAN MULESING. BOYCOTT SHEEP PRODUCTS'. Two sheep look on, with one saying to the other, 'It's Ms Townend. They say her brains are fly-blown.'

Despite the stress of being regularly vilified in public, Christine never for a moment considered giving up. 'They were very hard years, very strenuous years, in which I felt constantly criticised and ridiculed by the opposition. Nonetheless, there was a new certainty within me that at last I was doing something useful. The undirected power that had been bouncing about inside like fists in a sack was now directed and effective. I don't think I even questioned why I was doing it. I just thought, this is a job I have to do, and I did it.'

CHAPTER 6

TO MY SISTER, ANNE, ON HER BIRTHDAY

You once gave me your teddy bear and doll
beside the lake,
simply because you loved me.
I could make you do things,
had power over you.
I see you now, staring from the old picture,
round cheeks, round eyes, the pink knitted beret
pulled tightly over your ears,
and we are women with our grown children,
and we love still.
We rode ponies by the sea,
we were one being.
There was no one to hate and interrupt
the one stream of childhood.

You made me laugh so that I could not be closed,
although I would have liked it,
poking faces in Sunday school,
so that I was the punished one,
I the laugher while you, impassive, blue-eyed
watched.

Ever since she was a child Christine's sister Anne had wanted to live in the country. When she finished high school she completed a secretarial course in Sydney. She dabbled half-heartedly in one or two mundane jobs then went on a nine-month tour of Europe with her parents. When she came back she followed her dreams to a job as a governess at Eulo, near Charleville, in Northern Queensland. She loved country life. More governessing jobs followed in the same area, interspersed with stints at droving and as a jillaroo.

She had first met her future husband, Neil Kennedy, when she was seventeen, at Warren in outback NSW. The occasion was a Bachelors and Spinsters ball. Anne was attracted, she recalls, but, despite her glamorous attire of Thai silk dress and long white gloves ending above the elbow, he barely noticed she was alive. They met again three years later at a 'Warren Wolves Wossel' – translation: a party. Again, Anne was attracted, but, as Neil tells it, he thought she was 'a bit prim and proper' for him. When their paths crossed a few weeks later at the 'Ulundi Riot' – a woolshed dance at Ulundi near Coonabarabran, NSW – he evidently saw her in a new light. They married in 1968 when Anne was 21. Neil swept his bride away to the life she had always dreamed of in Coonamble in western NSW.

Coonamble is in wheat, sheep and cattle country, where dead-flat plains stretch to the horizon, and drought and dust and heat will break your heart if you let them. Neil's family had been on the land for six generations in Australia, and for as far back as they could trace before that, in Scotland and Ireland. Neil was lean, sunburned, direct, and capable. He castrated and branded his bulls, mulesed his sheep, and killed them when the household needed meat. He was, if you like, the embodiment of everything that Christine was fighting against. He was not one of your taciturn country men. He had opinions, and he didn't back away from an argument. Whenever the Townends visited there was trouble practically from the moment Christine walked in the door. Neil thought that his sister-in-law knew bugger-all about animals, and that she had a cheek trying to tell country people what they should be doing.

'We were always arguing,' he recalls. 'Our only conversation was about animals. I had a belief that I could persuade her, but I was wrong, I never swayed her one bit.'

Anne was in an awkward position. She loved her sister dearly, but she agreed with her husband that much of Christine's campaign rhetoric was plain wrong.

'Take mulesing. It looks awful but if you'd seen the sheep dying of fly strike out in the paddock and crows picking their eyes out . . . it's done when they're very young and it's one snip. They don't shear the living flesh as the animal liberationists say. It's a little fold of skin. They seem stiff for a little while and next thing they're over drinking from the mother and you'd hardly know anything had happened.'

Anne would tell Chris that she thought she was wrong, and try to leave it at that. Once, at Christine's request, Neil took her with him when he was going to kill a lamb. Christine wrote an account of the experience in her book, *A Voice for the Animals*:

When they were in the yard, and when he had kicked them, and shouted at them, because it was hot, and they did not move as fast as he wanted them to move, and when they were all pressed in terror into a corner, it was just a matter of which of them should die. To my brother-in-law it was a matter of no importance, for he had learnt that life could easily be taken, or lost. But because I had never seen death before, I wanted to beg him to stop, to drive to town to buy ten kilos of vegetarian sausages so that the blood and the dying could be halted.

A few paragraphs on she describes the death scene:

The sheep was hauled down from the ute and lay panting at my brother-in-law's feet. Its eyes were bulging from its head in terror. Its ankles were swollen with rope. It lay unmoving, frozen with apprehension. With a swift pass of the knife over the neck stretched backwards, the sheep died in spasms and jets of its own blood.

On another occasion Neil obligingly showed her how they castrated bulls. She later wrote a graphic description of him wielding 'a rusty knife'. This annoyed him when he read it, as he had performed the operations with a brand new scalpel, but he was most put out by a quote she attributed to him while campaigning against rodeos. Animal Liberation was against the use of flank ropes on rodeo horses to make them buck. Neil was closely involved with his local rodeo. He had spent a long time trying to persuade Christine that there was nothing cruel about the sport. Later, during a visit to Victoria, she quoted her brother-in-law as saying that 'rodeos were a dreadful thing'. The president of the Coonamble Rodeo Committee, Johnny

Lumden, happened to be in Victoria, and heard the remark on the radio. He telephoned Neil straight away. Neil was in the embarrassing situation of having to deny that he had said any such thing.

Such seemingly trivial indiscretions caused trouble in the close and sensitive community of which Anne and Neil were part. They avoided asking friends over when Christine was staying. Despite these difficulties, Christine remains extremely close to her sister, and she has a deep affection for her brother-in-law. She and Jeremy are welcome visitors at Coonamble whenever they are in Australia.

Christine sometimes failed to realise the effect that her single-minded passion for animals had on those close to her. If there was a demonstration happening and she had no one to look after the children, she simply took them with her. Miles and Cameron remember attending numerous demonstrations. In Melbourne, where she was campaigning against live-sheep exports, Cameron once watched wide-eyed as his mother and another Animal Liberationist, Patty Mark, engaged in a heated verbal battle with some burly farmers. When they turned on the TV news after a demonstration he used to wait with dread for his mum or, worse still, him to appear, knowing that he'd probably cop a ribbing from his schoolmates next day. As far as Christine was concerned it was all part of a proper education. As she says, 'In his book *The Extended Circle* Peter Singer argued how initially the family was considered as all-important, and humans beyond and outside the immediate family were seen as "the enemy" or as "other". Then, as civilisation advanced, the circle extended to include the tribe, the city, the nation, and then, beyond human interests, to the needs of the non-human animals and the environment. Of all the lessons

I would have liked my children to understand, it would have been this one. For this reason I tried to take them sometimes on marches, to celebrations, to demonstrations, on bushwalks, to see logged forests, and, yes, to see that chicken slaughterhouse, so that they could learn about individual responsibility and duties, about the injustices which needed to be redressed. I'm sad to see the way that children learn from their parents' example that consumerism, comfort, home-entertainment rooms and three cars are more important than giving some time, some compassion, some care to uplifting the downtrodden of this world, be it human, animal or forest.'

In high school Miles and Cameron both attended Shore, Jeremy's old private school. Cameron was apprehensive as there were a large number of rural boarders. As it happened, they did not give him an unduly hard time, although the school made him remove the SAVE THE FRANKLIN and ANIMAL LIBERATION stickers from his suitcase. Cameron got on well at Shore, but Miles was not so happy, not because of his mother's activities, it was just that he was a more sensitive and creative boy, and hated Shore's rigid approach. He pleaded with his parents to go somewhere else. After a year he moved to SCECGS Redlands, where he was much happier.

There was never any shortage of pets in the Townend household. There were always a few rescued dogs and cats – once even a pig – in the back yard. Sooner or later they always found new homes. Christine could never leave an animal that was sick or lost. Once when the family was driving on a back road near Coonamble they came upon an injured kangaroo that had been hit by a truck. They put it in the car and took it to

Neil, who ended its suffering with a rifle bullet.

What with Christine's activism and Jeremy's job, the Townends crammed a lot into their lives. Jeremy's law firm acted for some big property developers. The Eighties was a heady era. The economy was booming, banks were lending money recklessly, and fortunes were being made. Jeremy was the legal adviser to some multi-million-dollar developments. He often arrived at work at 7.30 in the morning and might not get home until eight at night – later if there was a big deal on. Because of the amounts of money involved it was stressful, exacting work, with no room for mistakes. He sometimes woke at four a.m. and paced the floor until daylight, worrying about work. When he arrived home in the evening he was usually exhausted and talked out. All he wanted to do was collapse quietly into a comfortable chair.

Christine travelled interstate frequently to attend conferences. They rarely offered to pay her expenses. Jeremy grumbled once or twice about how much it was costing them, but money was never a big issue – he was more unhappy about having to have take-away dinners with the boys when Christine was away. Many of the local meetings that she had to attend took place at night. She would often leave the house before Jeremy arrived home from work. There were times when they barely had a conversation for days on end.

It sometimes seemed as though Animal Liberation had taken over their lives. The media called at all hours. On some days the phone would start ringing at eight in the morning, and go on until 10.30 at night. Jeremy and Christine bickered about whether they should answer it. If it was after nine p.m. she would not want to pick up, but Jeremy scolded her that you could never not answer a phone.

In the midst of all this they had to bring up two lively young boys. In adulthood Miles and Cameron have different views about their childhood. As a child Cameron was never greatly bothered about his mother's busy life. In his late teens he left home to drive around Australia on a surfing safari. Perhaps he and his mates were discussing their parents at some stage, and awarded Christine a tick, because out of the blue one day he called her from somewhere in Western Australia to tell her he loved her and was proud of what she was doing. Miles, on the other hand, has always felt resentful about the missed school functions, her trips to India, the shaved hair, her maddening differences to normal mothers.

Christine worried about balancing her passion for animals with her responsibilities as a mother. She was strengthened by a conversation she had with one of Jeremy's lawyer friends, Colin Ferguson, who was very active in the conservation movement. Ferguson argued that far from being detrimental to their children, the time they put into these causes was for their good, because it was helping shape a better world.

Christine had first tried her hand at political lobbying shortly after joining the Colong Committee. The Committee had been involved in a campaign to turn Washpool, in the Gibraltar Ranges west of Grafton, into a national park, to prevent it from being logged. She arranged for a meeting with an adviser to the Minister for Land and Environment. It was a dispiriting introduction into how politics work. Christine had the idea that all she needed to do was point out how terrible logging was, and a change in policy would surely follow. Instead, the adviser had patronised her and treated her as if she was mentally deficient. 'This is a democracy,' he lectured. 'A democracy can't afford the luxury of indulging a small minority group. You want the place left as a wilderness? Well, who's going to see it then?'

In 1977, when the Australian Democrats had been formed as an antidote to the two major political parties, Christine stood for the seat of Grayndler. For a few frantic weeks she knocked on doors, handed out leaflets and made speeches. When the election was held she had garnered seven per cent of the vote. Her candidature helped elect Colin Mason to the Senate.

She went on to work briefly as an adviser to Don Chipp, who had founded the Democrats, helping shape the party's policy on animal welfare. In 1982 Senator Chip successfully called for a Senate select inquiry into animal welfare in Australia. The following year Christine stood, unsuccessfully, in the number-three position on the Australian Democrats' Senate ticket. She also found time to study for an arts degree at Macquarie University, majoring in politics.

While all this was going on she continued to lobby politicians, because, 'Animals have no votes. They're voiceless. They desperately need people to fight on their behalf.'

In those days she thought that politicians of goodwill could change the world. With the passing of time she has become more and more disillusioned. 'I don't think our political process works satisfactorily at all. I think the traditional parties, Liberal and Labour, are riddled with processes where you can't become a politician until you've worked your way through the ranks, and because of that selection process we simply don't get the best people. There must be some other way. For example, the majority of people don't want to eat battery eggs, they don't want to see pigs have their tails chopped off, or kept in iron crates all their lives, they don't want sheep mulesed, so why does it go on? Because the majority of people don't have the political power to change things.'

While the day-to-day battles were being fought she wrote a series of books about animal rights. *In Defence of Living Things* was published in 1980. It tackled the whole range of issues which Animal Liberation was fighting. There were chapters on factory farming, laboratory animals, hunting, rodeos and the destruction of the wilderness. In 1981 *A Voice for the Animals* was published, which was a history of Animal Liberation to that date. This was followed in 1985 by *Pulling the Wool*, a critical look at the wool industry, with a foreword by Justice Michael Kirby.

In 1978, two years to the day after Christine had founded Animal Liberation, a branch had opened in Melbourne, started by a local activist, Patty Mark. Peter Singer had returned from the United States where he had been a professor of philosophy. During a visit to Melbourne, Christine stayed with Peter and his wife Renata at their century-old Hawthorn home. They discussed what to do about unifying the numerous small groups around the country, each fighting their own battle for animal rights. They thought the fight could be more effective if they spoke with one voice. Talking late into the night, Christine and Peter decided to set up the Australian Federation of Animal Societies. Its founding in 1980 brought together under one banner 55 organisations involved in animal protection. Peter Singer was the first president, while Christine was secretary. With their involvement, AFAS grew rapidly until it soon had branches in all States. It is known today as Animals Australia. Christine is an honorary life member.

CHAPTER 7

In 1989 Christine received a phone call from a visiting animal-rights campaigner from India. Professor Ramaswami said he wished to speak to her about conditions in slaughter-houses in his country. She invited him to dinner that evening. Christine and Jeremy had by now moved to Gordon, another north-shore suburb. Miles had recently married and Cameron, after spending a year travelling around Australia, was studying coastal management at Lismore in northern NSW.

Jeremy arrived home from the office, exhausted as usual, to find Christine and a plump Indian man with long white hair and a white beard poring over photographs of animals being slaughtered.

'Would you like a beer?' said Jeremy.

'I am Brahmin, and Brahmins don't drink. But sometimes it is good to keep company so I will take whisky.'

Warily, Jeremy made conversation while Christine prepared

a vegetarian meal. Professor Ramaswami told him that he had founded an organisation in India to improve the design of bullock carts and to change cruel slaughtering practices. 'I have invited your wife to visit our family and to stay with us, and I will show her the slaughterhouses,' Professor Ramaswami said.

'I see,' Jeremy replied.

At the airport in Bangalore there was a man waving a placard which said, INDIAN HUMAN AND ANIMAL TECHNO-LOGY CENTRE. Christine went up to him, and he ushered her into the back of a large, comfortable car. Jeremy had been grim when she left Australia, and during the flight she had worried over a sense of impending marital crisis. 'I hated my pushing, storming self, which was always demanding and always being given something, so that everyone was serving me, but I never served anyone else.'

As she drove through the chaotic traffic her worries were submerged by the sights and smells of India. She felt once again the sense that she was where she belonged. Professor Ramaswami lived in a three-storey house in a well-to-do suburb. She removed her shoes and was ushered indoors to his study by a servant. The professor, looking like a cross between Santa Claus and a guru, sat behind a large desk. Speaking through a small microphone he welcomed her in a whisper. 'I use this microphone,' he explained, 'because the doctor says I'm losing my voice through shouting too much at everyone. I am trying to speak softly.'

The professor said that he planned a trip to Kerala, one of two states in India where it was legal to slaughter cattle. 'These Muslim slaughterers are very backward, uneducated people,' he said, with his eyes half-closed. 'The father teaches the son. They go with knife to the slaughterhouse. They do not like intermarrying with other occupations.'

'Are they a caste? Some writers say there's caste among the Muslims of India as well as among the Hindus?'

'They are seen to be low, like the sweeper caste, called untouchable because they handle the dead bodies and the filth.'

'Have you visited many slaughterhouses?' Christine asked.

'I have never visited any. I have a heart condition. But you can see these slaughterhouses, and go back to your country, and try to find assistance to have the situation changed.'

The professor handed Christine a red booklet. On the cover was a photograph of a white cow having its head twisted backwards over its neck.

'Why are they doing that?' she asked.

'Casting. You see, we cannot have pre-stunning introduced in this country. Therefore, animals must be pulled down while they're fully conscious. I can't tell you the things these poor animals suffer.'

'Is this because the Muslims do the butchering, and they only want to kill halal?'

'You're right. The Indian Muslims believe it's contrary to the Koran for the animal to be stunned before it's killed, and meat which is stunned is forbidden. The Muslims are the butchers, because no Hindu wants to slaughter animals. It's a very low job. They threaten to riot every time the Hindu managers try to introduce pre-stunning.

'Secondly, the Jain people, who are against all violence, do not want stunning introduced because they think if animals are killed more hygienically and more humanely, more people will buy the meat, and they want India to be vegetarian.'

'It must be a very difficult campaign then,' Christine said.

'With your auspicious presence, you will help us. I'm just a poor professor doing my duty, my karma yoga. Through work I will find union with God. Through my duty and because of the public ridicule I receive in trying to help animals, I will be speedily lifted.'

'And in that photo, why are they killing a cow? I thought cows were protected?'

'Cow is mother. She gives milk, she gives dung for fuel, and she gives the bullock, which provides the draught animal power. We worship cow, because she helped us build civilisation. Where would we Indians be without the cow? Europeans don't eat horses or dogs. We Hindus don't eat cows. But I am ashamed to say in Kerala and West Bengal it is permitted to kill cow and bullock. These are communist states. They say they are secular.'

Christine liked this odd little man with his gentle manner and his weary sense of despair. 'How did you first become involved in something so gruesome and difficult?'

'I was working for the United Nations as a consultant on appropriate technology. The bullock cart is an example of this. I began to realise the bullock suffers terribly. It is whipped, it is underfed, it is worked day and night, even when very tired. The wooden yoke is so badly designed, and presses on the neck, causing calluses and galls and cancers. The old wooden wheels do not roll well, and cause the animal further exhaustion when it has to turn. It is poor economics. The bullock owners do not get the return for their animal. I wanted to do something for the 80 million draught animals of India and their owners, so I started this organisation.'

After they had spoken for a while longer, the professor's wife, Rajan, appeared at the top of the steps. She was slim and tranquil with straight black hair made up in a bun. 'It is very kind of you to have a stranger to stay,' Christine said.

'We have many people to stay,' she replied resignedly, as though she would have liked to have refused, but could not disobey the professor. 'My husband built this house with seven bathrooms and seven bedrooms so he could accommodate travellers who wanted to learn about Indian philosophy.'

In the evening Professor Ramaswami drove through the streets, cursing the traffic, to his local temple. Small coloured lights illuminated the trees, all of which had simple altars beneath them in recognition of their sacredness. Outside the temple, under an open roof, a family had gathered. A priest in white robes, with his head smeared with ash, burnt sandalwood and incense while chanting prayers for them.

'Every detail of this ceremony is laid down in the Vedas,' the professor explained. 'If it is not performed exactly, it is said it won't work. For me, these rites are not necessary. It's the heart which counts.'

Christine watched the family sitting under a coloured awning, while a priest put offerings of coconut and lighted incense in front of an altar and began to chant. 'Actually, I know that man,' the professor said. 'He's a cabinet minister.'

It all seemed bizarre. Here she was watching a cabinet minister who made decisions about the governance of a great sub-continent, and who also believed that the chanting and placement of objects in certain positions was auspicious and necessary.

Two nights later they left Bangalore to drive to Cochin. The professor had bought a new car, a Contessa, with air-conditioning.

He said his son in America had sent him the money. He had been planning to leave in the morning, but the car had refused to start when he took delivery from the showroom. Later, when he did drive it back to his house, the steering wheel fell off, necessitating further rearrangements, some angry phone calls, and long stretches of waiting, during which Christine read some of his many treatises on draught-animal power. Finally they left in the new car, with a young, excessively enthusiastic driver travelling at top speed on the national highway between Bangalore and Mysore.

'These people do not have any idea of caution,' the professor said resignedly, as the car narrowly missed wandering animals, children, and roadside vegetable stalls. There were bullock carts that moved along the side of the road, and trucks painted in bright patterns and designs, which drove on the wrong side in order to overtake slower vehicles.

'These trucks overturn all the time,' Rajan said, as they passed the fourth smoking vehicle, its wheels spinning in the air.

They drove through villages with whitewashed houses and thatched roofs. There were women carrying water in earthenware pitchers on their heads. And all along the highway there were cattle, roped together by the neck, walking for two hundred kilometres to Kerala, where cows could be legally killed.

At dawn Christine went to the slaughterhouse. There was a shed divided into pens, in each of which about six to eight cattle were tethered. There were some young hybrid animals with jersey blood, and there was a strong young buffalo that bellowed in pain. He had been cast in order to pull him down to the floor so that his throat was accessible, and was struggling to stand up, although his legs were bound.

To cast the animal, two men pulled on ropes round its leg, while another man inserted his fingers into the nostrils, and jerked the head backwards over the shoulder. Another man twisted and pulled the tail, which was so mashed and broken it was like a twisted rag.

When the casters had pulled down the cattle, they would call to the slaughterer. This meant that some animals lay for a long time after casting before being killed. They lay in a state of extreme fear because they saw, heard and smelled their companions being killed all around them. Their eyes started and they defecated and urinated where they lay.

When the slaughterer was ready the casters stretched back the head roughly, then he swiftly cut a deep slash under the chin. The animal continued to gasp for breath, and the air gushed down the trachea, creating a hollow, moaning gurgle. This sound of dying went on for more than a minute until the cow's eyes fixed in death, and the head fell back.

Everywhere there were animals lying cast, or struggling and moaning as they were pulled down, or bleeding to death with twisted heads, blood beating from their throats, sides heaving as they struggled to fill their lungs with air. A dying cow blinked blood from her eye.

In another room sheep and goats were being slaughtered. The animals were dragged from outside with a rope round the neck. The goats were placed upside down onto a raised cement block by grabbing two legs and then throwing the animals down. They bleated and struggled, even while their throats were being cut. Then, while they were still gargling with life, they were thrown onto a pile of dead and dying animals. They

would thrash about, their eyes wild and deep, until death inter-
vened, and their heads fell back, and their lungs stopped
labouring.

When Christine had seen enough she said to the manager
that she would go. There was a car waiting outside, which the
professor had provided. The car was safe and padded. You
could slam the door and hide inside, and the killing was somewhere else. In Australia she had seen pigs slaughtered by
sticking a knife in the heart; she had seen frightened cattle
rolling their eyes as they were carried along a conveyor belt
towards their destruction; she had seen sheep electrocuted
between the ears in order to render them insensible to slaughter; she had visited ships where Australian sheep were packed
three to a square metre to endure the three-week journey to the
Middle East; she had seen hens crowded into battery cages,
and pigs kept most of their lives behind iron bars. But now she
began to understand the massive hidden killing which was
happening all over the world. She had not thought until then
about the significance to humanity of this calculated, callous
war between two kingdoms of nature, with one the permanent
victim and the other the eternal aggressor. The cattle, especially, touched her heart. The whipping, the shouting, the
pulling and pushing toward the noise and smell of blood, the
moans and grunts of dying, bleeding, shattered, ripped creatures – all this they meekly endured with their great, confused,
helpless, staring eyes. If they had fought or argued it might
have been easier, but their trust and their misery at human
betrayal seemed to render them immobile. They raised no
protest, no questioning voice. And they almost seemed to
redeem whatever was done to them by their soft meditative
eyes that were the gentle eyes of herbivores who had never

killed, never warred, never tortured; who had worked and served patiently and unquestioningly under the yoke that galled and marred. They were driven and whipped, always hungry, usually thirsty, always tired. Yet at the end of all this they were killed, without having been thanked once, without even one touch of love. She wondered if perhaps somewhere in a field, secretly, a peasant farmer had embraced those sweet-smelling necks for one last time. Perhaps once they had been loved, had been thanked, had known compassion. 'If I could have asked one thing it would have been that someone somewhere had loved them, that my own love could assuage a lifetime of human indifference. I loved them as deeply as it was possible for any person to love. They were my creatures, of me, my beloved animals, my God.'

At the hotel she met the professor and Rajan. They sat at a table in the dining room and ate idli and orange roast bananas and spinach curry and *pakora*. Christine picked at the food but she could not shake the images she had just witnessed.

'Why are you so glum?' the professor asked.

'I never imagined . . .'

'Even if you do something small it will help. Lord Buddha said, "Better to light one small candle, than to complain about the darkness."'

'But it's going to be difficult to help from another country.'

'We don't know our destiny,' he said.

'What do you think is my destiny?'

'To help animals.'

Jeremy came to meet her at the airport. While people wept and fell into each other's arms all around them, they greeted each other with their usual restraint. They were like old friends, where the value of years has more worth than any differences between them. But they were wary. Jeremy did not yet know what new fancies Christine may have seized upon while she was away.

'I took heaps of photographs,' she said.

'That's good. I hope you'll settle down now.'

The steering wheel did not fall off the car. At home the electrical appliances worked; water flowed from the taps; you could turn a switch and the hotplate would glow instantly. The house was spotless, the garden orderly and beautiful.

She rang her mother. 'You must appreciate your lovely home, dear,' said Suzanne, 'after all that sadness and poverty.' Sensitive to every nuance, Christine imagined she detected a veiled note of accusation. She felt that she could not talk to her mother or to anyone else about what she had seen. Everything in Australia seemed as before, except that nothing was, nor could it ever be again. As she immersed herself once more in work she was nagged by persistent images of India. She felt spiritually connected to the subcontinent. She longed for some reason or sign that she should return.

CHAPTER 8

Christine had written a treatment for a television series about the relationship between animals and humans. A producer showed interest and, in July 1988, five months after returning from India, she and Jeremy travelled to England for discussions with the famous zoologist and television presenter Desmond Morris.

Jeremy could only stay a week in London before he had to return home to work. Part of that time Christine spent lobbying British MPs. She had an idea that she might be able to persuade the British Parliament to boycott Australian wool, as mulesing was contrary to Britain's 'Protection of Animals Act' – a hopeless cause, as she now acknowledges. 'I met a few British parliamentarians who must have thought I was totally mad, and of course it was a complete waste of time.'

After Jeremy had left for Australia, Christine went to Morris's home in Oxford. Morris, a loud, charismatic, sexist charmer, took her for a drive through the countryside in his Rolls-Royce. 'My mother wanted to ride in the world's most expensive car,' he declared, 'so I bought it.'

Christine, the producer and Morris spent a week in the great zoologist's heritage house surrounded by artefacts from ancient civilisations, writing a treatment and discussing the program. It was eventually made as a three-part series but, despite them using Christine's ideas, she ended up having no part in the production.

For someone who is normally so stubborn and with such a highly developed sense of injustice, her reaction to losing control of the project was remarkably mild. Although legal avenues were open to her, she simply shrugged the loss aside. Her interest in the TV series by then had been eclipsed by two meetings which were far more significant in her mind. Friends at the animal-welfare movement in London had suggested that she get in touch with two people who had connections to India.

Crystal Rogers, a woman in her eighties, was running an animal shelter in Rajasthan. Hers was a remarkable story. During the Second World War she had been working in a library close to an RAF base in England. She had fallen in love with a Canadian pilot, Flight Sergeant Jim Pepper. The war was taking a terrible toll on the young men who flew out every night on operations over enemy territory. Every time Jim took off, Crystal was in a state of high anxiety until he returned. The night he did not come back she had not even known that he was flying. She thought he had the weekend off. Instead he had been ordered out at the last minute. A pilot friend broke the news to her that he was missing.

Crystal never got over losing Jim. He was her first and only love. After the war ended she decided to emigrate to New

Zealand to start a new life. On her way there by ship she stopped to visit friends in India. As she wrote in her biography *Mad Dogs and an Englishwoman*, she saw sights which shocked her to the core: a sick horse having its eyes picked out by crows; a street dog hobbling about with a broken leg; performing monkeys and bears; working animals half-starved and exhausted, being flogged along by their owners. She decided there and then to do something about it.

She started an animal shelter in New Delhi, and ran it for many years until she had a falling-out with the trustees. She then moved to Jaipur in Rajasthan where, with a faithful Indian family who had worked with her in Delhi, the Prasads, and practically no money, she founded a new shelter. It was called Help in Suffering.

In Jaipur, as in Delhi, Crystal became well-known for her eccentricities. She preferred to be called Mishy, 'as Crystal makes me sound like a film star'. Having no transport of her own she would commandeer rickshaws or taxis to carry injured dogs, cats, even goats or donkeys to the shelter. She also took in destitute humans. Two legs or four, it made no difference to her: if they were in need she would do all that she could to help. All the money that she raised back in Europe went to her patients. She herself lived in utter poverty, barely bothering to eat or attend to the infirmities that old age brought upon her.

One of Mishy's chief sources of funding was a Swiss animal-welfare organisation, Animaux-Secours. Its president, Janine Vogler, wrote in one of her newsletters an account of her first meeting with Mishy in 1983:

After crossing Durgapura, a hectic town of little shops along the very busy road leading to the airport, our motor rickshaw turned into a small road which, after some bumps, abruptly plunged into a ravine. There at the bottom two donkeys were happily rolling in the dust, their legs upwards. After endless minutes of blowing the horn and shouting a middle-aged lady suddenly appeared on the other side of the ravine. She unexpectedly inserted two fingers into her mouth to produce the shrillest whistle I ever heard, with an immediate result: the two donkeys at once leaped towards her. Our rickshaw followed them to the ramshackle heap of crumbling farm buildings that was at this time the headquarters of Help in Suffering. Some thirty human beings and countless species of animals crowded in it and we discovered with horrified amazement that the two lucky donkeys were the only 'whole' creatures of the lot. All the rest had something missing: a paw or two, one ear (and an ass had none left, both clipped off as punishment for stealing vegetables at a market stall), a leg or an arm (a handsome young man had lost his four limbs in a train accident). There was a blind old man patting a completely hairless cat, a boy coughing hard with TB, holding on his shoulder a tiny monkey with a burnt face, and a cancerous Ramon with practically no face at all. My son, who accompanied me on this trip, uttered what I was thinking: 'C'est la cour des miracles'.

All this misery was packed tight into the dilapidated buildings, humans and animals together to keep warm during the cold Rajasthan nights, and a few army tents had been lent to provide some more shelter.

When Christine called Mishy in London she sounded flustered. Some money meant for the shelter had gone astray, and she was on her way to the bank to try to sort out the muddle.

'I'm frightfully worried about it, and terribly busy,' she said. 'We must meet at the bank.'

Christine cannot remember where the bank was, but there is no forgetting Mishy. She was thin and wiry with a thatch of unruly, greyish hair. She was wearing badly stretched slacks and a ribbed, knitted jumper. 'Mishy had no money,' Christine recalls. 'She didn't care about money, she lived like a Buddhist monk. She was perfectly nice to us and I was rather in awe of her reputation.'

They sat on a bench seat in the bank and discussed the animals of India. Speaking in an imperious upper-class accent, in a tone that brooked no nonsense, Mishy told her all about Help in Suffering. Although she didn't say so directly, it was apparent that she was becoming too old and frail to manage the place. In fact, even as they spoke, Help in Suffering was at a crisis point, but Mishy made no mention of it then. Much later she told Christine, 'When I first met you I never thought you'd be interested in animals, you were standing there looking frightfully glamorous and I didn't think you'd be at all interested in coming to India, so I didn't ever broach the subject.'

Before parting they exchanged addresses and agreed to keep in touch.

During that same stay in London Christine met the Director (India) for the World Society for the Protection of Animals, Annabella Singh. An Englishwoman, Annabella had been the second wife of the Maharana – king of kings – of Udaipur. They had met when she was a twenty-year-old student on a visit to a wealthy Indian college. Annabella had ordered a taxi to take her back to her hotel, but, as is often the way in India, it had not arrived. A handsome Indian in a gleaming Mercedes had offered a lift. He was the Maharana, and despite a twenty-year difference in their ages, they had fallen in love and married.

When Christine met Annabella she had been widowed for several years and living most of the time in London. She had long been campaigning for more humane methods in the slaughterhouses. They met in Annabella's flat for an Indian lunch of rice, sweet-scented vegetables, dhal, curd and chapati. They liked one another immediately, and the lunch ended with Annabella inviting Christine to join her on a field trip she was planning to India.

In January 1989, they met in Bombay, and together inspected several slaughterhouses. Christine was assailed by the same charnel-house horrors that she had seen on her previous visit, and suffered the same disappointments. Nothing had changed.

Since her first trip to India Christine had kept up a regular correspondence with Diana, the Frenchwoman whom she had met in Pondicherry. She consulted her not only about spiritual matters but about decisions to do with daily life. Diana had encouraged her to join the Colong Committee. She herself had eventually gone back to France and, in 1991, a letter was returned marked *décédé* – deceased.

Christine had known Diana face-to-face for only a couple of months. Most of their relationship had been conducted via letters. Yet the enigmatic little Frenchwoman had profoundly influenced her life. 'What remained after her death, and still remains today, is a great and all-consuming love and gratitude for all the confidence she instilled in me.'

Not long after Diana's last letter was returned, a friend who had lived in Auroville introduced Christine to someone who had spent time with her in France before she died. She told Christine that Diana had admitted herself to hospital and died of natural causes.

'I told this woman that I had often wanted to visit Diana again,' says Christine. 'But when I asked her she had declined. This friend said that sometimes the teacher wanted the disciple to be independent. Somehow this conversation helped me to adjust to the reality that there would be no more communication with Diana.'

Despite her long correspondence with Diana, the question Christine had first asked her kindergarten teacher – 'Why are we here?' – had continued to trouble her all her life. For years her reading had consisted almost entirely of books about animals or spiritualism. She had studied the long history of spiritual enquiry which had originated in India thousands of years ago, when great sages were said to have taught the ancient wisdom that was later recorded by their disciples in the Vedas and the Upanishads. Historians thought they were at least 5,000 years old.

Tradition had it that when the Aryan people swept down into India, perhaps from Europe, and established a sophisticated civilisation in the Indus Valley, these great sages came from the Himalayas, where they lived in retreat passing on their understanding of life to those who would carry it down through the ages. Despite the pollution, the crush of traffic, the chase for material well-being among the affluent middle-class of India, this spirituality still existed. It was not to be found with the fake gurus who stood up before adoring, swaying fans, but rather with true 'realised beings' such as

Diana, who never proclaimed themselves, but who lived quietly, sharing their knowledge with those who came to enquire.

Before Christine had left India Diana told her about another so-called 'realised being', Vimala Thakar, who lived in Mount Abu in the Aravalli Hills in Rajasthan. Having read some of Vimala's books, Christine had become intrigued by her teaching. Vimala held that in order to reach spiritual fulfilment one needed to pass beyond the babble and clutter of everyday life, and enter what she called the 'state of silence'. To enter this state one needed to still one's constant thoughts and block out physical stimulus. Having a few days still to spend in India before she was due to meet Jeremy in Hong Kong for a week's holiday, Christine decided to go to Mount Abu.

Christine boarded a train in Ahmedabad. She pulled up the wooden slatted shutter and stared out the window at the earth of Mother India. There were clusters of small brick houses with corrugated iron roofs weighted down with rocks. There were three camels harnessed to carts loaded with firewood, their heads thrust proudly upward as they loped forwards. There was the golden light, which belonged only to India, draping and saturating everything. The train rocked and whistled. It slowed, sped up and slowed again. The sound of voices could be heard in other compartments when it stopped, for no apparent reason, in the midst of fields.

As the hours passed she continued staring out the window as a lover stares ceaselessly at the object of love. They passed an ancient white palace with fortressed walls overlooking a shrivelled river which was mostly sand. On the opposite bank, confronting it rudely, was a power plant with towering cement chimneys, belching grey clouds of pollution. Underneath there was a city of hessian tents supported by sticks. Everything was in total contradiction.

In the afternoon the train stopped at Abu Road, from where a bus wound up into the hills to the town of Mount Abu. After finding a hotel room with a clean toilet and shower, she went for a walk. There were rows of shops beside narrow winding lanes where merchants urged her to come in and look. While standing outside a shop a guide approached her. 'Do you want to see temples on the hills, Madam? I can show you.'

'Have you heard of Vimala Thakar?' Christine asked. 'She writes books. She has travelled the world lecturing on spiritual subjects. Do you know of her?'

It seemed unlikely that he would know what she was talking about. He stood for a while without speaking – an old man with a moustache and beard and a straight back. Finally he said, 'She lives in a house on the hill.'

'Would she talk to me?'

'She speaks to many peoples.'

He led her through winding lanes until they came to a house with a high fence and a gate. He opened the gate and they went through a garden and up a stairway to a verandah on which sat two women.

Christine asked the older of the two women, 'Are you Vimala Thakar?' Flustered, feeling as if she was an intruder, she stumbled on, 'I don't know what to call you or whether it is all right to be here.'

'Yes, it's all right,' the woman said. 'I am Vimala. Please sit. How can I help you?'

'I read your books, and I wanted to see you to ask about meditation.'

Vimala waited and said nothing.

'I had a whole lot of questions, but I can't think of any of them,' Christine said. 'I've been to the slaughterhouses. It's the most terrible thing.'

'Why did you go to the slaughterhouses, dear?' Vimala asked, as though she wished to give Christine time to pull herself together. But the more she tried the more flustered she became.

'There's an Indian, Professor Ramaswami . . . he's campaigning to have the transport and slaughter of animals improved. He asked me to help. He took me and showed me . . .'

Christine began to cry, because the love which emanated from Vimala was mixed with all the hate, the blood, the violence. All the tears which she had not shed suddenly began to flow uncontrollably, and she could not stop. Vimala just sat, quite blissfully and serenely. Finally, when the crying had finished, Vimala spoke.

'You shed tears for the state of the world.' She paused for a long moment. 'My tears have dried, but your tears have not yet dried. When I was young I campaigned against the cruelty of the slaughterhouse. I know exactly how you feel. It is caused by religion. Religion is the root cause. But you can do something. You can fight for change.'

'But it's so entrenched, and I don't live in India.'

There was more silence, which seemed never to end. Then Vimala said, 'You will return to India to work for animals.'

Christine did not answer. She could no longer speak. Everything seemed glorious.

'I've read your books,' she said when she was able. 'I've tried to observe myself but I can't control the thoughts.'

Vimala was again silent for a long time before replying. 'There are three stages. You see, once you were a beautiful young woman. Now you are older. First you watch yourself, and then this watching will melt into the state of observation. The thoughts will melt away, and you will enter the Silence. In the state of Silence many energies are activated. It is like growing older. It happens gradually.'

Christine did not understand at all. She felt confused. There were many things she wanted to ask, but none of them seemed important right now. She said, 'Well, I should go.'

Again there was a long silence.

'Well, I will go,' she repeated. Flustered, she left Vimala's presence and stumbled back down the hill.

Back in her hotel room Christine felt that the meeting had been a failure. She thought she had behaved stupidly by crying, and that Vimala had seemed cold and unresponsive. She did not realise then that this was the beginning of a strong pupil/ teacher relationship which has endured to the present day. In the following years she would visit Vimala again and again, becoming so conversant with her teaching that she wrote a book about it, *The Hidden Master*.[1]

While Jeremy had no interest in spiritual matters, he was always tolerant and supportive of Christine. Many of their friends were puzzled by her obsession with spiritual enquiry, but to her the need was clear. 'The important thing is, it becomes obvious once one starts to look at the workings of one's own consciousness and one's own mind that there's more than just consciousness. There's something behind and greater. Unless one can meet with someone who has experienced

---

[1] *The Hidden Master* published by Motilal Banarsidass Publisher PVT Ltd, Delhi, India.

another dimension, a leap in consciousness, a quantum jump, an "inner revolution", as Vimala calls it, or "enlightenment", as Buddhists have called it, unless one can meet such a person and understand that it's practically possible for all human beings to achieve such a state, you are really alone and isolated and there's no inspiration or teaching or guidance to help you along the way.'

Vimala had told Christine that in order to get in touch with 'enlightenment' she should begin with 'self observation'. This sounded so simple that it almost seemed ludicrous. 'How could it be,' she thought, 'that watching myself could ever lead to anything at all useful?' But this was what Vimala had said, and if she was to become a *sadakha*, an enquirer, she had to use the process which Vimala had recommended.

A few weeks after returning from India, Christine took leave from Animal Liberation and moved alone into a rented fibro cottage in Leura in the Blue Mountains west of Sydney. She had no idea what 'enlightenment' was, nor how it was achieved, nor what process it involved. All she knew was that she had to meditate to bring it about.

Sitting on her black Zen cushion from daybreak until dusk she tried to do as Vimala had instructed. 'I endured much rest-lessness, much confusion, and sometimes even fear and terror filled my mind. At other times the thoughts seemed to invade my mind so surreptitiously that I didn't even realise that I had stopped observing myself, and was absorbed in some other reverie. Sometimes I thought, What am I doing sitting here? This is utter madness! If I said to anyone, I'm sitting for two weeks trying to watch myself, they'd think I was crazy.'

Fourteen years and many retreats later, Christine is able to describe the process more clearly:

'One puts one's consciousness above one's head. You try to observe yourself by being above yourself, and that includes not only observing what you're doing at any minute but observing every thought that passes through your mind. At a certain moment if you go on doing that for long enough you'll finally be able to observe the thoughts as something outside, and then this extraordinary jump, which is a dimensional shift that is a really completely different way of perceiving, just suddenly happens. You can observe yourself and stop the thoughts in this way. That part of it is a huge effort. One's fighting with one's own mind if you like, and anything that involves your mind is an effort. There were moments of panic and at times it's even scary. You know how there's a moment between the time when you wake up and you don't know where you are? – that happens. You stop being Christine any more and you start looking at the world as you really are, not through this Christine thing but as a transcendental being. What you really are looks at the world.

'The first time it ever happened was in Leura. At first it's such an overpowering experience because it hasn't happened to you before. It's like being on a drug maybe. I think that's what Vimala calls "Silence" – a removed sort of feeling – but then in that state something very amazing happens. A person suddenly becomes aware of this pouring down of love. It doesn't come from inside, it comes from outside and it's everywhere. It permeates everything. You only have to be aware of it and it's pouring down and everything that happens is because of this love. What Vimala calls "Desire".'

One has to ask, 'Was this getting in touch with God?'

'You can't say that because it was always there. There was no ever getting in touch, but what you could say is you finally tuned yourself into what was always there. It's not as though you became anything different, it's just that you understood finally what you are. And it therefore became blissful. I think that's what Vimala and Diana could give.

'There were times in my life before I met Diana and Vimala when I thought I was going crazy, because I was having a lot of experiences which were unexplainable to myself, and I couldn't find what they were except in spiritual books. After having met these two people who had resolved this in their lives and who were at peace and who had come to understand the real source of being and life and existence, then I was able to realise I wasn't actually mad and it wasn't abnormal; I was mostly normal, and the other people who were just interested in buying a new car or getting a new carpet or careers, they were the ones who weren't normal, they were the ones who had made the mistake, they were the ones who were thinking this world is a material world and we have to build a material life with material comforts and material satisfactions, when in fact that's not what our world is at all, it's in a way a passing theme, and these two people have shown me the reality of life.'

CHAPTER 9

In 1990 Christine and Jeremy travelled to Switzerland to attend a conference of the World Society for the Protection of Animals, of which she was an Advisory Director. Among the delegates was Christine's friend Annabella Singh. After it ended they had been invited to stay in Geneva with a fellow animal-rights campaigner with whom Christine had corresponded but had never met. Janine Vogler, the president of Animaux-Secours, had known Annabella for many years; she had stayed with her in the palace in Udaipur when she was married to the Maharana, and they had campaigned together for animal rights.

Annabella arranged a dinner party at a restaurant attended by a who's-who of the animal-welfare world. It was hardly an auspicious beginning. The main course was a rich Swiss fondue of cheese laced with Kirsch. That night, when Christine and Jeremy went back to stay at Janine's house, Christine was violently ill. There was one bathroom which was right next door to their hosts' bedroom. She spent half the night vomiting noisily into the toilet.

The next day Janine, brushing aside Christine's apologies, took them to see her animal shelter, and to walk in the mountains near the city. After her first visit to India in 1983 Janine had continued to be one of the main sources of funding for Help in Suffering in India. As they went along she recounted a long story about Mishy. Because of her age and failing health, Help in Suffering had become too much for her. She had sent out a Swiss couple, Pierre and Marese Barcellini, to take over. They had proved to be a disastrous choice. For one thing they ate meat and drank, which was deeply offensive to the Indians with whom they had to work. They could not abide the Indian way of doing things which, to Europeans, can seem inefficient and wasteful. In addition, they had become embroiled in scandal. One day Pierre and Marese had turned up at the shelter with an Indian baby. They insisted that it was their own, which was a ludicrous claim considering their European complexions. It was obvious to all that some sort of back-door adoption had taken place.

The two Swiss had clashed repeatedly with the trustees and with Mishy, who could not bear to have her beloved shelter taken from her. In the end they had walked out, taking the child with them back to Europe. The shelter was in a terrible state, no one knew what was happening to the animals and there was no one who could be trusted to manage the money.

'What to do? What to do?' Janine cried.

Christine had a very good idea what to do, but she did not dare mention it as Jeremy was with them. They stayed in Geneva for another few days. Then Jeremy returned to Australia, and Christine went to London to stay with Annabella.

Naturally they discussed all that they had heard in Switzerland. Christine recalls that Annabella was very worried about the mess that Janine had found herself in. For all she knew, animals were dying at the shelter and she couldn't go there to see for herself, as she had a job as a teacher.

'Maybe I could ring her and talk to her,' suggested Christine.

Life-changing moments should be imprinted indelibly on the brain, yet Christine is vague about the details of what happened next. 'I'm not quite sure if I suggested I should go or Janine did, but she must have picked up on the idea that I wouldn't say no if she asked me to. She said she'd pay my air fares if I'd go for three months and see what was happening there.

'She said, "When can you go? I need someone immediately." I said, "I have to go back to Australia and tell Jeremy."'

Jeremy was a much bigger problem than Christine let on to Janine. Their marriage, frankly, was in disarray, and Christine knew this could well blow it apart completely.

'We were two ships that passed in the night. There wasn't really anything that we did together. He did his golf at the weekends. He was absolutely stressed out by the work. He couldn't speak at night. He just threw himself down in front of the television with a beer. I never knew what he was doing. He didn't want to speak about his work; he'd talked about it all day. And the fact that I was then telling him I was going off again was probably extremely awful for him because he'd have to come home at night and get his own meal and feed the three dogs and two cats or whatever was there at that moment and be alone, so naturally he wasn't happy about it.'

Jeremy was at work when Christine arrived home. She let herself into the house and had several hours in which to anticipate the prickly scene which was sure to take place. That evening she heard the car pull in under the carport. Jeremy came in through the kitchen door in his suit and tie. They hugged.

'I got your letter,' he said, 'about going to Help in Suffering. How can you say you're going there for three months when you've just been away for two months? How can I look after this house and these animals on my own?'

'I have to go, Janine needs me to go. She'll pay my fares.'

'It's the last straw. I don't want you to go.'

'I have to go. I was asked.'

'It's some tiny rundown shelter. What do you think you can do to help? What's the point of going? What about your work for Animal Liberation?'

'I'll have to leave Animal Liberation. There are other good people.'

'What about the boys?'

'They won't care. They have their own lives.'

'They might need you for something.'

'If so I could come.'

'I just can't see any future in this. I hope if you go this time, you won't need to go again.'

'We could go together. We could go and live in India.'

'I don't like India.'

'That time we stopped in Bombay, it wasn't a good example.'

'Faeces on the beach. Filth everywhere. I'd hate to live there. Anyway, I can't leave my work. I have a legal partnership which can't be broken except under exceptional circumstances. It'd be absolutely impossible for me to come.'

It seemed to Christine that all of the portents had for years been leading her to this point – her first trip to India where she met Diana, her work with Professor Ramaswami, Vimala's prophesy, the serendipitous links between Mishy and Annabella and Janine. She felt as if she had really played no part in it, that destiny had been leading her all along. Jeremy was not pleased, but, in the end, he went along with Christine's wishes.

Two months later, she went to India.

BOOK TWO
INDIA

CHAPTER 10

New Delhi was like a sauna. Christine caught a taxi from the airport through parklands past the parliamentary buildings, Connaught Circle, with its central park and concentric rings of white-columned, expensive shops, rows of diplomatic and ministerial bungalows with verandahs and gardens, the sprawling market made up of stalls with hessian roofs, the hospital with crowds sleeping and cooking on the pavement, shops with a plethora of mad signs: 'SOUTH INDIAN FOOD PARADISE', and 'GET CHOOSY FOR YOUR NEXT CUP OF TEA – TEA CITY'. When the taxi stopped a woman with a clinging child begged through the window, her bangles clicking on the glass. There were men on motorbikes with their wives clinging on behind in blowing saris, buses going against the lights with passengers leaning from the doors.

At three o'clock the next morning the porter knocked on the door of her hotel as arranged, with a pot of coffee and two pieces of toast. It had been pointed out to Christine by another guest that she had to request two toast, or one toast, or three toast. Each was itemised quite exactly. Also, there was never enough butter supplied, so you had to ask for two butter. Additionally, it was not assumed that jam was automatic. Therefore you needed also to remember to request the jam. It was a strange, jelly-like pink and yellow substance, tasting like bubblegum.

When it was time to leave, the porter blew a whistle and a driver, who was asleep in the back of his taxi with his feet protruding from the window, woke and coaxed the engine reluctantly to life. After establishing a price of one hundred rupees they drove back through the same darkened route to Airport Terminal One National.

The flight to Jaipur took only half an hour. Janine had told Christine she was paying a veterinary manager, Dr Bajaaj, 3,000 rupees a month to look after the shelter. The arrangement was that he should visit once a week to ensure everything was in order. At the airport she was approached by a dark, good-looking young man who introduced himself as Daya, the son of the Prasad family who had been Mishy's long-time assistants. He was accompanied by a plump man with a short moustache called Deepak, the shelter's manager.

Daya plunged through the crowd to seize Christine's bags then led the way outside to a battered white ambulance vehicle with the words 'Help in Suffering, Durgapura' painted on the side. With the engine roaring and the bodywork rattling and squeaking, the ambulance moved out into the traffic. Motor cars, buses, auto-rickshaws, bicycles, motor scooters and trucks proceeded through baking, potholed streets with horns blaring as if engaged in some mad race. There seemed to be no rules:

smaller vehicles gave way to the larger, although occasionally one more daring than the rest would dash recklessly forward to claim a small gap in the flow, setting off a cacophony of screeching brakes, blaring horns and shouted Hindi.

Christine asked Daya how long he had been working at the shelter.

'I was there when Mishy started it ten years ago, with my father who worked for her. Now he has gone to another animal shelter.'

He was concentrating on driving, shouting above the roar and rattle of the engine. Once he said, 'Please put out hand' when he wanted to turn left, and Christine waved out the window to indicate to the cars behind.

'You speak English very well,' she said.

'I learnt it since I was a child, from Mishy. She loved me too much.'

The streets were full of animals. Now and then they saw a cow grazing on the median strip. Towering above the ambulance stood a great camel, waiting at the traffic lights, nonchalantly chewing its cud while its driver smoked a *beedi*. Beside him, among a bevy of cyclists and scooter riders, was a bullock cart pulled by two strong white beasts with long horns painted green. Along the side of the road a small boy drove a flock of black and brown goats. A grey cow was being shooed away by a vegetable vendor with a broom. Some monkeys sat on the roof of a house, peering down at the shoppers below. A family loaded into the back of a pony cart was dressed in gold finery and swaying slightly in time to the prancing of the small fat pony which pulled them. A man rode a tall white horse with frothing mouth and arched neck, haughty in red and gold harness, on the way to a wedding somewhere. Vultures circled over the carcase of a bullock which lay in an empty field. A pack of dingo-coloured dogs rummaged in a garbage heap. An elephant plodded sedately along the side of the road with a *mahout* under an umbrella seated on his neck. The elephant was decorated with red, pink, white and blue, and a tinselled shawl hung over his back with swinging tassels.

'It's beautiful,' Christine said.

'Pierre did not like India,' Daya replied.

'Why did he leave so suddenly?'

'He came to me with tears in his eyes one night. It's the only time I ever saw him cry. He said he had to leave because he couldn't bear it any more. He said I was his dear son and that I was to manage the shelter after he left. But Dr Bajaaj appointed Deepak as the manager when I was in London.'

'Is he a good manager?' Deepak, sitting in the back behind glass, could not hear their conversation.

'There are many problems,' Daya answered. 'You will see.'

It was a twenty-minute drive to Durgapura, a ramshackle village consisting of a row of shops on either side of the main road with the original village behind. Turning off the main highway, they drove down a dusty road until they came to an inky river. They travelled alongside it for a while then turned in through two whitewashed pillars, coming to a stop outside a cement-rendered, whitewashed building.

The shelter was situated on about one and a half acres of land. The grounds were filled with neem, acacia, bougainvillea and palms. A large white-pillared verandah ran the length of the office block, from which French doors opened into the staff kitchen and three offices. The buildings were all flat-roofed and whitewashed, with thick cement walls and wooden windows painted dark green. Behind the shelter the land fell away to the river, which ran grey with froth and stink.

The staff came out to meet them. Daya introduced Christine to each one – Birmalal, Manju, Babulal, Ramdayal, Rajendra, Sunita, Sumitra. And there were five human patients – Kailesh, Ramprasad, Koonarai, Sankalal and Sambu.

After the introductions had finished, Daya took Christine to a small cottage surrounded by a dusty rose garden and a number of shady trees filled with birds. The door was locked and he had lost the key. Unperturbed, he prised the lock from the bolt with an iron rod. The damaged door was flung open, revealing a small, dusty room adorned with cobwebs and water stains on the whitewashed walls. Terrazzo shelves were inset into the thick walls. The floor and walls were cement. Daya flicked a switch and a squeaking fan began slowly to turn in the ceiling. An iron-framed double bed in one corner and a stool and desk were the only furniture. There was a bedside light that looked promising but did not work. The bedroom opened through panelled wooden French doors onto a kitchen, which consisted of a long terrazzo slab for a cooking bench, into one end of which was sunk a terrazzo sink with a cold-water tap. These cell-like accommodations looked wonderful to Christine.

She was left alone to unpack. It was evening. A small grey-hound-like dog nudged at the wire screen door until it came open, crept into her bedroom and curled up on the bed with a shifty expression on its face. He had a black patch over half of his face giving him a lopsided look, legs that were too long, comic, knowing eyes and a mouth that seemed set in a crooked grin. Soon two large and friendly cats appeared, walked all over the sink, and having assured themselves that no food was available, settled down to sleep on the folded clothes.

Christine tried to sleep, but it was difficult. At four thirty in the morning, when it was almost light, she went outside to the cold tap and washed, squatting on her haunches. She lit the kerosene stove and put on a saucepan of water to boil.

At nine o'clock Daya knocked on the door. She asked him if they could inspect the shelter together. First they walked down to a row of ten kennels at the back of the shelter. They were very dark and it was hard to see inside. As her eyes adjusted to the light she saw a large red setter-type dog lying in a fetid pool of excrement.

'We can't leave this dog like this,' she said.

'He's dangerous,' Daya said.

She opened the door and stretched out her hand. The dog allowed her to touch his head. There was a chain round his neck, so she led him outside and tied him under a tree. His coat was covered in faeces, so Christine washed him in the sun with medicated soap.

'We have to clean out these kennels,' she said to Daya.

Continuing their tour they came to another room which was full of puppy cages made of wire. In these divided cages there were about twenty puppies, all of which were thin and covered in diarrhoea and vomit.

'The dogs all need to be fed and their kennels need to be cleaned urgently,' Christine said. 'Do we have meat?'

'The trustees don't allow any meat to be fed. We give bread and milk and vegetables and rice only.'

'These puppies are dying. They need meat.'

'We could ask the trustees,' Daya said.

Christine realised she had no idea how to supervise staff, nor how to run an animal shelter. She began to feel panicky knowing that animals that were suddenly her responsibility were starving and dying. They moved on to another cage where an emaciated kitten lay, obviously starving.

'What are the animals being fed?'

'You see that chapati on the fire? That's the food.'

'That flat bread? No meat?'

'You see, Deepak is a Jain. They're strict vegetarians who don't feed meat to animals either.'

'But cats have to eat meat, and sometimes puppies, if they're weak.'

She went to Deepak, who was sitting on the verandah drinking a cup of *chai* and reading the paper.

'The dogs and cats must be fed meat.'

'Yes, madam.'

'So will you arrange it for tomorrow?'

'Yes, madam.'

That night Christine lay awake. Mosquitos buzzed in her ears. The fan turned and rattled but it was not enough to drown the cries of the hungry animals. The small greyhound-shaped dog climbed onto the bed and lay beside her, the semi-wild eyes staring into hers. Then, like a cat, it jumped onto the windowsill where it curled up and slept.

At nine o'clock the next morning Christine went up to the office.

'Did you buy the meat?' she asked Deepak.

'Madam, there is no money.'

Christine resolved that she would go to the bank and cash traveller's cheques, and then go to see Mr Jain, who was one of the trustees. Cashing the cheques necessitated one or two hours of standing in queues waiting, then sitting in chairs waiting, and finally being ushered into an office where she presented a brass token with a number on it. With her handbag stuffed full of rupees, Daya drove her to Mr Jain's house.

He came to the front door, straight, unsmiling, staring at

Christine with cold eyes. 'How good of you to come from so far to help,' he said. 'Please come in.'

Workmen were coming in and out of the house carrying cement bags. Mr Jain explained that he was renovating. He gestured to Christine to sit on a mattress, which was the only piece of furniture in the room. She noticed that Daya and Deepak had remained outside with the vehicle. A man who was sweeping the floor came grovelling on his hands and knees. At first she thought he was crippled, but then she realised that he could stand, for he straightened his legs as he exited from the room.

'I'm worried the animals aren't getting enough food,' she said. 'The dogs need meat.'

'No meat,' said Mr Jain emphatically. 'We do not want to encourage the butchery of the slaughterhouse.'

'I've been a vegetarian for twenty years, and I've been to the slaughterhouses and campaigned for their closure, but if the animals are sick and weak they have to have meat. They can't just have bread and milk.'

'Just give them more and they'll grow fat.'

'But there's already wasted chapati rotting in the cages.'

'They must not be fed meat.'

There was no more she could say. She repaid the six thousand rupees that he had lent to the shelter. Daya and Deepak were waiting outside, bemused and uncertain because of this new, pushy arrival from foreign parts who could not be predicted.

'He told me not to feed the animals meat. So we'll have to feed it secretly.'

Daya did not say anything. They were about to drive off when she saw a camel with flies covering its nose, and asked

Daya to stop. He leant out of the window and spoke in Hindi to the camel driver. Then, starting the engine again, he said, 'I've asked this man to bring the camel now so we can treat it.'

An hour after they had arrived back at the shelter the camel came through the gate led by a small man. It was hard to believe that such a powerful beast would allow itself to be bullied by such a little creature. With one command its knees bent and, as it gently collapsed, its legs folded neatly underneath. Its owner grabbed its lip and, while it grumbled in pain, Daya prised the wooden peg from the nose.

He held it up. It was caked with pus and blood. The camel's nostril was black with baked pus and congealed scabs. A large gaping hole with yellow fluid running from it remained. Daya mopped it with cotton wool and disinfectant, while the camel-*wallah* watched anxiously, holding the halter and the bottom lip so that his beast could not bite. When the flaps of loose and decaying skin had been severed by the scissors, and the wound covered with yellow Loroxene cream to keep away the flies, the camel was released and allowed to stand.

'In Australia they don't use these pegs at all,' Christine said. 'It's so cruel. It must get infected all the time because the wound would never heal if it's always being pulled.'

'We're trying to get the camel drivers to use harness,' Daya said. 'But these people only use peg, because they say it's the only way to stop camel bolting.' He went away and came back with a leather halter, painted pink and decorated with bells. He handed it to the camel owner.

It was early afternoon and they had not yet had lunch. Although no meat had been forthcoming, Christine wanted to feed the animals with the new supplies of Farax baby food they had bought. She carried round bowls of gruel to all the cages.

Only the kitten refused to eat, and continued to cry and climb the wire of the cage.

A little later she was sitting in her kitchen writing a list of things to do when Dr Bajaaj arrived. An elderly, dignified gentleman, he accepted the offer of tea, and sat. 'What's this I hear about no meat for the animals?'

Christine didn't know how he felt about meat. She explained her meeting with Mr Jain and his order that they were not to have meat at the sanctuary.

Dr Bajaaj took a sip of his tea. 'He's a Jain so he cannot endorse the feeding of meat. If he finds it detrimental to his status to be associated with a sanctuary that serves meat then he should retire as a trustee. As long as I'm a vet here the animals will have meat. I was in charge of Jaipur Zoo once. Do you feed a tiger grass?'

With some relief Christine asked him if he was a vegetarian. He was not, but he explained that he could never eat beef because he was a Hindu. She thought how strange it was that in her own country it was radical to be a vegetarian, but that in Rajasthan it was radical not to be a vegetarian. Here she was not an outrageous non-conformist but part of the established order.

'The meat should be cooked in a gravy with the chapati and some vegetables,' Dr Bajaaj said. 'It should be allowed to cool before it's given to the animals. It should be given last thing at night. In the morning you give the puppies and kittens bread and milk.'

Christine told him about the kitten dying of starvation.

'Meat will not be available now for today,' Dr Bajaaj said. 'Except for goat, which is very expensive. But you could buy a little for this kitten.'

Birmalal was despatched on a bicycle to buy some goat

meat. When the starving kitten saw the meat it fell upon it, growling. As Christine watched it eat she thought of all the animals she had rescued throughout her life, the puppies she had hidden in hotel rooms, and others she had been forced to pass by. She felt a sense of elation because now, whenever she saw an animal that was in need, she could collect it and provide it with shelter. And because of this, at least some of the animals of India could now be rescued and know human love, perhaps for the first time ever.

On her second night in the shelter Christine slept with six dogs in the room. She had diarrhoea all night. The bathroom smelled and the flushing mechanism did not work. Insects flew against the plastic bucket, their bodies making small clicks in the silence of the night. A dog howled. She was doubled with cramp in the hot, breathless room, but she was in heaven.

'I've never been happier in my whole life,' she recalls a decade and a half later. 'It was totally wonderful, I was living like a monk, which was what I'd always wanted to do.'

The next day she was busy all morning organising new equipment. It was afternoon before she had time to take a break. Deepak was sitting as usual on a chair in the garden, watching Daya and Birmalal mending a cage. She could not understand why they should be mending cages when the animals had still not been fed. She was mindful that she should try to reign in her impatience, but she could contain herself no longer. She burst out, 'This is ridiculous!'

They all stopped working and looked at her. Deepak stood up and pretended to rummage for some betel in his pocket.

'This is ridiculous,' she cried again. 'I've tried not to interfere, but we're meant to be an animal sanctuary. We're meant to give life to animals, but the animals are dying in prison from starvation. I've tried to be patient but I can't bear it any more. This is absolutely unacceptable. I'm going to phone Janine in Geneva. I'm going to ring Dr Bajaaj.'

Christine didn't know how they would react. She only knew that she had tried patience and it hadn't worked. 'Who's responsible for organising the feeding?' she demanded.

'I am, madam,' Deepak said. 'I'm very sorry, madam. This is very wrong, madam, I know. This will not happen again.'

Deepak hurried off, presumably to organise meat. When he had gone, Daya, looking smug, said, 'Thank you for doing this.'

Christine stamped off to the telephone and rang Janine in Geneva, promptly bursting into tears. 'The shelter's in the most terrible mess,' she sobbed. 'All the animals are dying. The cages were filthy, and they weren't being fed any meat. It's disgraceful.'

There was a pause while the line hissed and crackled. Then Janine said, 'Oh Christine, are you going to go home?'

'No, I love it.'

'You should become managing trustee, so you can have power to change things.'

'No, you can't make me managing trustee. I have a house at home and a husband. There's the boys, there's my mother, there's Animal Liberation . . .'

'Well I'm not going to send any money if you're not there.'

Soon Deepak came back; fires were lit, pots stirred, and in the dark the staff ran round feeding the animals. Dish after dish was placed on the lawn, and in the cages, and the hungry animals devoured them until nothing was left.

CHAPTER 11

The office was a sparsely furnished room with two steel filing cabinets, a couple of laminex-topped desks and a few wobbly iron chairs. A young man called Nirmal came at weekends to do the books. He worked during the week as an accountant at a company that made refrigerators. Nirmal had a high forehead with dark, sunken eyes and black, swept-back hair. He hardly spoke as he worked diligently all day at his desk. He was reticent to the point of shyness.

One morning soon after she had arrived, Christine was discussing some accounts with Nirmal. When they had finished he gave her a serious look, and said, 'You please stay.'

'I can only stay three months,' Christine said. 'I've got a husband.'

'Things here are not good,' said Nirmal.

'What things?'

'There is something. You will see.'

'If you don't tell me how can I do anything?'

But he just smiled, and said, 'You stay.'

Before she could question him further the door opened and a middle-aged Indian gentleman entered. He wore a polo shirt and perfectly tailored cotton trousers. His hair was grey and his complexion was almost European. 'How do you do,' he said in perfect Oxford English, 'I'm Raja J. K. Atal. You must be Mrs Townend.'

Raja Atal was another trustee. He had served as an ambassador for India in Yugoslavia under Tito, as well as in Greece and Africa. He had been in Pakistan when the war broke out with India, and had been held prisoner for a week. He had the straight shoulders of a rider, and the upright bearing of a ruler; his whole manner showed that he was used to giving orders and being obeyed.

'Now,' he pronounced, 'having spoken with Janine, we've come to this conclusion. We'll make three new trustees – yourself, Dr Bajaaj and a prominent businessman of Jaipur called Bipan Desai. You and I will be joint managing trustees.'

'I'd be delighted and honoured,' said Christine. 'But there's a problem. I won't be able to be here much. I have a husband and family.'

'That's all right. You do a bit of fundraising overseas and you come to India for half the year.'

Christine doubted that her marriage would survive her living half of her life in Jaipur and the other half in Sydney. What sounded simple to Raja Atal she knew was fraught with complications. Nevertheless, she heard herself saying that, yes, it sounded like a good idea.

They chatted a while longer about the shelter, then he left in a car with a uniformed chauffeur. When Christine returned to the office, Nirmal said, 'That is very good. Now all problems will be solved.'

Christine thought to herself that when she had time she must try to find out from Nirmal what these problems were that he kept talking about.

Christine immersed herself in the life of the shelter. She had the buildings whitewashed, and she went often with Daya in the ambulance to attend to sick animals. Although he had no formal veterinary training, Daya was quite able to diagnose illnesses and prescribe treatment for minor cases. More complicated ones were left for Dr Bajaaj.

As the days went by, continual closures and curfews were making it difficult to do the work. The papers were carrying daily stories about a politician, Mr Advani, who had rallied 10,000 Hindus to march to Ayodhya in Uttar Pradesh, where they wanted to build a Hindu temple on the site where a mosque had stood for centuries. According to the Hindus, invading Moghuls had destroyed a Ram temple that had been on the site originally. Now the Hindus wanted it rebuilt. Muslim leaders had threatened that unless the government stopped the march they would take matters into their own hands.

Violence was spreading across the country, including Jaipur. One day Christine asked Daya to drive her to the Post Office to send out the shelter's first newsletter. They had been sitting in a corner pasting on stamps for a while when Daya said, 'We must hurry, they want to close.'

Looking up, she realised that the Post Office was empty. The superintendent was hovering over them anxiously. 'Why is it closing now, in the middle of the day?' she asked.

'Mr Advani has been arrested,' Daya said.

'You mean the man who is marching to Ayodhya?'

'The government has arrested him, because he was going to make trouble and cause riots. But he has 10,000 people who were following him.'

'Is the postmaster afraid?'

'Everyone is afraid. Everyone is going home.'

Hastily, they stuck the stamps on the last envelopes, and thrust them into the hands of the waiting postmaster. As they hurried from the building, up and down the street shopkeepers were bolting their windows and doors. A stream of traffic was emptying from the city. Police stood on every corner, some holding guns and truncheons. A fire engine went past, siren blaring. An overturned truck lay smoking on the bitumen, and further down the road piles of tyres were burning. Beside them angry men were standing in groups shouting and singing.

'What are they saying?' Christine asked.

'They say they want to kill Muslims so they can have their temple.'

The next day all the shops were closed. Christine and Daya decided to take two monkeys into the jungle to be released after having been brought in with injuries that were now cured. In Durgapura village Daya stopped and talked to some friends. They told him that a man had been murdered overnight and his body was down on the railway line. 'People are killing each other,' Daya warned. 'It's dangerous to drive anywhere.'

'Do you think we should go back?'

'We shall see,' he said.

They drove on. The road into the city was empty. There were no camel carts, or bullock carts, or painted trucks, or motor scooters, no crowded *tempos* or buses. Daya turned off onto a side road so that they wouldn't have to go through Jaipur. This alternative route was crowded with traffic with the same idea. In the distance they could see billowing smoke rising from the city. Christine was suddenly struck by the bizarre nature of what she was doing. Nearby, people were killing each other, and they were driving about the countryside with a couple of monkeys.

They continued out into the country until they came to a temple. The monkeys stared from the cage, their little hands clutching the wire. Outside, gangs of large macaques roamed the road. Daya carried the cage down a path and set it down. He lifted the monkeys out onto the ground. They peered about for an instant then ran into the forest. A zoologist had warned Christine that the other monkeys might attack them, but it seemed to her that the risk was preferable to spending life in a cage.

In the distance a family was bending over the engine of a Jeep. They spoke to Daya in Hindi.

'They are Muslims and they are frightened,' he said. 'They want to go back to Amer, without going through Jaipur. I told them I knew a way, and they could follow me.'

They set off with the family in the Jeep following. When they reached the outskirts of Jaipur there were tyres burning on the road. Daya pointed, and the people who had been following took a turn to the right.

'We will be safe now,' he said, but it seemed to Christine that no one could really know that they were completely safe.

The following morning the paper reported that nineteen people had been killed in riots in Jaipur, so they spent the day among the animals. The next morning they read that the violence was continuing and more people had been murdered. They made one or two trips to attend sick animals nearby, but for the most part stayed in the shelter.

That evening, Daya came down to Christine's house. 'Today three men were killed on that roundabout we passed yesterday,' he said. 'It's not safe for you to be down here alone. You are to sleep in the office. It's nearer my house. Tonight they're making trouble. There're armed gangs of hoodlums driving round in Jeeps. They've set fire to houses in Durgapura. There're no policemen because they're all in the walled city, so there's no law and order any more. We're going to organise our own group. We'll have armed men on every corner to protect our houses and our women.'

Birmalal and Daya carried Christine's bed into the office, and she brought all the mats and rags on which the dogs slept. She had a pressure-pack can of deodorant, which came from Australia, which a security guard had once told her she could spray into an assailant's eyes. She locked her room, and left all the lights burning. On the roof of the office building Daya had erected a floodlight that illuminated the garden, so they could see if anyone came out of the forest towards them.

Before wishing her goodnight, Daya said, 'I must tell you another thing. We've secretly hidden a Muslim family in here who were afraid.'

Christine lay awake in the office looking at the light shining through the mosquito wire onto the walls, listening to the small grunts of the animals as they dreamt and twitched. Outside on the road, youths shouted. She had no idea if they were killing each other, or if they would come charging into the shelter to murder her and the rest of the inmates.

At about midnight there was a knock on the door. Two of the

female staff, Sumitra and Manju, stood holding Sumitra's two children clasped to their hips, with blankets under their arms. 'Please madam, we're afraid,' they whispered.

She ushered them inside. 'You can lie on the bed.' But they shook their heads and sat on the floor, swathed in rugs, clasping the children to their breasts, whispering together and crying. Outside, across the *nulla* (river) there was shouting, and they could see in the distance the orange glow of a fire. The men stood on the verandah, holding knives and poles. Their eyes were glowing and their faces were flushed. They were laughing and jostling each other, charged with excitement.

In the light of day everything seemed normal. Christine went down to her house, unlocked it, turned off the lights, fed the puppies and kittens, and made coffee for herself. Sambu brought the paper, and she read that bombs and lethal weapons had been seized and sporadic incidents of violence and arson had continued. The death toll was now officially stated to be 44; according to unconfirmed reports the number was around 70.

Sambu, one of the patients who was mentally handicapped was, in theory, the shelter's security man. He would occasion-ally walk round the grounds during the night, blowing a whistle loudly outside Christine's window, and thumping a heavy rod on the earth or against the stone walls. He wore a tattered khaki blazer and cap, and in his night-time ramblings he startled dogs, woke Christine with a jump, and generally created mayhem. However, as the nights grew cooler, he was reluctant to leave his bed.

Because of the dangerous situation in Jaipur, Dr Bajaaj one

day decided that the shelter needed a proper security guard with a uniform and a bit more attitude than Sambu. He turned up one day with a thin, tired-looking man with black circles under his eyes. In the absence of any knowledge of English the man smiled at Christine and bowed.

'This is Sambu,' she said, so that Sambu would not feel superseded. 'He's the protector of the sanctuary.'

Sambu smiled widely, jiggled his feet, and looked at the ground. Still trying to be diplomatic, Christine instructed through Daya that the new security guard would be allowed to rest if Sambu was walking round, and when Sambu was resting the security guard should patrol. The guard nodded vigorously.

That night for the first time she went to sleep quickly, secure in the knowledge that she didn't need to listen for intruders. At about three in the morning she was woken by the dogs barking loudly. She unlocked her door and cautiously eased outside. Three of them were chasing a small grey calf that had been brought in for treatment. She yelled at the dogs and threw stones at them until they ran off. Then she hugged the calf, pressed her face against its soft, wet muzzle, and put it back in the cow shed.

She walked all around the shelter but the new security guard was nowhere to be seen. She knocked on Sambu's door for several minutes until he emerged tousled and rubbing his eyes.

'Sambu, security guard *kahan hai?*' she said, and shrugged expressively to make up for her bad Hindi.

Sambu picked up his torch, wrapped a blanket round his shoulders and together they walked round the garden. Finally, when they had gone everywhere, and she thought the guard must have run away, they looked in through the office window and saw a pile of blankets heaving on the divan.

'Security guard,' Christine shouted triumphantly to Sambu, and tried to open the door, which was locked. After repeated pounding, the pile of blankets began to stir, and from underneath staggered the security guard, swaying and stumbling towards the door. He opened it and put his palms together in a *namaste*. 'Sorry, so sorry, memsahib, very sorry.'

Christine was assailed by a billowing cloud of alcoholic breath. It was hard to remain angry in the face of such absurdity; she had to see the funny side. But although they gave him another chance, the guard was drunk again the next night. After that they did not employ any more security guards but simply left the night to the burglars and ghosts and men with knives to do what they would.

Christine had forgotten all about Nirmal's enigmatic warning until one morning when they were alone in the office, he once again fixed her with a serious expression and said, 'You must stay here. Coming and going is not good.'

She agreed it was not good, and it would be difficult to keep everything running smoothly when sometimes she would be here and sometimes in Australia, but her husband would not want her to stay permanently.

'You will see, Deepak is taking the cow food for feeding his own cow.'

'How do you know that?'

'I have seen. Staff have told me.'

'Then we'll have to do something,' she said. But Deepak presented another diplomatic problem. He had been appointed by Dr Bajaaj, who was a friend of Deepak's family. She was not at all sure that she would be able to sack him.

A day or two later when she was out on a rescue with Daya in the ambulance, they saw Deepak with his father in the shelter's Jeep.

'Where's he going with his father?' she asked Daya. 'He told me he was going to collect a dog.'

'You see, he does this many times,' Daya answered.

Christine decided to enlist the help of Raja Atal. She was by no means confident that the trustees would support her request for Deepak's dismissal. She prepared a written statement listing his misdeeds, and Daya drove her to Raja Atal's house.

Situated within acres of lawns, great trees and gardens was a beautiful century-old bungalow with wide verandahs and flat roofs. Christine had been enchanted when she first saw it. As they arrived, earth-moving machinery was digging a huge hole, while other equipment was lumbering about smashing down shrubs and trees.

She walked over the marble verandah and knocked on the door. A servant appeared, smiled and vanished. Soon Raja Atal emerged.

'Apologies for all this,' he said with a disgusted expression on his face. 'It's too terrible. I can hardly bear to watch. They're destroying my garden.'

'But why's this happening? It's so beautiful.'

'The government has said we have to divide our land. There are too many people and not enough land for them. Either it could have been sold for housing or else we could have a hotel. I decided on the hotel because at least it would not turn into a slum.'

'So they're building a hotel, here in your garden?'

'Yes,' he answered. 'A five-star hotel. See the well of pure water? It will be smashed. Every rose, everything will go.

There's nothing I can do about these socialist people. Come inside away from the noise.'

In a cool interior courtyard Christine produced her document listing Deepak's shortcomings. She was worried about how he would react to an outsider who, having barely arrived, wanted to summarily fire people.

'Oh, I'm so sorry,' he said. 'How frightfully unpleasant for you. We won't tell his family he's been dismissed for stealing. We'll just say we don't need him any more because you've come.'

'Should I say it?'

'No, we'll ask Dr Bajaaj to say it.'

It was one more sign to Christine that she had been accepted. More than ever it seemed to her that her destiny was linked to Help in Suffering.

CHAPTER 12

One day, unannounced, Mishy came on a visit from Bangalore where she was starting yet another animal shelter. After two days travelling by bus, her clothing was crushed, her hair was awry and she needed a bath. Her born-to-rule manner and upper class British accent were as strong as when Christine had last met her in London.

Christine was delighted that Mishy would come but a little concerned about how she would feel about the changes that had been made to the shelter. Leaning on a large stick, Mishy allowed herself to be conducted on a tour. When they came to the room where she used to live she noted with approval its Spartan furnishings, the lack of hot water and the simple kerosene cooker.

The little dog that slept in the room every night came up to them wagging its tail. When it had first arrived it had been half-starved, with patches of hair falling out. Now it had put on weight and its coat was glossy with good health.

'Oh this one's lovely,' said Mishy.

'He's my favourite,' said Christine.

'Does he have a name?'

'I love him too much. I'm afraid to name him.'

'Call him Funny.'

'He sleeps in my room.'

'I know,' Mishy said. 'You get fond of them and they die, and it breaks your heart.'

Christine showed her the room where the cats had been kept. They had cleaned it out, put in a fan, a divan, a table, and some books. Over the door was a painted sign, 'MISHY'S ROOM'.

'Why did you do this?' she demanded, pleased.

'So you could stay here.'

They put her bag in the room and continued the tour. Christine told Mishy that she was struggling to learn Hindi.

'There are only two words you need to know,' she said. *'Mat maro* – don't beat.'

In the evening Mishy declined a proper meal. Instead, she drank some tea and ate a few crushed rusks, which she carried in a bag, and a banana. While it was still quite early she announced that she would like to retire. 'What do you do about going to the toilet in the night?' she asked.

'Well, I use a bucket, because the toilet's outside.'

'Well, give me a bucket too,' Mishy said, and they laughed like two old friends who had known each other for years.

The next day they drove Mishy into town and put her on the bus to Bangalore. They watched as she climbed aboard, admonishing her fellow passengers in Hindi and elbowing them as they tried to beat her to a seat. The bus started with a roar, there was a blast of the horn and behind the dirty window Mishy raised her hand for a moment before disappearing down the road in a cloud of black diesel smoke.

Now that some practical changes had been made, Christine was able to enjoy more fully the life of the shelter. It was blissful to be living close to so many animals. There was a cow outside her window, a camel in the yard, two or three pigs, numerous dogs and cats, assorted birds, donkeys, and even a tortoise. She enjoyed being able to hold and pet them, but perhaps the beasts that gave her most pleasure were the cattle.

'I used to go and sit in the cow shed for long periods of time. You know, they've found now that cows release endorphin when they chew their cud. Cows are in a state of prayer or meditation, you could say, and they surely impart that to people who are in their presence. That's why they talk about bucolic milkmen. I think if you could allow stressed people or schizophrenic people to sit in a cow shed for a week they'd come out sane. I loved sitting with the cows.'

She was beginning to be included in the personal lives of the staff. Nirmal was getting married to a young woman chosen, as is customary, by his parents. All the staff members had been invited to the wedding at his village, three hours' drive from Jaipur. The shelter was abuzz with excitement as the big day approached, yet Christine felt strangely divorced from the mood because, for several days, Funny had been refusing to eat.

The night before the wedding she lay awake listening to his laboured breathing. From the small neighbourhood temple the sound of chanting drifted across the worn old fields with their dried stubble and yellow dust. At about two in the morning when the chanting had stopped, Christine was seized with agonising stomach cramps. She vomited and staggered to the toilet where she bent over double for a while. When she made her way back to her bedroom she saw that Funny was dying. He had caught distemper from one of the other dogs. With each breath she could hear fluid rattling in his lungs. He could no longer even whine, because all of his energy was focused on the act of staying alive. She knew she could not hold on to him any longer. She went to the clinic, unlocked the cupboard, took a phial of sodium pentobarbital and, holding him on her knee, injected the merciful drug below the ribs into his stomach. Because of the pain of his breathing he could not even struggle against the insertion of the needle and he lay, gasping and bubbling, until his eyes closed and he became unconscious. When he had died, and blood and fluid had flowed from his mouth onto the floor, she lay on the bed, sobbing bitterly.

For the next couple of hours she kept vomiting and having to go to the toilet. A little before five she put on her ironed dress and walked shakily up to the office where Daya and the staff were loading the vehicle.

'I can't go,' she said.

'But you must go, Nirmal wants you to go so much.'

'I'll just be vomiting all the way, and I have diarrhoea. There won't be any toilets to stop at. And Funny died in the night. I had to kill him with my own hand, alone.'

'You loved that dog too much,' said Daya.

Christine went back to her room. After a while Daya appeared and said, 'You take this pill.'

'What is it?'

'Pierre left it. It's very good Swiss medicine.'

She was too weak to refuse, even though it might have been

anything. Daya watched her swallow the pill, and said, 'Now you come. You'll see what we've done.'

She walked up the path to the ambulance. The staff had taped all the back windows with newspapers, so nobody could see in, and they had covered the floor with mattresses, blankets and pillows, and placed a bucket inside.

'Now you can lie there, and you can use that bucket if there's nowhere else to go,' Daya said.

'But what about all of you? How will five of you fit into the front cabin.'

'We will fit.'

'I love you, Daya.'

'I love you too. Now, even if you have to vomit you just tap on the window, and we will stop, but no one can see you.'

They left and Christine dozed in the back, lulled by the churning engine, until it was light. She only had to ask him to stop once so that she could stumble into a field and go to the toilet unobserved.

They drove past men and women squatting and defecating in the drainage ditches beside the road. There were rippling fields of ripened wheat where women worked with scythes, their coloured skirts swinging with their movements. They passed a village well where a girl in an orange sari with long black wet hair sticking to her back vigorously pumped for her brother who scrubbed his head under the flowing water. A man went to elaborate measures to change his clothes inside a garment, which he held around his body like a tent, and Christine wondered why Indians were always so modest in bathing, yet so brazen in acts of defecation.

In the village they were welcomed by Nirmal's parents, and sat sipping coffee and nibbling sweets. Then they drove on through winding lanes, past an ancient fort, fields of mauve flowering crops, and mobs of black-faced sheep treading daintily over the stony soil, led by a shepherd all in white except for the red turban on his head. At the bride's village they waited again until her family came and said she was ready. Nirmal, after praying with the priest, mounted a white horse and rode through narrow, winding streets, followed by the guests dancing and rejoicing to the sound of an out-of-tune band. At the wedding location two thrones had been prepared. Seated side by side the couple exchanged vows of love forever, then Daya said they could go, and they drove through the darkness back to the shelter.

Alone in her room, Christine thought about the little dog who had died in her arms, and how he used to run to her whimpering with joy whenever she appeared. Funny had gone, and it was time for her to go too – back to Australia to decide her future.

CHAPTER 13

Any hope by Jeremy that Christine's stint at Help in Suffering might have been a one-off event was dispelled the moment he saw her. She was glowing like a woman in love; and over the next few days as she related to him her adventures it was clear without having to be said that this animal shelter in faraway India was going to be part of her life – if not his – for a long time to come.

For Christine the last three months had been full of wonder and discovery. Jeremy, on the other hand, had been running on the same old treadmill, pacing out a stressful round of commuting to the city, long hours of work, lonely TV dinners and weekend golf. He had visited his parents occasionally to talk about rugby and politics with his father and to relate the latest news of their grandchildren. He had seen Miles and his wife once or twice, but the truth of his existence had been inescapable – he was alone and missing his wife. Cameron, studying in Lismore, showed no sign of returning to Sydney. Miles, a videotape editor, also led a busy life, but at least he lived in the same city.

Rather than bringing things back to normal, Christine's return made Jeremy realise that he would have to resign himself to her making further regular trips to India. For the foreseeable future they would probably be spending half of their lives apart.

Christine was still torn between two responsibilities – to her marriage, and to the shelter. She told Jeremy that she just could not leave the place running on its own. A less tolerant man might have called for divorce there and then, or else thrown down an ultimatum. Not Jeremy. He was, as Christine acknow-ledges, unshakeably loyal. 'I was very lucky to meet and marry Jeremy. He's a very stable person, and probably without him I'd be in the loony bin by now.'

While she continued to work for Animal Liberation, Chris-tine remained in regular touch with Janine Vogler in Geneva, who urged her to return as soon as possible to Help in Suffer-ing. Two or three months after coming home, she again boarded a flight to India.

A few days after Christine's return, Daya told her that a woman who had been severely burnt had been brought into the shelter by her family. The public hospital would not take her as she was dying. She had been given a small room next to Koonarai, the elderly patient whom Mishy had taken in a year or so pre-viously. Sala was her name. She was about 30 years old. In despair after years of abuse from a cruel husband, she had tried to throw herself in front of a train. Although severely injured, she had failed to die. She had then jumped into a fire.

Sala was lying on the bed covered by a blanket. Even though there was a heater turned on she was shivering. Despite the smoke from burning insect coils, flies swarmed over the bed and crawled along the shelves set into the wall. Under the bed there was a pool of urine.

Gently they drew back the blanket. Sala's breasts, shoulders, legs and arms were covered in deep lesions from which pus and fluid leaked. One foot had been completely severed, and the thigh of one leg was all but denuded of flesh. Only her face was untouched. Her arms and legs had become frozen in one position. As she was unable to move by herself the staff had made a hole in the mattress for a toilet.

Christine's gorge rose as she fought to conceal her emotions. 'You'll be safe here,' she said, 'and you'll grow well.'

They arranged for a doctor to see Sala. He wrote some prescriptions, and instructed them to burn more incense and to wash the whole room with disinfectant to keep the flies away. She was to be given plenty of water as she was losing so much serum from her wounds. Outside the room Christine asked him, 'Is she going to die?'

'She'll almost certainly die,' he said. 'Maybe it's better that way. If she lives she'll be very disfigured. She'll be a cripple.'

They did as the doctor had instructed. Every day Sambu fed Sala spoonfuls of dahl and rice. After a week or so he reported that she had smiled at him once or twice. It seemed as though she was getting better. Then one day when Christine was sitting in the office doing accounts, Sambu came running, shouting in Hindi for her to come quickly.

Sala was lying in bed retching with foaming yellow froth running from her mouth and nose. Sambu stammered that she had asked him to pass her a bottle of Savlon detergent that was on the shelf; before he could stop her she had drunk it.

'We'll have to take her to the hospital and have her stomach pumped,' Christine said, but already Daya had run from the room and was reversing the ambulance to the door.

They put her on a stretcher covered with a sheet, and drove at reckless speed to the hospital. Birmalal and Babulal carried the stretcher into the casualty ward. It was a large room in an old stone building, with high ceilings. Crowds of people hung about, some wailing, some shouting, some simply standing in silence. Down one side of the room there were cubicles, into which you could see, because the tattered curtains did not pull shut. There were groaning women and thin men and pale, shaking children and clusters of concerned relatives standing about with no notion of how to help.

At a desk three people in uniform were filling in forms. Daya talked for a long time to various people but no one wanted to admit Sala because it might be a police case. No one seemed to be in charge.

At last, when Christine was about to start screaming, a woman in a dirty white coat came and said that Sala could be put on a bed in a side room. They carried her in. There were two beds. On the other one a boy was lying. His feet were swollen and bright red and black. While he moaned and writhed with pain his father sat beside him without displaying any expression at all.

'What's happened to that boy?' Christine asked Daya.

'He was working on the road and he sank into hot tar,' Daya said.

The boy continued to moan and cry. No one came to tend to him, or to give him an injection to lessen the pain.

133

Sala lay on her back with foam continuing to pour from her mouth. Eventually, after what seemed an interminable time, two men came. Without any explanations nor any effort at delicacy, they forced open her mouth with a plastic rod and pushed a plastic tube through one nostril down into her stomach. They attached the other end to a tap and turned it on. While she writhed and tried to call out, yellow water and froth began to flow from her mouth through a hose into a bucket beside the bed.

When the bucket was half full with stained lumps and foam they pulled the tube from her nose and left. Christine and Daya stood for a long time while the boy with the burnt feet continued moaning, until two men came and wheeled the bed away.

'She's going to be admitted,' Daya said. 'This is very good, because here she can get proper care.'

The ward to which they took Sala was a long narrow room with stone walls on one side and open windows on the other. Along both sides there were rows of beds filled with patients and surrounded by clusters of people.

By now two hours had passed. Christine had to leave for an appointment with a visiting French film crew. She and Daya left Birmalal with some money so that he could watch over Sala until the evening when they could return. Before she left, Christine bent over Sala and touched her arm. Sala frowned furiously, and Christine realised that they were forcing her to live when she did not want to.

The next day Sala was sent back to the shelter. The hospital would not keep her. Nobody wanted to change the dressings on her wounds. Birmalal had needed to bribe them to do it even once. Then, when a few more days had passed, Daya came to the office in the morning and said, 'Sala died in the night.'

Christine went down to look at her body. Sala lay on her back with her eyes closed. She had a small, peaceful smile and her hands were folded on her chest. Christine felt glad that their efforts to force her to live had been thwarted and that Sala was free.

Kailesh had been a patient at Help in Suffering when Christine first arrived. He was stick-thin and sallow, and often had to fight for breath when he walked up the path to visit the office. Because he had no way to occupy his mind she had bought him a new red radio, which he listened to at night. She had also asked him if he could teach her Hindi, and paid him for the lessons. They would sit in the office and Kailesh would speak slow Hindi sentences from a textbook, which Christine would struggle to understand.

Once he said, 'Madam, I fear I will not be in this world much longer.'

When Christine had returned to HIS from Australia, Kailesh was still just 'in the world'. But he had grown so thin and frail that he was not interested in anything that happened outside his room. He sat struggling for breath, crouched on his haunches on the floor. His room smelled bad because he was too weak to walk, and he was urinating in the corners.

After seeing how ill he was, Christine said to Daya, 'He'll die very soon, won't he?'

'Yes,' Daya said matter-of-factly.

It was obvious that Kailesh needed more professional care than they could give him. They lifted his stretcher into the shelter's ambulance and drove him to the public hospital. Nothing had changed since the visit with Sala. In the corridors groups of families squatted or leant against the walls, waiting, always waiting. Kailesh waited too, for someone to tell them there would be a bed for him and, as they waited, it occurred to Christine that each individual in India was one small nothing in the mass of one billion people. Each humble life seemed inconsequential; each would live and die without being noticed at all except by those closest to them. People such as Kailesh, when they died, were not even recorded in the statistics. They were just the 'unorganised sector' in the parlance of political scientists – those who were so un-noteworthy that officials did not bother to record their illness or death.

After three hours of waiting they were told they could take Kailesh to a bed. They carried him into a large room with windows that opened onto the outside corridors. There were rows of beds along the walls. Around the beds, families were camped, with stainless-steel food containers, packets of biscuits and supplies of medicines. A man was being lifted from a bed and rolled onto a trolley. The bed had a torn black vinyl mattress.

'This is for Kailesh,' Daya said.

'But it hasn't been wiped. We can't put him on it until it's been wiped.'

'Here there is no wiping,' Daya said.

They lifted Kailesh onto the sticky mattress, where he squatted, gasping for breath. He weighed only about 30 kilos now. His eyes were huge and frightened. He could not speak. The breath whistled and moaned through his trachea. Under the bed a cat searched among filthy bandages and paper bags for remnants of food. A woman came in with a broom, but she only swept the centre of the room and left the rotting food untouched.

While they were waiting for a doctor to examine Kailesh, Christine went to the toilet. She walked up a sloping ramp for two floors then through a ward. There were dying children with drips attached to their wrists, and grandmothers bending over them. A little boy lay with a broken leg set in plaster, the traction provided by two bricks and a rope that hung over the end of the bed. In the toilet there were faeces all over the floor and sanitary pads lying in piles in the corners. It was impossible to avoid treading in excrement. Christine walked back through the ward leaving polluted footsteps behind her.

Kailesh was still squatting on the mattress, his hands pressed to his sides to keep him balanced, gasping for breath. Eventually a doctor came and held a stethoscope to his chest. When he had finished examining him, he said, 'We will give him oxygen.'

He wrote some instructions on a piece of paper and said to Daya, 'You go across the road and purchase these medicines.'

Christine followed the doctor into the corridor. 'Please tell me, I know you're very busy, very over-worked, but what's wrong with Kailesh?'

'He has TB,' he said. 'If he'd been treated early it could have been cured.'

'But he told us it was asthma, and incurable.'

'Maybe he thought you would ask him to leave, since TB's a communicable disease.'

Christine looked at the doctor's exhausted face, and noticed that he was not wearing a mask. When she commented on this he merely shrugged. 'We go from bed to bed treating patients with infectious diseases. The government can't afford masks.'

'Kailesh is going to die, isn't he?' she said.

'We'll do all that we can, but his condition is serious.'

Christine had a sense of helplessness, of inability to alter the events of life in India, where to resist the flow of happenings seemed only to lead to frustration and exhaustion. Perhaps, she thought, it was this yielding to things rather than fighting against the impossible, this feeling of swimming in a great ocean whose tides and currents directed all movements, that was the attraction of India, as well as its greatest exasperation. And so with a feeling of fatalism she and Daya took it in turns to sit beside Kailesh as he slowly faded. By the third day his breathing was almost imperceptible. He seemed to be dead, but when Christine touched his forehead and said, 'Hello, Kailesh,' he regained consciousness and mumbled something she could not understand. Some people who were visiting patients in adjacent beds gathered round to watch the death. Daya called a doctor. The doctor injected massive doses of drugs into the stretched, withered arms. Then Kailesh's breathing simply stopped.

The doctors suddenly threw themselves into a frenzy of activity, punching his chest so that his stick-like arms flew into the air and his shrunken body vibrated with the blows. It was so fruitless that after days of neglect they now saw it necessary to disturb the peace of his dying by a final display of medical defiance. Christine hoped fervently that Kailesh would remain dead and not respond to their violence.

When it was clear that he was truly dead, and the doctors had left, Daya said, 'We'll take the body now.'

'But aren't there forms to fill in, things to sign?'

'Nothing like that,' he said.

Daya and Ramdayal wrapped the body in a sheet, carried it to the Jeep, and put it in the back. Kailesh was now just one of the unknown, unrecorded statistics.

The next morning after the woodmen delivered some logs, they took his body to the burning ground next door and cremated it. As the body burnt, Daya smashed the skull to allow the indwelling spirit to escape. They put Kailesh's few possessions, except for the red plastic radio, into a cardboard box and left it beside the ashes so that poor people could come and take what they wanted. Then they went away, up the worn path covered with goats' droppings, past the temple with the pipal tree, back to the shelter, and cleaned the room of every last trace of Kailesh.

CHAPTER 14

It had been Mishy's vision that Help in Suffering would cater for human patients as well as animals. After the experience with Sala and Kailesh the trustees pointed out to Christine that this policy was too risky to continue. Kailesh could easily have infected staff members with TB. And in cases like Sala's the shelter, having no doctor or means of providing proper care, could leave itself exposed to legal claims of negligence. She was relieved when they advised her not to take in any more human patients.

There were still some of the original ones left, however. Ramprasad, who had been dumped at the shelter by his family, was mentally ill. He used to go out begging outside the main public hospital, returning to Help in Suffering for food and shelter. There was really no reason why his family could not look after him. Daya contacted them and asked them to take him back.

Not long before Kailesh's death, a patient who was a family friend of Daya's had arrived. His name was Sapadeen and he was schizophrenic. He had started a small fire in one of the kennels one night, and another time he tried to burn Koonarai's room. Sapadeen was also returned to his family.

Sambu and Koonarai had nowhere else to go, so they remained as valued icons of the shelter. Koonarai was known to everyone as Goat Baba. When his family had brought him to the shelter he had been suffering from leprosy. His leprosy was cured now but the family refused to take him back. Thin, ancient and without a tooth in his head, Goat Baba lived in a small concrete room with a collection of goats, some of which slept on his bed with him. The floor was covered in their hard little pellets and there was a strong smell of goat urine.

Christine often told Goat Baba that it was not acceptable to breed goats at the animal shelter and sell them in the market for meat. He laughed his toothless laugh and went right on doing it.

During the month when the castor-oil trees seeded, Goat Baba hobbled round the grounds collecting fallen seeds. Because there was hardly ever rain, the leaves and sticks that fell from the trees did not rot to form a layer of protective litter over the soil, and when the hot winds of April came the dry vegetation was blown away. Goat Baba would stoop over, resting on his stick, picking the smooth brown-patterned seeds from the ground with his claw-like hands. He would put the seeds in a crushed, dusty plastic bag, and sell them somewhere for a small amount of cash.

There was never any shortage of animal patients. In Jaipur there was a vast population of camels, horses, donkeys, bullocks and mules who pulled carts laden with anything from building materials to furniture to produce for the market. Each morning men and beasts rose early to toil in the baking summer heat or the bitter winter cold, typically earning just enough to keep themselves and their families alive for one more day. The animals, like the people who worked them, were half-starved and prone to a litany of ailments that their owners could not afford to treat. The shelter saw animals that were sick with colic, riddled with worms, with ankles swollen from being hobbled, abscesses from ill-designed harnesses, toothache, foot-and-mouth disease, heat stroke, fly strike . . . sometimes they were suffering simply from sheer exhaustion, having worked all their lives until they could work no more.

Christine tried out several local veterinarians without finding one who was any good. They were either too arrogant and thought they knew everything, or else completely incompetent. One had operated on a dog and reported that the ovaries had been removed. The trouble was, it was a male dog!

They would have been lost without Daya. Although he had no formal training, the Swiss manager Pierre had taught him how to do quite complicated operations. Daya's amputations, spayings and stitching of wounds, carried out under full anaesthetic, were always successful. Strictly speaking it was illegal to use someone without qualifications, but they could never find a real vet who was as good as him.

They cared for creatures great and small. Often they would come across a street dog which had been injured in a traffic accident. No matter how badly injured the dog might be or how much pain it was in, people rarely showed any concern. The ambulance would pick these creatures up and take them back to the shelter, where they would be treated if it was possible, or else put painlessly to sleep.

Putting animals to sleep, or PTS as it was known, was a humane and necessary part of their daily work. But for Christine it was never an easy decision. She grieved deeply for each small life lost.

TO THE GREY CAT

For three days you were given.
From the rubbish heap where you lay
I lifted your frail body into my arms.

Your purring, kneading, pressing love
extracted my vow to heal.
No doctors here, in these mountains,
but I gave you a small meal which you ate.

You lay on my bed,
a tiny, fragile, grey-furred thing,
squatted in pain, back arched
your relentless yellow eyes
forever asking why?

Your body had forgotten food,
expelled nutrition undigested.
You continued to die
as we watched each other
in the lonely room of our confusion.

All the love was not enough.
I gave you death through a needle
even though you tried to purr.

Alone in the night
I held you on my knee
while you left quietly.

All I could give was three days.

Like the rest of India, Jaipur had a growing middle class, with a middle-class predilection for pets. If a pedigreed dog was surrendered there was always a long queue of people begging to adopt it. They had to be careful about who they gave it to. Only a very wealthy person could afford to keep a large dog like a German Shepherd or a Doberman. Purebred dogs did not have the constitution of street dogs. In summer when the temperature regularly reached 45 degrees Celsius they needed to be kept in an air-conditioned room, so they could not give a large, delicate dog to a poor person.

Some wanted a dog just to resell it. When the shelter rehomed a dog they charged only the cost of vaccinations – about 200 rupees. If the dog was worth 4,000 rupees there could be a nice profit to be made.

It was a different story with mixed-breed dogs. A person who took one of them did so because they loved dogs, rather than because they wanted a status symbol.

Finding a new home for a dog was always a happy experience. On the other hand the surrender of dogs was often distressing. One day some people brought in a very old dog of mixed pedigree. Gypsy had no teeth left and was constantly dribbling. They did not leave a telephone number, only a distant address.

The old dog whimpered forlornly when his owners left. He barked frantically for hour after hour, gazing at the staff through the bars of his cage with an expression that said clearly, 'I want to go home.' He became so distressed that Christine decided to take him back to his former owners to see if they would keep him for the last few years of his life.

With some difficulty they located the apartment. Gypsy, on hearing his mistress's voice, leapt from the vehicle and ran to a spot at the foot of the stairs where an iron ring and chain showed what must have been his living place.

When they informed the owner why they were there she burst into tears. She took them inside and showed them a photograph of her husband. He had been killed in a car accident a month before. The dog had been his. He had owned Gypsy since he was a pup, and now she did not want the dog any more.

They took the distraught Gypsy back to the shelter. They knew they could never rehome him since he was much too old, and most of his teeth were missing. For a while Christine tried to keep him in her garden, but he stood by the gate all day whimpering for his master. Gypsy was too old to change his ways now. She decided to release his loyal soul from his body.

In the old city of Jaipur there were still troupes of monkeys, and they met with frequent accidents. One day the ambulance arrived at the shelter with a half-grown macaque monkey that had been found lying in the gutter covered with burns from swinging on power lines.

Daya had had some bad experiences with monkeys. Because they are wild animals they are difficult to treat. Even monkeys that have been reared as pets can be unpredictable and can suddenly bite someone who is trying to handle them.

This monkey was different. His wounds were deep and painful but he seemed to understand that they were trying to save his life. Instead of baring his teeth he sat quietly without any sedative while his wounds were dressed and bandaged. The procedure had to be repeated every day for several weeks. By the time his wounds were healed everyone had grown extremely fond of the little fellow, but they knew they would have to release him before he became too domesticated. They could not keep him in the shelter because he might become dangerous to humans, or else be killed by the dogs.

Christine was driving past a temple in a nearby suburb when she had an idea. They stopped the car and approached the *saddhu* sitting cross-legged under an old peepal tree. He agreed that they could leave the monkey there. The next day they brought the monkey to the temple and released him. He walked quietly to the *saddhu* and sat on his lap!

They returned a few days later to see the *saddhu* sitting as usual under the tree. The monkey was nowhere in sight. They assumed that he must have fled. The *saddhu* smiled and quietly lifted his blanket to reveal the monkey asleep underneath. In the peace of the temple the little creature had found a safe refuge for life.

It was the middle of 1991. This second stint at Help in Suffering lasted, like the first, for about three months until Christine decided that she should once again return home. One of the things she had to do back in Australia was to tell Animal Liberation that she would no longer be available to play a leading role. Christine was sad to sever her links with Animal Liberation. She had given the organisation fourteen years of her life. She had formed deep friendships with other volunteers, and she had enjoyed the richness and fun of their meetings but since becoming involved with India she had devoted less and less time to the organisation. The administrators accepted her decision with reluctance and wished her well.

The decision to devote herself fully to Help in Suffering hardly made life easier. She now settled into a pattern where she spent three or four months in Australia, alternating with similar periods in India. It was unsatisfactory for both her and Jeremy. She knew that they could not go on this way for much longer and still remain married. As strong-minded as she seemed about her commitment to Help in Suffering, she was still often beset by doubt about whether she was doing the right thing. She wished that there was some way she could remain involved and not have to be apart from her husband. As for Jeremy: 'I did wonder whether the marriage would survive our separations . . . I felt something needed to be done as I found the situation to be emotionally draining, and the "here again, gone again" situation was unsettling.'

One morning early in 1992 during one of Christine's stints in Jaipur, Sambu told her he was going to pray at the little temple near the shelter. He asked if she would like to come with him. Together they walked the hundred or so metres up the road and entered the grounds. The temple, dedicated to the god Hanuman, had a simple little open-air altar, built around an ancient stone which was rubbed smooth from years – probably centuries – of touching. Christine knelt before the stone and prayed: 'Oh Lord Hanuman, I want to serve animals; please show me the way that is right. Should I stay here or should I return to Australia?'

After she and Sambu had finished their devotions they

returned to the shelter. As Christine entered the office the telephone was ringing. It was Jeremy calling from Australia. He sounded in great distress.

'We can't go on like this,' he said. 'I've decided to resign my partnership and we can live in India together.'

Christine could hardly believe what she had heard. 'I thought maybe I'd misunderstood what he said. I didn't want to ask him again in case I had. We hadn't been arguing about it, it just came out of nowhere, which made it all the more special. It was his proposal and his suggestion. He was very intuitive. It was a very great and generous thing that he did.'

Without letting even Christine know, Jeremy had been mulling over his future for a long time. 'I found myself going to work, I'd park the car in the car park and start walking to the office, and I'd think, What on earth am I doing this for while Chris is over there? The thrill of the law had worn off, and I couldn't see any point in persevering. When I told my partners this was what I was going to do I said, "If I don't do it this could well be the end of my marriage".'

Jeremy, in his practical way, had already worked out the financial details. When Christine arrived home he told her that after they sold their house and helped Miles with his mortgage and Cameron finish his studies, there would be very little money left. She told him that she didn't care, she had never wanted material things anyway.

But here's the funny thing. When the time came to sell the house it was Christine, not Jeremy, who had second thoughts. 'I always thought I was a rather detached Buddhist and didn't care about those things. I was very upset when we had to sell the house. I was almost in tears because this was where we'd lived, and we'd furnished these rooms, and made this house, and there were the things of our family and of our past. It seemed outrageous that it shouldn't belong to us forever.'

Lying in bed one night she said to Jeremy, 'We don't have to go if you don't want to go. It's not too late to change our minds.'

'I've made up my mind,' said Jeremy, 'and I'm going.'

Jeremy's partners were understanding, although legally they could have made things difficult. His father, on the other hand, was not. 'First of all he didn't think I was serious, then when he found I was serious he became quite upset about it. Maybe he thought I was dropping out, not living up to my responsibilities. It wasn't the sort of thing persons of his generation and background would normally do. He tried to dissuade me, and as time went by he became stronger about it. He just didn't think it was the right thing to do. He felt I was letting down clients who I'd built up a relationship with. And I wasn't going to be there while the kids were making their way.'

Sita, their blue-heeler cattle dog whom they had found pregnant and abandoned, was evidently put out too. On the morning that half a dozen real-estate agents, slick in their suits and ties, came to value the house, Sita deposited a large, soft turd in the middle of the white-carpeted sitting room. It was only discovered when Christine showed them in.

'Does your dog normally do this?' asked one, with a handkerchief held to his nose.

'She's never done anything like that before in her life.'

After Sita's statement Christine felt slightly better about selling the house.

Jeremy suggested that they put their furniture into storage. It would be expensive, but they might be glad of it some day if their plans changed.

After all the arrangements had been made – the house gone,

thirty years' worth of possessions sold in a garage sale, old friends farewelled, they calculated that they would have enough money invested to live a very frugal lifestyle.

Cameron was in Lismore when the time came for them to leave. Miles came to the airport to say goodbye. He was embittered and angry. He had always felt that Christine put work before family. He was opposed to his parents going to India. He felt, like Jeremy's father, that they should be around for their children and grandchildren.

It was a wretched farewell. After Christine went through the immigration check she sat on a seat, sobbing for the life that she was leaving irrevocably behind, and for her alienated son.

TO MILES

There was a prayer.
You came from far heaven
like ceilings of trumpets and blue cherubs,
fat hands, small toes.

I remember how you held
a whole roomful of people
as you danced, golden curls,
plump knees, small shoes,
the yellow smock.

You slept in my lap,
in the darkness of the late-night car,
tiny body, great being,
filling the plastic, metal shell
with wings in clouds.

Sometimes you ran to me,
even cried for me.

Beloved, angry son,
who will not see my smile,
who speaks police words,
made short to clip the love.
I was young when I left
to seek myself,
to know the truth of life,
I found my God in an old temple,
beside a ghat,
the stone fixed with heat.

Your righteous, childhood eyes
turned from seeing
the mother-place unfilled,
and, when I returned,
you still refused to look.

I see the light in your hair,
your eyes, your being.
I ask only that
you turn to me once more,
and share that light with me.

CHAPTER 15

For Jeremy and Christine, this new life in the small cottage in the grounds of the animal shelter, surrounded by animals, seemed wondrous. They spent time attending to basic things. They brought the electric wiring in the shelter up-to-date, installed a new bore and pump which had been donated by one of the trustees, improved the plumbing, whitewashed and repaired rooms, gardens, cages and the dispensary. They devised a daily work schedule, assigned tasks to specific staff members and generally tried to organise the shelter so that it ran more smoothly. Jeremy worked out a budget. He calculated that it cost US$750 to run the shelter for three months, although with growing demand that figure soon escalated.

The major work was still the rescue of street animals, which they treated if there seemed to be hope, or else euthanased if their prognosis was hopeless. Euthanasia, however, was often not a simple matter, as few owners would directly ask for an animal to be put to sleep. Instead they might say, 'I want you to look after my dog. I can't provide for it properly.'

'What's wrong with it?'

'It has a tumour,' they would answer; or, 'It's dangerous'; or, 'It's vomiting and passing blood.'

Once an owner brought in a small white dog with a grotesque growth on its side, which was bright pink and crawling with maggots.

'It would be kind to put this dog out of its misery,' Christine told the owner.

'Destiny should decide whether it lives or dies,' he replied. 'It's for God to decide, not us.'

'Then you should sign the book that you surrender it to us.'

The man signed and walked away without once looking back.

'We'll put it down,' said Daya, 'and say it died a natural death.'

Another time an owner surrendered an ancient, purebred black Labrador retriever – a rarity in India. Unusually, on this occasion the owner specifically asked for it to be put down. The old dog was stick-thin, her breathing was laboured and she was so weak she could not stand. Christine thought she recognised the symptoms of distemper, in which case she knew that it would not have long to live. If by some miracle the dog did recover from distemper she would almost certainly have neuro-logical damage, which could result in seizures or permanent spasms. Christine decided to follow the owner's wishes. She asked one of the ground staff, Ramswaroop, to bring the needle.

Ramswaroop came and Christine bent down to perform the final act of mercy. As she did so, the dog, with a great effort, slowly lifted her head so that she could look into Christine's eyes. As they gazed at one another Christine felt that the dog was asking for one last chance. She put the needle aside and vowed to herself to do all she could to help the Labrador recover.

She fetched a small bowl of milk and put it under the dog's nose. The creature showed no interest, but continued to lie without moving. It was critical that the dog receive some nourishment so Christine prepared an IV drip for her. She was about to begin the procedure when she was seized with a sudden impulse. She walked out the front gate and up to the temple, where there was a very old image of the Hindu monkey god Hanuman, a symbol of the love between human and animal. She offered prayers for the dog's recovery, then returned.

The Labrador was still lying there, not moving. Again Christine fetched the bowl of milk and held it under her nose. This time she slowly lifted her head and drank the entire contents of the bowl. Christine was delighted, although she still did not really believe that it was possible for her to live.

Every few hours she fed the dog small measures of food – baby cereal, raw egg, some bread soaked in milk. Each time she fed her she marvelled that the dog was still breathing. Over the next 24 hours the dog's strength slowly returned. As the days passed and it seemed the animal might live, Christine worried that the dog would be left with a legacy of convulsing limbs or a permanently nodding head, which she had seen so often in other victims of distemper.

After a couple of weeks with still no sign of neurological damage, Christine knew her patient was out of danger. The dog was able to wag her tail vigorously, walk stiffly and smile a crooked dog-smile that seemed to say, 'Thank you for saving my life'.

Christine decided to name her Silky and to adopt her as her own. She took her to the cottage. To her surprise, as soon as

Silky walked into the bedroom she jumped onto the bed.

'No Silky,' Christine said, and went to pull her off. As she tugged on her collar Silky growled furiously and snapped at her. Christine snatched her hand away just in time to prevent it being bitten. She was shocked. It had not occurred to her that there might be an aggressive side to Silky's personality. Clearly someone had mistreated her, and she thought that Christine, too, was going to brutalise her.

'Silky?' she asked in a soothing tone. The dog snarled and bared her teeth in response.

'I have to show her who's boss,' she thought. 'She must obey me. We can't keep her if she's dangerous. It's crucial that she pass this test.'

The two locked eyes again. Suddenly Christine realised that it was she who needed to pass a test. Others had mistreated the dog; now Silky wanted to know whether Christine, too, would be a bully or treat her with kindness.

She stood a few feet away speaking gently. Christine explained to Silky that she would never be hurt again nor need she ever fear again. As Christine spoke she consciously held loving thoughts and images in her mind. She believes that this is the way animals communicate with one another.

Silky watched her with her large brown eyes. The moment had come to discover whether Christine had passed her test. She leant forward and took the dog's collar. Silky lay with front paws extended forward, slightly to one side. She seemed to be thinking, watching. Christine held the collar and tugged gently.

'Silky, come.'

Without hesitation, as though she had never been anything but the most loving and obedient dog, Silky jumped down from the bed.

'Good Silky,' said Christine, patting and fondling her ears. The dog's tail began to wag.

Silky never again jumped on the bed.

Nirmal still came on Sunday to do the books. He always arrived precisely on time, on a motor scooter which he carefully covered against bird droppings. He prayed, lit incense, then polished his shoes before starting work on the accounts. Christine loved his thorough, precise manner – the way he sat at his desk working through the figures, exasperated but laughing when Daya failed to present him with the necessary receipts. After talking it over with Jeremy and then with Janine and the other trustees, she summoned up the courage to ask Nirmal if he would come and work full-time at HIS.

He looked up sweetly from his desk. 'I will think and I will inform,' he said.

She asked him about his salary, and offered to pay him more than he was receiving, because they could not promise to give superannuation.

It was a difficult decision for Nirmal to make, because he held a very good job in a large enterprise. But he was a Jain, and his religion taught that helping animals was a prerequisite in life, so he agreed to sacrifice a secure future in order to work at a small, unknown shelter.

His coming changed everything. He began to organise the staff, took over all the book-keeping and accounts, researched government and legal requirements as to the auditing of charities and employment of staff, answered the phone and even posted letters.

This last task was not as simple as it sounds. You had to

stand in a queue to have the letter weighed, after which a man would write on the envelope the stamps that you needed. Then you had to stand in another queue to buy the stamps. After that there was a third queue where a clerk imprinted the stamps, so they would not be stolen.

Christine and Jeremy did not have television; the phone mostly did not work; there was no air-conditioning; they cooked on a small gas cooker. Behind the shelter the *nulla*, which once had been clean and which had cooled Jaipur on the hot summer nights, had now had most of the water pumped from it, and what remained was stinking grey sludge.

On the other side of the *nulla* was a government farm with acres of fruit trees and paddocks where prisoners being rehabili- tated were given jobs. Because of the trees, scores of peacocks came every morning to eat the leftover rice in the dog bowls. Their haunting, cat-like call evoked all the mystery of the East. There were also many varieties of birds, particularly crows, which feasted on the fruit. The first time they heard a cacophony of shouting from across the *nulla* they thought it was the prisoners fighting, but they soon discovered they were simply scaring away the birds. They identified over 25 varieties of birds which visited the river and swamp-land next door, and which also rested in the trees of the shelter. In the steep red-earth river banks, flocks of swallows nested, and the cliffs were full of the holes in which they bred.

In 1992, while the middle-class revolution was beginning to transform India, there were no supermarkets as yet in Jaipur. Christine shopped for groceries at a dimly lit store a short drive from the shelter. You asked for something and an assistant climbed a ladder or disappeared into a dark corner, then the shopkeeper weighed out the purchase on old-fashioned scales and handed it over in a brown paper bag.

For meat they went to the Muslim quarter, where the butcher sliced the cuts by holding the knife between his toes and pulling the flesh backwards and forwards across the blade. Flies rose in swarms. Jeremy needed little persuasion to decide that as long as he was in India, he, like the Hindus, would be vegetarian.

Christine and Jeremy decided that they needed to buy a car, as the shelter's ambulance always seemed to be in use whenever they needed to drive somewhere. There was no such thing as a second-hand car dealer or advertisements in the newspaper. You simply asked around and let it be known that you were in the market for one.

At ten p.m. one evening a dealer arrived with a small Maruti 800. The radio was blaring and its dashboard was covered with synthetic, fluffy tiger-print material. When asked why the car was for sale, the dealer said his grandmother wanted to sell it. As dubious as this sounded, Jeremy agreed to take the car for a test-drive around the block. Or, rather, Daya did, as Jeremy did not yet feel he was ready to face the challenge of driving in Jaipur.

The 'block' consisted of a new housing development that the Rajasthani State Government was building in an attempt to house its rapidly expanding population. Former fields, paddocks and orchards were rapidly being covered with ugly cement buildings. The sewer was not yet connected, and the roads were unpaved mud. Navigating through the potholes was an excellent test of roadworthiness. The Maruti failed.

They next test-drove a Maruti Gypsy, an Indian version of a four-wheel-drive Suzuki. It was a three-year-old model, already showing signs of rust, with torn upholstery and the dashboard cracked by the sun. When they drove it they discovered there were also serious deficiencies on the mechanical side. The air-conditioning did not work and the transmission made expensive-sounding noises.

In its favour, though, the price was not dear. After negotiating a sum that was considerably less than the one being asked, the seller agreed to take the car to a mechanic, who would quote for the needed repairs, which would then be deducted from the final amount.

After it had been examined, despite the best efforts of the mechanic the car failed to start. By now, buying a second-hand car did not seem to be such a good idea. For an extra A\$2,500 they could have a new Gypsy, which they could assume would be reliable. Leaving the hapless seller with his mechanic head-down under the bonnet, Christine and Jeremy proceeded straight away to a Maruti showroom where they asked a salesman if he had a brochure for the Gypsy. He vanished for fifteen minutes on other business and finally reappeared to announce he did not have a brochure. They asked if they could test-drive a vehicle, and he vanished again. At this stage, thoroughly exasperated, they left and took an auto-rickshaw to another Maruti agency close to the shelter.

There they found a more accommodating manager, who not only had a brochure but was happy to sit and discuss it with them. Unfortunately there were no Gypsys in stock; if they wanted to see one they would have to wait until one arrived at the dealership to be delivered to another customer. Even then a test-drive was out of the question. If they wanted to buy one they had to sign an order form, pay the full price and wait for the factory to deliver it. They could not say how long it might take.

With a feeling of resignation they went to the bank, returned with a bag full of cash, and prepared themselves for an indefinite wait. Three weeks later they took delivery of a new vehicle, which did everything that they could wish – even showing a willingness to start in the morning without complaint.

Jeremy drove at first using his international licence. The next step was to obtain Indian driving licences. The government department that looked after licences was located in the old city palace, which had once belonged to the Maharaja of Jaipur. Outside in a big open courtyard there were perhaps a hundred desks behind which sat a hundred clerks. Peons hurried about carrying files to and fro.

Christine and Jeremy went there one day with Ngaire, a Scottish volunteer vet, who was working at the shelter temporarily. Daya found someone on one of the desks whom he knew. Over the next few days they were given forms which they filled in then dutifully returned, only to find that they had not been completed exactly to requirements, or that there were other forms which had not been mentioned before. At length they were directed to an official in the office building behind the courtyard. They negotiated winding stairways with red betel-spit in the corners, and entered a maze of offices containing more desks piled high with dusty folders.

They were ushered into a room by an official. He politely asked them to sit down. They handed over their forms and waited while he studied them closely. He looked up with an apologetic smile.

'I'm very sorry madam and sir, but I need to ask you some questions.'

Before, whenever they had enquired whether they needed to learn any road rules the clerks' eyes had rolled in their heads as though they had never heard of anything so strange. Now it seemed they did indeed need to know some rules. The official produced a folder with a series of greasy pages. On each page was a symbol, which he asked them to identify. Some they could guess at, such as a circle with a line through it; others, with esoteric Indian symbols, were completely unknown to them. With these Christine mumbled nonsense and hoped for the best. Being too polite to say that he could not understand her English, the official ticked the question and moved on to the next.

It was then time for driving tests – except for Jeremy. 'I don't have to give you one, sir,' said the examiner, 'I have already seen you driving.'

Christine was asked to drive around the block. The examiner declined to accompany her, perhaps out of fear.

Then it was Ngaire's turn. The examiner asked her to drive to the end of the street and back. She put the car into what she thought was first gear, released the hand-brake and began to move – backwards. After some crunching of gears she found first and kangaroo-hopped up the narrow dead-end street, coming to a halt with the front bumper a couple of metres from a wall.

'Reverse, reverse,' shouted the examiner. Christine, Jeremy and the examiner waited. The car moved forward and stopped once more. Through the back window they could see Ngaire wrestling with the gear lever. They all waited in expectant silence. After more delay the Gypsy at last began to reverse towards them. Ngaire had got the four-wheel-drive control mixed up with the gear lever.

Anticipating failure they followed the examiner back to his office. 'You are to be congratulated,' he said. Signing three pieces of paper, he handed them over with a smile – not just any old bits of paper, these, of which there had been so many, but special ones bearing the longed-for signature which, after just one more visit to one more desk, would entitle them to be issued green cardboard documents with Indian squiggles on them saying that they were allowed to drive.

If there were road rules in Jaipur it seemed contrary to the Indian temperament to obey them. Near Durgapura there was a railway crossing which was closed whenever a train came through. The man in charge always shut the gate well ahead of time because of the objections which inevitably arose from thwarted drivers. As he began his task people would push with their motor scooters, camel carts and little Marutis and shout at him, attempting to intimidate him into allowing them through. Even as the gate began to swing some still darted across the track. When he finally managed to close it a great jam of cars, buses, trucks, auto-rickshaws, motorcycles and scooters would build up on both sides of the line, like water against a dam – not in an orderly queue, but two, three or four abreast at the gate, spreading out fanwise as the queue lengthened.

At the very front the scooter riders waited like a brigade ready to go into battle, jostling and swaying against each other, sometimes edging slightly forwards as they juggled for position. Many of the trucks came from far away. They bore signs such as HARYANA, WEST BENGAL and ORISSA, and were decorated with gaudy coloured logos of flowers, gods and animals. Some had a sign on the back bumper bar – '*Awaz do*', which translated to 'make noise', meaning 'If you are caught behind me, blow your horn'.

Despite the invitation on the signs, no one blew their horn. Instead the truck drivers cut their engines, and the large, decorated machines waited in decorous silence for the train to pass.

When the train at last came into view, drawn by a puffing steam engine, with passengers hanging out of the carriage doors and seated on the roof, a frisson of expectation would ripple among the waiting drivers. Engines would start and the air would turn opaque, filling with the stench of diesel as each driver revved in anticipation. The gate man would stroll from his little stone hut, the traffic would inch forward, he would pause for a moment, raise the bar, then a glittering phalanx of metal would advance from either side of the railway track – and come to a dead stop in the middle. Then the air would reverberate to the sound of horns and indignant shouts. Sometimes it took half an hour for the gridlock to sort itself out and for the traffic to begin moving again.

Driverji, the shelter's ambulance driver, was a well-built man whose most prominent facial feature was a luxuriant moustache. His appearance, allied to a certain dashing, devil-may-care style, gave him the air of a Cossack horseman riding into battle. And indeed, when Driverji mounted the lumbering ambulance, and with curses and imprecations urged it forth into the traffic, it was as if he were engaging in an activity in which no quarter would be countenanced. Giving way to other vehicles was, in his eyes, tantamount to surrender. When confronted with larger vehicles than his own he displayed the courage of a true warrior.

Knowing Driverji's style it was with some trepidation that Christine asked him one day to take her to the airport, as

163

Jeremy was busy elsewhere with the Gypsy. As luck would have it they came to the Durgapura railway crossing just as the gate was closing.

Undeterred, Driverji hauled the wheel and made a U-turn, explaining that he knew of another small crossing a few kilometres away which might still be open. The ambulance set off through a sandy desert track roughly parallel to the railway line. Driverji was hunched over the wheel, wrestling now and then with the gears as the Jeep slid and bounced into potholes and around small hillocks. Soon they were racing a little white Maruti sedan. The track split in two; the Maruti took one fork, and Driverji took the other. As Driverji urged on his lurching, swaying vehicle he stole occasional glances at his rival. When the tracks again joined into one he was just in front of the smaller car. He did not consider that perhaps his driving might have been dangerous, and possibly frightening to his passenger. He saw himself rather as the valiant rescuer using lateral thinking and knowledge of the neighbourhood roads to deliver his charge to her destination, despite all the obstacles which confronted him.

Just when it seemed that he had triumphed over the Maruti, he was faced by another threat. Ahead, where the road crossed the railway tracks, a man was closing a solitary gate. The odds against arriving at the gate in time seemed remote. A less courageous driver may well have chosen to slow down, but instead Driverji urged the vibrating ambulance to even greater speed. Christine gripped the dashboard and watched in silent fear as the gate began to swing. It seemed impossible that they would get there in time. Still Driverji's foot remained pressed to the floor. Christine closed her eyes and the ambulance sped through the gap, bounced wildly over the railway tracks and onto the road on the other side. She glanced back. The gate was shut and the Maruti was left stranded in a cloud of settling dust.

At the airport, trembling, she thanked Driverji and alighted with her rucksack, only to find, as she hurried into the air-conditioned coolness, that the plane had been delayed and would not depart for another three hours.

CHAPTER 16

Janine Vogler had arranged for Christine and Jeremy to be provided with accommodation within the shelter and with food. They drew no salary while Cameron was still at University in Lismore and they were contributing about A$170 a week to his living expenses. They had income coming in from two investment properties in Australia, but the margin of income over expenses was extremely fine, and they were only just managing to get a small return. When they bought the Gypsy they were worried that they might not be able to afford to run it; and they also worried about where the money would come from if either of them were to fall ill or have an accident.

Jeremy calculated that they had about A$100 a week to live on, which at the time translated to 2,100 rupees per week or 300 rupees per day. They could afford to go out once a week, but as Jeremy found that Indian food did not agree with him they did not overdo it. Supplementing the shelter food with fruit and western-style 'luxuries' such as jams, baked beans, cordials and so on was expensive. They tried hard to avoid alcoholic drinks; even ice cream was an extravagance. With no TV or radio, reading was their chief form of entertainment. In order to keep within their budget they recorded all personal expenditure in a notebook.

While they were living on 2,100 rupees a week, Jeremy is quick to point out that their staff were getting by on less than 1,000 rupees per month, and feeding their families. 'To them our 2,100 rupees would have seemed a huge amount. We weren't complaining. It was a happy time, and it was really our non-Indian expenses that were the problem.'

Six months after they had arrived they received a shock which dented further their already meagre budget. Jeremy had known before leaving Australia that a tax bill was due. He had asked his accountant to pay it for him when it arrived. Unfortunately, the amount was far in excess of what he had expected. As a result they were practically broke.

The amenities in their new home were hardly luxurious. In the morning they would rise at dawn and take a bucket to the outside laundry, where there was a uniquely Indian device known as a 'geyser' attached to the wall. If they were lucky it would give forth hot water; if the power was off, as often happened, the water would be cold, or perhaps there would be no water at all, as it had to be pumped by an electric pump from 300 feet underground into holding tanks on the roof of the dispensary, which might have run out. If the taps were dry they would take a bucket across the street to the communal pump and fill it by hand. They would then carry it into the bathroom, which had a concrete floor sloped so as to drain through a hole at the base of one wall. Squatting naked they would ladle water over themselves; showers or baths were a forgotten luxury from a former life.

Strangely for such spartan appointments there was a bidet. It had never worked. When you turned the tap it squirted water over the wall, and where it landed there was an unsightly stain.

Apart from mosquitos, they shared the cottage with large daddy-longlegs spiders, which made webs in the corners of the ceilings. They did not kill them except in the little room beside the kitchen where visitors sat. Lizards clung to the walls and ceiling. They were skilled at catching insects. With their large, black eyes, Christine found them so appealing that even though they dropped little black deposits filled with insect shells all over the house, they, too, were allowed to thrive.

Termites built earthen tubes that climbed the walls and intertwined with shoes and clothes if they had not been disturbed for a while. Sometimes little edifices sprouted from cracks in the cement floor like strange castles in the middle of the room. Christine was loath to spray them with insecticide but the termites had voracious appetites, and secretly ate the complete interior of one wooden door, leaving only a shell of paint. One day when she pushed it the paint gave way, and all that was left inside was crumbling dust.

Then there were the snakes. There was a type of yellow and green striped snake which liked to hang from trees in the garden. At night it was unwise to walk anywhere without shoes and socks, in case they trod on a viper. Short and brown-coloured, they looked like fallen branches. Once in the night one came into the house and Christine walked within a few centimetres of one in the darkness on her way to the bathroom. When she turned on the light it slid across the floor in fright and out into the garden through the hole in the wall where it had entered.

The cottage had a minimum of furniture and decoration. On the walls hung four or five oils of flowers and animals which Christine had painted, and a picture of a cat given to her by her mother. There were four pictures of the god Hanuman, and a statue of Hanuman covered in pieces of mirror. There were some pots which Christine had painted in patterns and glazed, and a pair of wooden Rajasthani chests, upon one of which rested a brass Buddha holding an injured swan. Apart from the bed the only furniture was a glass-topped wrought-iron table in the small room adjoining the kitchen, with two chairs.

Christine and Jeremy's relationship had changed. For the first time in years they were communicating easily with one another. Christine remembers: 'It was quite a radiant time in our lives because we started to be together again. After the awfulness and after the weeping at the airport saying goodbye to Miles, which was very bad, it became a very liberating experience.'

Liberating, too, for Jeremy, who had been freed from the relentless stress of his old job. 'In lots of ways it was all something new. We were able to do things because we enjoyed doing them rather than doing them because we had to, with the stress of what might happen if you didn't do them or if things went wrong.'

Jeremy developed skills that he had never known he possessed during thirty years as a solicitor. He learned how to drain kennels and mix cement in the correct proportions; he designed cages and dealt with the intricacies of Indian bureaucracy. 'If I'd have been at home I'd probably be still at Gray and Perkins, which is where I'd been all my life, and I probably would have done the same thing until the end of my working life. Here I've learned all sorts of different skills, and I've seen some fascinating things, and it's very satisfying. I've met people that I would never have had the opportunity to meet. The relationship between Chris and myself has changed, and it's something to have a wife and friend who you can be sure you're going to go through the rest of your life with.'

While Help in Suffering was now purely dedicated to helping animals, Christine was always mindful of the human dimension to their work. A man from a migratory tribe of gypsies brought a seriously ill camel into the shelter. Although they did what they could, it died. They went to his camp in an empty field on the outskirts of the city to tell him the bad news. The hut in which he and his family had been living had been destroyed in a fire. His daughter had been badly burnt, and he would have to take on crippling debt to pay for her medical fees. Now their means of livelihood, the camel, was gone. The only food they had was two potatoes, which the man's wife was cooking in charcoal.

The shelter gave him money for the medical fees and bought material for a new hut that he could disassemble and take with him when he had to move. And they gave him another camel.

'There are lots of stories like that,' says Christine. 'It's very satisfying to be able to help someone. He had other children too. The thing that's always tragic is that the help is not a final solution, it's only temporary. Maybe for a few years the camel will help that family, but a much larger solution is needed for these people.'

Every day she would deal with some new and touching case. Sometimes an animal would make a special impact. One such creature was a poor old pony that the staff had rescued from the road where she had been abandoned after falling down from exhaustion. Her owner had removed the harness, pulled away the wooden cart, and left her lying in the sun to die of dehydration and starvation. Luckily a passing stranger who knew about the shelter phoned and told them of the pony's predicament.

After they had unloaded the pony from the ambulance and given her food and water, she struggled to her feet and stood pitifully before them. Her feet were so crippled that she could hardly take a step. This crippling of the feet was a common problem in Jaipur, for the tendons swelled and became inflamed from constant trotting on the hard, hot roads. Bad shoeing compounded the problem. The leg near the hoof would become shortened, losing its elasticity. In bad cases such as this one the rear hooves actually started to turn backwards, so that the horse was walking on the front of the hoof itself. The damage was irreversible, and they felt that the kindest thing would be to put the pony to sleep.

Joy, a volunteer vet from Britain who specialised in equines, examined the old horse thoroughly. 'She's been worked until she couldn't take another step,' she said. 'See here on her shoulders – the gall marks from rubbing. And here around her fetlocks, the scars from hobbling with ropes.'

Christine rubbed the old pony on the forelock. After having led such a hard life, she fully expected that the horse would lay back her ears and try to bite her. She had known nothing but cruelty from humans, so why would she behave otherwise? But as she touched her forelock and murmured gently to her, the horse slightly quivered her bottom lip and gazed affectionately from large brown eyes.

Joy examined the horse again. 'With careful trimming of the hooves, we might be able to slightly correct the situation,' she said. 'She'll never be able to work again, but she could lead a comfortable life for a few more years.'

They called in the best '*jutewalla*' (shoeman) they knew, and Joy directed him as to how to cut the hooves. They called the pony Tattoo (the Hindi word for pony). Over the following weeks, with a carefully balanced diet, her coat began to shine and her bones became covered with flesh. She began to walk and, although she was very crippled, she did not seem to suffer pain, for they gave her the run of the shelter, and she would often go out the gate, ambling for long distances down the road, returning in the evenings.

Tattoo was affectionate and clever, more like a dog than a pony. She would come and stand on the verandah outside the office door near the cooler when it was hot. If she had a chance she would even walk into the office to scrounge for stale biscuits and bread, which a local bakery donated. Having been starved all her life she was always interested in food. She would lick the tea out of the tea-cups should anyone leave one lying around. Vegetable curry, dahl, and anything vegetarian would vanish down her ever-ready throat.

The *kooti* (chaff) for the shelter animals was delivered by a man who came with the sacks on a cart pulled by a small, fat, chestnut stallion. This little pony was very friendly, and also greedy. While the sacks were being unloaded he liked to help himself to whatever fodder he could find in one of the cows' or donkeys' bins. He enjoyed his short sojourns at the shelter so much that he used to visit at night after the day's work was finished. They often had to ring the *kootiwalla* and ask him to come and collect his charge.

It became apparent that the *kootiwalla*'s pony had other things on his mind besides food. Soon they noticed that Tattoo was growing fatter than ever, until one evening she gave birth to a beautiful little chestnut filly. Her long life of suffering had now been replaced by a new life of happiness and fulfilment. Joy called the filly *Basanti*, the Hindi word for 'spring', for she seemed full of newness and promise and beauty. With great tenderness and love Tattoo cared for her baby. She never left the shelter now – the two of them were inseparable.

One day they noticed that Tattoo was unable to walk any more. Her feet were clearly giving her terrible pain. Basanti was now six months old, and able to care for herself. They knew that at last they had to euthanase Tattoo.

The pony died peacefully and her body shivered. One moment her muscles and bone thrilled with her life force, but with the departure of consciousness her old body became just an empty corpse. They allowed Basanti to come and say her farewells. She walked over to the body and sniffed it all over. Christine wondered whether she understood what had happened.

Basanti was too valuable to be allowed to roam freely. They kept her in a small run. She was so friendly and pretty that everyone liked petting and talking to her. But as she grew into a yearling she began to grow restless. She started to kick and bite and charge around the enclosure. They taught her to wear a halter, and took her for walks along the streets where once her mother had wandered, but she liked to play games and to rear in the air if she had an excuse. A passing tractor or camel would be enough to send her into a frenzy.

Basanti was as clever as her mother. She knew how to lift the latch with her mouth and pull the bolt on the gate to open it. Once free, she would tear around the shelter at a gallop, kicking her back legs out behind her, wild with the taste of freedom.

Basanti obviously wanted to experience the outside world. She wanted to smell new scents, to touch new surfaces, to see new sights; she wanted to use her inquisitive, intelligent mind. Christine knew all too well what life would probably be like outside the shelter for her. Nearly every day she saw horses suffering from common diseases such as babesiosis, a debilitating illness caused by a parasite spread by ticks; she saw cuts and wounds from road accidents, and bloated stomachs from worm infestation. But most of all she saw the incurable results of over-work – the tight tendons and straight, inflexible fetlocks, the crippled, stiff legs caused by years of labour on the hard, hot roads while shod with small, badly fitting shoes. She was torn between Basanti's boredom in confinement and the cruelty of the outside world.

One day an old, white-bearded Muslim man brought his horse to her for treatment. The horse was as small as a donkey and all its ribs and bones protruded. It could barely stand on its tiny, twisted hooves. There were hardly any teeth left. The man used the horse to carry people from the railway station to the hotels. Overloaded with passengers and their luggage, these little *tonga* ponies were a cheap form of taxi. Joy told the old man that his horse was too old to work any more.

'I very poor man,' he answered, patting his old pony's head, his eyes filling with tears.

That night Joy and Christine discussed what to do. Basanti needed to be broken in or she would become even more difficult to manage. She might even become vicious if she was very bored. At eighteen months of age she was ready to begin work. If she stayed at Help in Suffering all her life, she would never experience anything beyond the confines of the shelter. They thought that if they gave her to the old man he would look after her kindly, and her life would be meaningful.

The man agreed to take Basanti on the strict condition that he would care for her properly and break her in gently. While Basanti was being trained he could continue to use his old horse, as he said he could not survive without his daily earnings from the *tonga*. The shelter would pay for Basanti's food for three months, then the old horse was to be surrendered, and if Basanti was in good condition she would be formally given to the old man.

Three months later Basanti returned for her check-up. Christine hurried from the office to see her. The beautiful chestnut pony was harnessed to an old cart with wobbly, worn wooden wheels. She no longer stood with her head held proudly, with flared nostrils and bold eyes. Now her head hung down, her whole demeanour was dejected and broken. She seemed already old and exhausted. Christine could hardly believe it was the same horse.

'Basanti!' she said. 'Do you remember me?' She stretched out her hand, but instead of nudging with a velvety nose, the horse snorted, rolled her eyes so that the whites showed, and flinched away.

Christine looked at the bridle. At each side of her mouth there was a deep, weeping red wound. The bit was spiked, with deep, sharp ridges that had cut into her lips.

Indignation and anger rose in her. They had given their greatest gift to this man: they had entrusted him with a young pony, had handed her over on the understanding that she would know no cruelty at his hands, and now he had broken his promise to them.

'Why did you use this bit when we asked you not to?' she asked.

'She was being very naughty in the traffic, so the people told me I should use it.'

'Those wounds could easily become infested with maggots,' Joy said. She looked at Basanti's back legs. Sure enough, the tell-tale signs were there. The pasterns had become quite straight. 'She's been overworked,' she concluded. 'There was that genetic tendency there from her mother, and this man has compounded it.'

Christine asked the owner to unharness Basanti. She explained that Basanti could not be worked until the lips had healed, otherwise they might be permanently damaged.

The old man put his head in his hands and began to sob. For a moment Christine felt tempted to give Basanti back to him with a new, smooth bit, but then she thought of those tight legs and the deep mouth wounds. When Basanti had left the shelter her lower limbs had been soft and flexible, her mouth was smooth and unblemished. Now, on each wither there was a rubbed, bare patch which had been caused by friction from the harness.

Then she noticed that around each back fetlock there was a deep indentation in the hair, and in one place there was a bald, exposed line. The man had hobbled her. Perhaps he had tied the back legs together for days at a time to force her to stand still, or perhaps he hobbled her every night and turned her out. In any case it was a cruel practice, which led to wounds that soon became fly-infested. Once the maggots hatched the whole leg could be eaten away. On many occasions they had rescued donkeys and ponies from the street with the bones of a leg exposed, the hoof attached but unable to move due to the absence of muscle, while the animal was still living.

Christine thought of the old mare that the man had

surrendered. Was this how Basanti would end up?

The process of rehabilitation began again. Within ten days Basanti's lips had healed and her pasterns had become more flexible. Every time she saw Christine she would lift her head and nicker.

They asked the milkman if he needed another pony, and he said yes. Basanti now lived near the shelter. She was glossy and friendly. Sometimes, breaking free, she would still come charging down the road, to stand outside the fence whinnying to announce her presence.

CHAPTER 17

Christine took a personal interest in the lives of everyone who worked at the shelter. To her they were more than just employees. They made up a family of which she was a part. Manju, the shelter's cook, was married to Babulal, who was in charge of the dispensary. Manju had been looking radiant lately. After trying to have a baby for a long time she was pregnant. The baby was due in about two weeks' time.

One day when she had finished her day's work cooking and sweeping at the shelter a medicine man came to visit her. He was a swarthy man of about thirty, dressed in a white shirt and pyjamas. He said magic words and gave Manju a potion to swallow. About ten days later Christine was driving back from buying stores in Durgapura, when the Jeep from the shelter passed in the opposite direction. Daya stopped and ran across, his face tense. 'Manju's baby has died inside her,' he said. 'We're taking her to the hospital at Durgapura now.'

Babulal was standing beside the Jeep, his shoulders drooped forwards, his face knotted, and as Christine touched his arm he began to shudder with great sobs. Manju was sitting in the front of the Jeep with her mother. Christine hugged her and they cried together, clinging to each other with despair.

This hospital was a clean, freshly whitewashed building. In the front room parents with desperately ill children drooped over their shoulders crowded about. In the wards were moaning women with families clustered around their beds. Everywhere there were small dramas of life and death.

Manju was given a room on her own. She lay on the bed with a drip connected by a plastic tube to her arm. She wore a brightly patterned sari with a blue blouse underneath, and a *bindi* jewel on her forehead. Her mother bent over her, a strong, proud, dark-faced woman with the same high cheekbones as her daughter, and the same large eyes. Her sister stroked her forehead, brushing the hair back from her temples. Half a dozen people from the shelter crowded into the room, standing in silence.

Soon the doctor came – a small, stout, efficient woman in a blue sari, carrying a notebook.

'Is the child definitely dead?' Christine asked.

'It's definitely dead. It's been dead about ten days. There was no sound of heart beat about ten days ago. I asked Babulal to take Manju for further tests. Since Manju was so healthy he didn't think anything could be wrong.'

'Why did it die?'

'We cannot know.'

'So how will you get it out?'

'First we'll try to induce labour through administration of a drug. It's best she should give birth naturally. The onset of labour could take from twelve hours to two days. If this is unsuccessful we'll have to do a caesarean.'

There was little space for the crowd of visitors in the small room. They all stood around a little longer, then told Manju they would come back in the morning, leaving her in the care of her mother and sisters.

When Christine went to visit her in the afternoon the contractions had begun. Numerous staff and relatives were clustered about. It seemed to make no difference that some were male and some were female. All together shared in the mourning and the pain.

Manju squatted on the floor, her hands clutching at the sheet on the bed, her head resting on a pillow. Her hair was knotted and wet. She rolled her head backwards and forwards, moaning and crying with the pain. She stopped crying for a moment when she saw Christine, and composed herself enough to say, 'Memsahib, thank you for coming.'

They stroked her arms, held her hand, caressed her forehead. '*Dard, dard,*' she cried, 'pain, pain.'

After a while everyone went back to the shelter. Two hours later, Rajendra came running to Christine's door. 'Memsahib, memsahib, baby come. Hospital now.'

They all piled into the Jeep once more, and raced down the road through the darkness. Small lights twinkled in the dwellings nearby. Some migrant tribal people were camped by the road with their goats and camels. It was about nine p.m. and the shops in Durgapura were closing. Manju was inside a door that was marked, 'Labour room. Dark room.' Babulal stood outside, exhausted and expressionless.

'The baby has been born dead,' Daya said. 'Babulal is going to get it to show to us.'

Christine's father, Harold Woolcott, in army uniform, October 1940.

Christine with her grandfather's dog, Josie, at her grandparents' home in Cheltenham, Victoria.

Christine cuddles her new little sister, Anne.

Christine and Anne sample country life at a family friend's property in Toowoomba, Queensland.

Mother and two reluctant daughters preparing for one of Suzanne's lavish dinner parties.

Christine and Jeremy at a ball in Sydney shortly before they married.

Proud parents with the bride, 23 October 1965.

Christine with Miles in the Townends' first flat at Cremorne.

Two young mothers share a laugh at Anne's home in Coonamble.

Cameron (left) and Miles.

Christine confronts wharfies at Port Adelaide in 1982 while trying to prevent live sheep exports. Moments later she was forcibly ejected.

On the steps of the Sydney Opera House addressing animal rights campaigners, 1998.

Christine and the philosopher, Peter Singer, share a break during a meeting of the Australian Federation of Animal Societies.

Christine with Badal.

Mishy on a visit to Help in Suffering shortly after Christine took over as managing trustee.

Mishy, Daya and Christine on Mishy's last visit, February 1996.

Jeremy at work in Jaipur.

Rescued street dog, Jaipur.

Dr Ashok Tanwar (left) and compounder, Shiv, treat a Brooke program patient.
Photograph Anna Little.

Dr Devi Shankar treats an injured eye.
Photograph Anna Little.

Capturing
a street dog
for the Jaipur
ABC Program.

Photograph Anna Little.

Dr Naveen Pandey operating during a Himalayan field trip.

Photograph Anna Little.

Dr Jack Reece on a field trip in Rajasthan.
Photograph Anna Little.

Jaipur vets prepare to excise a massive tumour on the right hand side of the horse's stomach. The patient made a complete recovery.
Photograph Anna Little.

Dr Madhulal Valliatte and Munna treat an infected tusk.

Photograph Anna Little.

Madhulal with a
very special patient.
Photograph Anna Little.

Elephants wait their turn
to carry tourists up to the
Amer fortress-palace in
Jaipur. The finery often
hides painful injuries.
Photograph Anna Little.

Christine on a social visit to Her Highness the Rajmata of Jaipur.
Photograph Anna Little.

Some of the thirty Jaipur staff. *Back row L to R*: Akloo, Jeremy, Raj, Nirmal, Christine, Sunil, Iti, Sambu, Jack, Ramnivas, Driverji, Feliram. *Front row*: Rakhee, Babulal, Dulichand, Suresh, Nandu.

Photograph Anna Little.

Four Cows Resting – from one of Christine's Australian exhibitions.

There was an old cardboard carton on a wooden table outside the room. Babulal went into the labour room with the carton and brought it out again, carrying it with great reverence. He laid it on the table and everyone clustered round peering into the open box. It was a grocery box, slightly crushed at the sides from previous use. Inside lay a small baby like a pink doll. A thick umbilical cord was attached to its navel. All its skin had peeled off in sheets, and around its eyes and nose the skin had puckered, so there were just clogged holes. Christine thought that it looked beautiful in its stillness.

Babulal did not cry any more now. He seemed to be less hunched, his eyes purged. He had seen his child, and it had died. He had fathered a living being, had produced a son, even though that son was now dead.

Manju came from the labour ward, weeping, 'Mera baccha, mera baccha,' 'my child, my child,' leaning on the shoulders of a nurse and her mother. She lay down on the bed, exhausted, sobbing, and they pulled a blanket over her.

'She wants to see her baby,' Daya said.

'It's good that she should see it,' Christine said.

'If she doesn't see it she'll always wonder, and never be at rest,' Daya agreed.

Babulal carried the box into the room and opened the lid so that Manju could look. She stopped crying at once and became very calm and peaceful.

Christine went outside and asked the doctor, 'Why did that baby die?'

'We cannot know,' she said, 'but many, many people go to a guru to take drugs because they think he can make it be a male child. Manju took drugs from a guru. In the West it's known that any sort of drug is extremely dangerous to a pregnant woman, but here there are no books in Hindi that say those things.'

'Have you seen other babies die from this then?'

'Many babies all the time, even among the middle classes. They take these traditional plant medicines.'

'Can you have an autopsy?'

'It's not possible. In the West every baby that dies has an autopsy. There are statistics available, causes are known. Here so many babies die. There is no one who is interested. There's no one to do an autopsy. We'll never really know the cause, but my guess is that it was the drug she took. This sloughing of the skin shows the baby has been dead approximately ten days.'

The lane was quiet and dark when Christine went outside. She waited for Daya and when he eventually came he said, 'They're going to bury the baby.'

'But it's a Hindu. Shouldn't it be burnt?'

'No, not baby. We thinks with diseases and with dead baby not to burn, since the bad things go into the air.'

'Shall I come?'

'Woman cannot come. You stay with Manju.'

Christine went and sat with Manju. She was quite peaceful. She was a woman. She had carried a child full term and given birth to it.

'I'm glad I saw the baby,' Christine said. 'It was beautiful.'

Manju spoke to her mother in Hindi, and the mother rummaged in her bag to produce a small yellow baby suit. Christine spread it out on her knees and looked at it. For one moment Manju wept, then she stopped again.

'The pain has finished now,' said Christine. 'And you are very brave.'

'Memsahib,' she said in Hindi. 'You must not wait here. You should go back home. I am all right.'

'I like to be with you.'

'But I am worried about you, memsahib,' she said. 'No dinner.'

Christine said she did not care about dinner. Manju told how the doctor had removed the dead baby with forceps, which she called big scissors. She explained how she had had six miscarriages before. Then she said she would like to go home, back to the shelter.

'You can't go yet, because you need special treatment,' Christine said. 'But tomorrow we'll come to see if you can come back.'

Soon the men returned from the burial. Babulal said he would stay the night with Manju. Christine hugged her and squeezed her hand. Her mother sat on the end of the bed, straight-shouldered, calm, powerful, of the earth, one who had seen so much labour, birth and death. They drove home in the ambulance. Somewhere, in an empty paddock, the small body lay underground.

CHAPTER 18

When Jeremy had decided to come to live in Jaipur the plan had been for he and Christine to use their holidays to see different parts of India. In May 1993, about a year after they had arrived, summer temperatures were soaring daily to around 45 degrees Celsius. In colonial days the British used to escape the plains at this time of year to cooler places such as Darjeeling in the Himalayas. The Townends had been working hard for a year. In that time they had both suffered from several debilitating bouts of illness as their systems rebelled against the local food and water. They needed a break, and following the British tradition seemed a good idea.

Daya and Ngaire happily agreed to look after the shelter while they took three months off. They could not afford to fly to Darjeeling, which was the easy way. Another difficulty was their blue heeler, Sita, whom they had brought with them from Australia. Whenever they began packing to go anywhere, Sita put on such a show of misery, slinking around with her tail between her legs and waiting beside the car to make sure they didn't sneak away without her, that they felt they couldn't possibly leave her for three months.

Perhaps if they had realised how hard the journey was going to be they might not have attempted it. However, they loaded their luggage into the Gypsy, along with an esky full of luke-warm mineral water, installed Sita on the back seat, covered themselves with wet towels to withstand the searing heat, and set off.

On the first day they travelled between Jaipur and Agra, where they stayed the night with an Indian friend, Lal, and his family. The second day was a long and arduous journey to Alla-habad, 400 kilometres away – not an unduly long day's drive by Australian standards, but it took twelve hours to get there, crawling along a potholed 'national highway' bullied by trucks, weaving in and out of camel teams, cyclists, pedestrians, bul-lock carts, and several times becoming lost in labyrinthine towns.

From Allahabad they went on to Varanasi, where they were caught in a traffic jam for an hour in the full heat of the day, sandwiched amid a throng of buses belching diesel fumes. It was a relief to arrive at the Government Tourist Dak Bungalow, which had a leafy, tree-filled garden, the vegetation reducing the searing temperature by at least ten degrees. Sita went mad with joy, chasing her ball with such exuberance that she had a nose bleed.

The next morning they set off early for Bodh Gaya. It was one of the places Christine had always wanted to see, because it was here, so it was said, that, sitting under a peepal tree, Buddha had gained enlightenment. Again, progress was slow. Each time they had to pass through a town or city they became hopelessly lost in the maze of streets. There was no such thing as a road directory – Christine was obliged to lean out the car window, shouting in bad Hindi at passers-by. Once, after an elaborate Hindi sentence, the recipient stared at her in a puzzled way and replied in halting words, 'Sorry, I don't speak English, madam.'

Whenever they stopped crowds gathered around the Gypsy and peered in the windows, once or twice even opening the doors so that they could have a closer look. Sometimes they became so lost that they found the only solution was to pay a rickshaw *wallah* to lead them through the town to the exit at the other end.

When they finally reached the place where Buddha had sat as He awaited the downflow of spirit that was to cause a total mutation in His being, they discovered it had been built over with gold thrones and fences, and was plagued with tourist touts trying to sell postcards or guidebooks. By now they were so exhausted from three days of driving that they took a room at the Ashok Gaya Hotel. This was wanton luxury but they were desperate for an air-conditioner. The management said dogs were forbidden, but then proceeded to make arrangements for Sita to have boiled meat for dinner and a suitable room was selected where she could have full and undisturbed access to the gardens.

As they were unloading their dusty supplies of melted paratha and squashed bananas a group of Japanese tourists arrived in an air-conditioned bus. For once Christine envied their ordered journey, with a guide who knew where they would be going next, and cold drinks and comfortable seats and an assured arrival time.

The tourists fussed over Sita, as did everyone, rather as if she were a small child. 'What is her breed?' people would ask in lilting English.

'Australian dog.'

'Ah,' with a knowing nod. 'Australian dog. Does she have passport?'

Sita, of course, enjoyed the attention, looking at any admirer with her head cocked on one side and the corners of her mouth pulled back to make a smile just like a human's. Then Christine would say apologetically, 'She thinks she's a human being,' which, if they were Hindu, they understood.

Ahead of them were still three days of driving across the Gangetic Plain to reach their destination. Their next stop was Purnia. Leaving there the next day they saw on the road a large crowd of people marching towards them waving banners displaying the hammer and sickle. Among them were half-naked tribespeople with bows and arrows, and angry-looking peasants with black, burning eyes wielding *lathies* (heavy canes that the police use for crowd control). They were clearly Naxalites, the dreaded and murderous communists of Purnia, who killed those who did not comply with their dictates.

What to do? Should they retreat to last night's hotel and sit in the room all day; or wind up the windows, put one hand on the horn and force their way through; or, leaving the windows open and smiling happily, wave like royalty and try to bluff their way through the oncoming crowd?

With smiles fixed in place, they continued slowly forwards. Some of the marchers tried to stop them, shouting in the window, grabbing hold of the door, pointing to Sita on the back seat, but fortunately their leaders came up, calmed their companions down and indicated that if Christine and Jeremy would wait a few minutes the march would pass by and they could proceed on their way.

As they emerged thankfully from the melee they saw

another crowd ahead on the road, this time blockading it completely. They were shouting angrily at a villager who was trying to drive his tractor through on his way to market. Intimidated, he turned back. Christine and Jeremy waved out the window, called out 'Good luck,' and were once more relieved that the leaders beckoned them through.

The rest of the journey was very pleasant. The countryside grew increasingly lush and tropical, with tea plantations, thatched huts, and small shacks along the way selling golden cubes of pineapple which was crushed into juice while they waited. In Siliguri they took an air-conditioned room, sorting out and washing their dusty things for the final journey the following day to Darjeeling. Sita, after a languorous day spent lying on the back seat of the car, now demanded a ball-throwing game. As she leapt into the air, contorting herself to catch the ball, a crowd gathered to watch this curious Australian custom. 'Alan Border,' they said, and laughed.

The next morning they began the seventy-kilometre journey to Darjeeling. The air cooled as they wound slowly upwards along a road flanked with rainforest, rushing streams and views of plunging valleys, purple and green. All the tension of the long journey began to evaporate. It was raining softly and there was a swirling mist, so that they seemed to emerge from behind a curtain into a scene and then, going behind another curtain, the scene would vanish. Finally they could see Darjeeling on a ridge beyond the valleys.

They had arranged to stay in a room owned by the principal of nearby Kalimpong College, Dr Yonzone. Negotiating the steep, narrow streets of the town they parked outside a house made of stone, surrounded by a white picket fence. It must once have been owned by some British government functionary who would have used it to escape the heat of summer. They would hardly have been surprised to see the door opened by a pale Englishman in a tweed jacket; instead a small Mongolian-featured man came out, extending his hands, smiling in greeting.

'Welcome, welcome,' he said. He told them that, being a Buddhist, he supported their animal welfare work. The flat, which was available for a hundred rupees a night, consisted of three tiny rooms with low ceilings, a small toilet, and a kitchen that was like a cupboard. After Dr Yonzone had showed them through he left them to think about it.

'I can't stay here for three months,' Christine said.

'Do you think you can find anywhere else for a hundred rupees a night?' Jeremy asked.

'Anything would have to be better than this.'

But after a sleepless night in a hotel on a damp mattress with bedding that was quite wet, Christine saw Dr Yonzone's flat in a different light. After agreeing to move in, they walked up through the narrow streets until they came upon the Mall, a wide open square at the highest point looking out over a spectacular vista. The mist had cleared and for the first time they saw the Himalayas floating in the sky above a blue haze, as if they were not joined to the earth at all. Stark above the range was the snow-capped peak of Kanchenjunga, the third highest mountain in the world.

In the Mall, thin, badly shod ponies stood about waiting to take tourists for rides.

'I'd like to get them fixed up,' Christine said. 'They all need worming.'

'You've already got an animal shelter,' Jeremy said. 'For goodness sake, don't start any more.'

They had an introduction to an expatriate American, Pilgrim, who had just opened a restaurant, 'Madam Frog'. Pilgrim looked to be in his 50s – tall, thin, practically toothless, with long, yellowish-grey beard and hair. His skin was yellow too. He wore a pair of cream knit-cotton pants that looked like long underwear, holed and fraying at the ankles. Above this was a multi-coloured T-shirt and on his feet were leather sandals.

Christine had planned to do a lot of reading and meditating, but Jeremy was keen to find something to occupy his time. They began to help Pilgrim with his restaurant. Often they bought the ingredients for the apple crumble, which they then made on a wooden table in the kitchen. Then they would take the dishes of apple crumble to a nearby bakehouse, where they were baked for a modest fee. Because Pilgrim always had three or four pies baked at one time, and he did not have a refrigerator, Christine wondered whether a hapless customer would die of food poisoning one day.

In the kitchen a pot of stew continually simmered on the kerosene stove. The stew was a mixture of various vegetables and, when it diminished, more vegetables and water were thrown into the pot. They served this to the customers with two thick slices of brown bread in return for 'a donation'.

One day a young German woman came in looking for the two Australians. Hearing that they ran an animal shelter in Jaipur, she wanted some advice. Angelika lived at a monastery about half an hour's drive from Darjeeling. She had befriended the dogs that hung about there, and she was hoping Christine and Jeremy might be able to tell her what was wrong with one of them whom she was feeding and allowing to sleep in her room.

Angelika explained how its jaw had dropped open and stayed open for about two days; how it was salivating and walking round the room in circles; and how she had opened its mouth and tried to see whether it had a bone caught there. As she talked they both realised with horror that she was describing the classic symptoms of dumb rabies, something they had seen frequently at the Jaipur shelter.

'You must be vaccinated straight away,' Christine told her. 'Even a small lick could infect you, you shouldn't take any chances.'

Angelika was a trained nurse; she knew how deadly rabies could be. She thanked them profusely for possibly saving her life.

Later Christine mentioned the incident to Dr Yonzone. He reacted with typical nervous excitement, declaring that he had thought for a long time that Darjeeling needed an animal shelter, and this incident only showed that the time had come.

Dr Yonzone arranged a meeting of Darjeeling's decision-makers, including the chief vet of the West Bengal government, the chairman of the municipality, and a vet from the Ghorka Hill Council, which was the local government body. Christine and Jeremy also attended – Christine with a feeling of excitement, Jeremy with a sense more like dread.

The meeting resolved to start an animal shelter. In response to letters from Christine, Annabella Singh quickly contributed 10,000 pounds from London, while another A$10,000 came from Animal Liberation in Australia.

'This is madness,' said Jeremy. They were sitting in the front room of Dr Yonzone's flat. 'We can't start another animal shelter. Have you thought it through? How will we cope? We're already working flat-out in Jaipur. The plan was to have some time together, time to travel and see India, but if you start this we'll be tied to coming here too. It's a massive, impossible task.'

As ever, Christine was not about to be swayed by such practical concerns. 'Buddhists say you have to have worldly engagement,' she said.

'What does that mean?'

'You have to build something. You have to give something. You can't just live for yourself. You have to save all living beings.'

'That's all very well,' said Jeremy. 'But in this case there's no one to help. You're committed to Help in Suffering.'

'Things will work out.'

Practically, of course, Jeremy was correct. But Christine had never acted according to practicality. She had a strong sense that fate was leading her to this new venture. 'That's the way I conduct my life,' she says. 'I try to listen to that inner voice. There seems to be some guiding being. That's how I try to do it, although I don't always know that I listen that well.'

With Jeremy in reluctant agreement they began looking for land. They quickly discovered that anything in Darjeeling was beyond their means. The town was crammed together on a narrow ridge surrounded by tea gardens and forest. Every spare piece of land was being subdivided and built upon. Prices were the same as in Sydney.

Dr Yonzone told them that land in Kalimpong would be much cheaper. To get there they had to drive back down the winding mountain road and cross the Teesta River on a swaying suspension bridge. The road then snaked back up again, past banana and bamboo groves, and small village houses made of bamboo and mud, brightly painted like dolls' houses, with flowerpots at the doors and gardens of azalea and hibiscus and flowering trees and papaya and mango and pear and apple.

Kalimpong was a hill station like Darjeeling, with similar labyrinthine streets and laneways snaking up and down a steep-sided ridge. There was plenty of land for sale, but, to Jeremy's relief, none that they saw was suitable for an animal shelter.

It was late July. They had been away from Jaipur for three months. Dr Yonzone said he would ask his students to let him know if any suitable land became available. They planned to come back again in November. For now, it was time to make the long drive back to the plains.

CHAPTER 19

THE STREET DOG

Your yellow eyes confront me.
You lie curled under the bush,
the only hiding place
among the roar of cars, the train's rattle.

Your pups, tiny and wriggling,
whimpering with new life, crawl at your breast
among the plastic bags and old bottles.

Your eyes are from caves and ancient artisans,
gold as temple gods which glow in black niches,
with circling smoke.

You fought to find this place,
heavy with birth,

were kicked from doorways.
You are the poem of curses.

Your ancestors held pact with mine,
roamed the forest, shared the hunt,
sentinel at the fortress gate.
Grew adjusted, you the eyes,
in trust, forever following,
taking the morsel, forgotten but needed.

From my pocket I offer
one crushed biscuit,
which I lay before you
in homage to your line.
But you, expecting just another trick,
like an old queen with traitorous courtiers,
teeth bared, coiled in motherhood,
thicket eyes,
decline my gift
and, burdened by that ancient tryst,
the old bond of the jungle,
wanting to love, but too afraid,
turn your golden eyes, your golden head, away.

During the street dog-breeding season in Jaipur, which peaked in the winter months of December and January, boxes of puppies were delivered to the shelter. When the staff explained that the puppies could not survive without their mothers, and that they would therefore need to euthanase them, they would be greeted by a long silence.

'Please take them and return them to the place you found them,' they would ask, 'and we'll spay them all for you when they're older.' However, the deliverer of the pups invariably replied that the mother had died. The staff knew only too well that the mother had probably given birth to the pups outside the family home, or perhaps she had even dug a hole in the small front garden, and the inhabitants did not want eight stroppy puppies soiling the street outside their house.

During those winter months when the temperature dropped to five or six degrees Celsius the weakest of the street pups died of pneumonia, or exposure, or starvation, or disease. Often pups were attacked and killed by other street dogs, or else they were seriously injured on the road and crawled away to die slowly. The mother dogs often could not feed all the pups. You would see litters of six or eight tiny pups but, by the time the pups were four or five months old, there would only be one or two still alive. This was nature's way of controlling the population, because if all the pups had survived there would have been a dog plague. They had to die, but in dying they suffered much.

Indian street dogs are quite different to domesticated dogs kept as pets. Wild and free-spirited, they are descended from pie dogs. Often they look like dingos, with tawny hair and yellow-green eyes. They have a dingo's temperament, more governed by instinct than their pet cousins. They can climb a five-foot wall like a cat, they will defend their territory savagely, and they hunt in packs to pull down and kill any stray animal that is weaker than they are.

Outbreaks of rabies are common in the street-dog population. In India 20,000 to 30,000 people die each year from the disease, and India accounts for half the known cases of death by rabies in the world. When Christine and Jeremy first went to

Jaipur street dogs were everywhere, owing to the fact that there was no municipal rubbish collection. People simply threw their rubbish into the street, where it was picked over by hordes of hungry dogs. Every year in Jaipur 70 people died of rabies.

HIS staff had often rescued rabid dogs as the result of a complaint. Although they were skilled at catching the animals and very careful, as an additional precaution they were all vaccinated against rabies. A rabid dog was usually fairly easy to identify, although sometimes distemper or a head injury could also affect the brain of an animal and make it appear rabid.

There were two types of rabies – furious rabies and dumb rabies. The dogs with furious rabies were very dangerous and tried to bite everything they saw. Once Babulal had been charged by a rabid dog when he was simply standing looking at it, and it had sunk its teeth into his arm. Dogs with dumb rabies were more apt to walk around in circles, drooling at the mouth, or cringing in the back of the Jeep.

They had been called out once to put down a horse with rabies. The villagers had tied each of its four legs to a separate tree. Even so, it tried to charge whoever went close to it, and it was very difficult to euthanase. Daya finally managed to achieve the desired result with swashbuckling bravado by quickly jabbing the lunging horse's flank with a needle loaded with sedative. He then stood back and waited for it to collapse before administering the euthanasia agent into a vein in the neck. At that village there were several dogs that the villagers had thrown alive down a dry well because they were rabid. The staff bravely retrieved these animals, which they euthanased later.

On several occasions they had also been called out to kill rabid cows. Once Daya gallantly climbed on top of a fence, held a captive bolt pistol to a cow's head and pulled the trigger.

Bits of brain splashed over his face. Christine was concerned, as the brain almost certainly would have contained the fatal virus. Daya, however, threw back his head and laughed. But still they bought him a rabies booster, which he then asked Christine to administer.

In September 1993, three months after returning from Darjeeling, Christine and Jeremy received a message from two representatives of the World Society for the Protection of Animals in London, asking for a meeting. They were touring India looking for suitable places for animal birth-control (ABC) programs.

Most Indian cities regularly eradicated large numbers of dogs by poisoning or electrocution. Quite apart from being cruel, it did nothing to reduce the numbers of dogs. So long as there was food in the form of rubbish, the dogs survived, filling a biological role in the city.

The two representatives asked to meet at the hotel in Jaipur where they were staying. Their description of the barbaric slaughter of street dogs was quite familiar to Christine. At the city palace where many tourists went there were always plenty of dogs, yet just before the start of the tourist season she had noted there was not a single one. They had obviously been poisoned. Then about a month later the place was swarming with dogs once more.

She told the visitors that a large percentage of the animal suffering in Jaipur involved the street dogs. The population had evolved for thousands of years alongside their human companions, unsupervised, breeding randomly, and being poisoned when the numbers grew too large. The municipality used strychnine mixed in sweets called *burfi*, which were appealing to a hungry dog. The sweets were thrown from a vehicle into the street. Once it ate the bait the dog took about ten minutes to die, writhing and convulsing and choking, its mouth turning blue as its breathing system failed to function.

'We have a proposal for you,' Johnathan said. 'The World Health Organization and WSPA have produced a publication called *Guidelines for Dog Population Management*. These guidelines argue that the scientific way to reduce the incidence of rabies is not by poisoning and electrocution, but by sterilisation and vaccination. The idea is to stabilise the dog population. Evidence suggests that rabies is spread by instability in the population. Dogs fight. There's inward migration and the ones that come in are the weaker ones that haven't established themselves in the territory they came from. Weaker animals tend to have more diseases, one of which is rabies. The aim is to have a stable population, which will be pretty much the carrying capacity of the environment, consisting of food, shelter and water.'

Christine thought it was a wonderful idea. It wasn't good to be killing healthy dogs who had lived for thousands of years in the company of humans. They had a right to exist as much as people did. This was very much the Indian philosophy too.

'Would you be interested in doing such a program?' Jonathan asked Jeremy.

'We don't have the funds.'

'You could prepare a detailed budget and submit it to WSPA,' said Jonathan. 'You'd have to think the whole program through, from start to finish, write a protocol, draw up a budget, a time-frame, and so on.'

Christine thought an ABC program would give the shelter a real purpose, and it would get to the root of the terrible problem of dying pups, exhausted bitches, rabies outbreaks and poisoning. Jeremy was attracted to the idea of having a positive program to plan and execute, but there were many questions to be answered. For instance, how many dogs would they need to sterilise every week? Christine thought that she would ideally like to do a small number of dogs and make sure they were properly treated. They would need more kennels than the twelve they had at present, and an operating theatre; they'd have to form a committee with officials from the municipality so that they could work in co-operation with them. It would be pointless to spend time and money operating on the dogs if the municipality then went and killed them.

'There's one thing that your budget should include, which will make your program different from any other,' Jonathan said. 'You have to count the street dogs.'

'Count them?' said Christine. 'How would we count them?'

'The guidelines show various methods of counting wildlife populations.'

'We're not biologists or wildlife experts. We'd never worked at an animal shelter before we came here. We can try our best, but we can't promise anything,' Jeremy said, formulating a disclaimer, as good lawyers are trained to do. 'And how would we ever catch the dogs? They're semi-wild. They run whenever they see a human.'

'You'll have to work out all those things,' Jonathan replied.

Driving back to the shelter, the reality of what they were contemplating began to sink in. There were thousands of dogs in Jaipur: it seemed impossible that anything they could do would make any difference.

'We'll never be able to catch them,' said Christine. 'It's all a grand idea which will totally flop because it'll be utterly impossible to catch the dogs.'

Jeremy agreed. 'They're not stupid those dogs. You just look at them and they run.'

'How embarrassing. Imagine if we spend weeks preparing a proposal, and then they give us the money and the whole thing's a total failure because all the dogs run too fast.'

Back at the shelter they spoke to Daya and Ngaire about everything that had been discussed. Despite all the obvious difficulties Christine was drawn to the proposal. If it worked it could be a small contribution – a small act of non-violence as a counter to the unspeakably cruel methods used in the third world to massacre dogs. She knew that there were other ABC programs in Bombay and Madras, and that the Animal Welfare Board of India was encouraging them. Just possibly, with their help, India could lead the way. She asked Daya what he thought.

'We could do it,' he said.

'But how could we catch the dogs?'

'I can catch dogs. Don't worry. We will catch.'

Jeremy, labouring long hours at his desk, produced a protocol for WSPA which attempted to account for every eventuality that they could imagine. It called for an additional fifteen kennels to be built and a small operating theatre. The protocol must have impressed because WSPA agreed to fund a pilot program lasting three years.

Ever since taking over the shelter Christine had had trouble finding competent veterinarians. The cherished aim of most vets after graduating from university was to get a government job, which guaranteed a lucrative income for life no matter how lazy or incompetent they might be. She had hired a succession of government vets on a part-time basis. They had proved so unsatisfactory that she had turned to western-trained volunteers who were prepared to work for a few months for food and accomodation only, in order to expand their experience. One of these, an Australian, David Paxton, specialised in animal dynamics. During a six-week stay David taught them how to count animals. They selected three specific areas that were representative of the city of Jaipur, containing both intensive and spread-out housing, markets and commercial shopping areas.

Starting at six o'clock in the morning HIS staff would spend three or four hours walking the streets counting dogs. They soon realised that the number of dogs in the city had been over-estimated. People thought that there were more than in reality because they saw them in packs rummaging through garbage, or they saw ten or twelve dogs congregating round a bitch in heat.

The HIS staff, who knew the pilot areas well, had thought they would find at least 3,000 dogs. The dog officer from the Municipal Corporation guessed there would be around 5,000. After driving and walking up each alley and street for many hours, day after day, they found in their first count a total of 585 dogs. They were amazed. Even if they had missed counting one third of the dogs this still gave a figure much lower than they had expected.

David spent a lot of time with Daya teaching him how to do a variety of operations. When he left he was replaced by another volunteer, Ann Rodgers, who had taken six weeks' leave from her job as chief executive officer of the Animal Welfare

League of South Australia. Back in Australia her shelter conducted about 30 sterilisations a day using one vet and two veterinary nurses. Spaying was done by the 'keyhole flank' method. WSPA had recommended the method to HIS but until Ann arrived Christine had not been aware that spaying could be done using keyhole surgery. Ann brought with her an instruction video. She explained that in most cases a bitch would recover in three days. This was a revelation to Christine and Jeremy. The local vets had using the so-called mid-line approach, making long incisions. There was generally blood all over the place, the bitch was swathed in bandages and it was usually a day at least before she could even stand up. They had expected to have to hold a dog for ten days or so post-operation. To be able to release the dogs after five or six days would dramatically reduce the expected duration of the pilot project.

Ann offered to assist Daya in a spay operation using the new technique. At his first attempt things did not go well, and Daya opted to stop the procedure and sew up the wound. The next day he announced he had thought about it all through the night, had worked out where he had gone wrong, and was now certain he could do a keyhole-flank spay. The second operation went according to plan, the dog recovered beautifully and was released after four days. Jeremy then reworked the tender documents allowing for the average dog to occupy a kennel (pre and post operation) for a maximum of seven days. Ann also helped with the design of the operating theatre.

And so it began. After Ann left, Daya worked under a couple of local vets, but it quickly became obvious that he could do the operations better than they could. Eventually he took over.

When Christine and Jeremy were happy that things were running smoothly they invited Mrs Maneka Gandhi to launch the program. The widow of the late Sanjay Gandhi, who had died in a helicopter crash in 1980, Mrs Gandhi was a tireless campaigner for animal rights. The opening was a grand affair. A large marquee was erected in the grounds and the new kennels and theatre complex bore a brass sign which said, 'Opened by Mrs Maneka Gandhi on 27th November 1994'. A choir of school children sang. Mrs Gandhi, Johnathan Joseph from WSPA, and the Municipal Commissioner gave speeches.

While the medical side of the program was in place, the business of catching dogs was not so easy. One method was 'scruffing'. While one man distracted the dog by offering a scrap of food, his partner sneaked up and caught it by the back of the neck with one hand, lifting it with the other hand underneath the belly. The trouble was that with street dogs there was a pretty good chance of being bitten. Some tried wire loops and chains, but nothing was really satisfactory. After being bitten a few times catchers started to lose their nerve and, in trying to avoid further bites, they tended to be rough with the dogs.

The problem was solved with the arrival of another volunteer, Kathy Nolan, from Britain. Kathy had made a study of dog-catching methods in Mumbai, where they used the so-called 'sack-and-loop method'. A team of three people – two catchers and a driver for the Jeep, which had a cage on the back – would go out at dawn. When they saw a likely dog the Jeep would stop and one man would approach, offering a scrap of bread. When the animal's attention was diverted the other man would sidle up behind and quickly throw a sack over the dog. A drawstring at the mouth of the sack could be tightened to prevent escape.

Watching a skilled catcher at work was like watching a matador reacting with a bull. It required judgement about

which were the most likely dogs they could catch; they had to
know when to approach and when to hold back; and then they
had to throw the sack with accuracy and perfect timing. It was
a lot harder than it looked. After many failures and much frustration the staff got the hang of it, and the method became
standard.

So, with hope and optimism they groped their way through
this unfamiliar veterinary territory. They had few scientific
sources to draw upon. Practically nothing was known about
Indian street dogs. They were entering a new area of investi-
gation about which the animal behaviourists and population
biologists were largely ignorant. The measure of their success
would be if the dog population stabilised or diminished, and if
the incidence of rabies declined. But it was early days yet. It
would be years before they could make that assessment with
confidence.

CHAPTER 20

A young vet who had recently graduated from college came to the shelter one day looking for a job. Sunil Chawla said he did not want to work for the government as all the vets did was sit around all day. He wanted to work for the private sector. Sunil was slim and quiet, with soulful eyes. There was an air of composed confidence about him. His family had come from the lowest caste – butchers who, for generations, had earned their living by slaughtering animals. By sheer hard work and determination his father had managed to break free of the ageless cycle and become a schoolteacher. Sunil's choice of career, giving life to animals, could not have been further removed from his heritage.

Given his background, it was a brave decision to seek work with Help in Suffering. Sunil would be turning his back on a lifetime of security for a job where there were no guarantees of permanence. With a government job, even when he died his wife would continue to draw his salary until she died. Pressured by his family, who thought he was being foolish, Sunil held out for a salary that was equal to the one he would earn with the government. Christine was not at all sure that they could afford him, but there was something compelling about Sunil. He had a gentle presence, and his obvious compassion for animals attracted her.

When Sunil began working with Kathy Nolan she reported that he had excellent surgical skills. She taught him to do the flank-spay operation, which he had not learned at veterinary college, and he proved adept at all manner of emergency surgeries.

As time went on Christine often found herself calling upon Sunil to help deal with some of the peculiarly Indian difficulties which arose from time to time. One such occasion was the case of the baby elephant. Following a visit by the chief minister of Jaipur to the Maharaja of Gwalia, the Maharaja had sent him the gift of an elephant. It so happened that the elephant was pregnant and, in due course, it gave birth to a healthy baby.

The cute little newcomer was dubbed 'The Pride of Jaipur' by the newspapers and, for days, they milked the story for all it was worth. Unfortunately the happy tale soon took on a different tone. The baby had been entrusted to the care of some owners of working elephants. These elephant owners were a stubbornly traditional clique whose animal-welfare methods often did more harm than good. They believed that it was necessary to starve the mother of a newborn elephant. They fed the mother an improper diet and gave the baby some concoction that they had made themselves. Without proper nourishment the baby soon succumbed to diarrhoea and pneumonia.

Although Help in Suffering had nothing to do with elephants at the time, a volunteer vet from New Zealand, hearing about the plight of the baby elephant, paid it a visit. The baby was in a distressed state and clearly gravely ill. Close to tears the volunteer called Sunil, imploring him to send the ambulance and bring it to the shelter for treatment.

Sunil knew the elephant would certainly die and, if it happened at the shelter, they would quite likely be accused of euthanasing it. The whole question of euthanasia was a political, religious and legal nightmare at the best of times. Throw into the mix the beloved Indian icon of an elephant – The Pride of Jaipur – and you had all the ingredients for a damaging controversy.

Sunil said no, and breathed a sigh of relief at having avoided a potentially disastrous incident. But the volunteer, in the grip of emotion, took matters into her own hands. Commandeering another vehicle, she arrived at the shelter and presented Sunil with a fait accompli.

Reluctantly they coaxed the little patient from the vehicle. No one knew anything about elephants. They did not even know what its temperature was supposed to be. While they pondered how to begin treating it, the little animal lay down on the ground and died.

Worried about the damage that might ensue once the story of the death got out, Sunil rang a friend, Rashid Khan, who was the secretary of the Elephant Welfare Association. Khan advised him to perform an autopsy and to make sure he had a government vet as a witness.

This is what he did. During the post mortem Sunil and two government vets found that the elephant's lungs were filled with pus. It had indisputably died of pneumonia. There was no way it could have survived.

The funeral was bigger than for most humans. An enormous crowd came to mourn; a band played, speeches were made, and the body was ceremoniously cremated.

Thanks to Sunil's wise action the shelter escaped any hint of controversy.

Unknown to Christine, Goat Baba had found a bitch with five puppies and had been feeding the animal in his room. She only found out about it when he brought the bitch to the dispensary to show Daya. It was a golden dog, with ribs showing, heavy teats swollen with milk swinging from her stomach. Her back foot had been eaten away with maggots to the knee joint, and all of her body was so poisoned that maggots had also begun to eat the flesh around her lip.

'She can't be saved,' Daya said. 'To amputate this leg would be a difficult and cruel operation.'

'We should put her down,' said Christine. 'Will Goat Baba mind?'

'He will not want us to destroy her. He thinks she should be treated.'

Daya spoke to Goat Baba in Hindi. He stood, a thin, old man, with black skin falling in withered folds from his body, and his face crumpled. He was bereft because he had kept the dog in his room and had not told anyone about it until it was too late. Daya took a needle and injected it into the vein on the dog's leg, and she lay her head on the cement floor and died with a small sigh. The old man's eyes filled with tears of puzzlement. Christine took bowls and Farax down to his room and showed him how to mix it and how to feed the puppies, and soon he was laughing again, saying, '*mota, mota*', which meant 'fat, fat', as the puppies fell about his feet and crawled under the bed and left piles of soft poo on the floor. But one by one the puppies began to die from distemper, and one by one they had to euthanase each of them. Goat Baba, left alone with only his goats, vowed he would never keep a dog again.

A little while after Goat Baba lost the dogs he fell ill. An abscess near his shoulder socket had become infected, and he lay in his filthy bed with pus pouring from the wound. They had to forcibly remove a kid from his pillow to take his sheets and wash them.

'You have to sell your goats,' said Christine. 'You're too old to look after them.'

'Sell them,' Goat Baba replied.

They gave them to some of the staff who took them to their villages, and they kept the most co-operative one to be tied up outside Goat Baba's room. Never wanting to repeat their experiences with the public hospital they took Goat Baba to a private hospital, where staff members took it in turns to sit beside his bed and to go out and buy the medicines he had been prescribed.

After a while he came home, but they could tell that his life was slipping away. He no longer laughed, and when greeted he complained of pains. Summer passed and the monsoon came, but it held itself back, giving only a few drops of rain which quickly evaporated in the dust. Goat Baba still managed to hobble out of the gate in the evenings when the sun had retreated in a fiery red orb setting alight the world, so that the palms flared and the neem trees were orange and everything hung breathless, dusty, suspended, burning, before the great flaming ball vanished behind the distant flat-topped roofs.

Then winter came and the days grew shorter. Goat Baba was

so feeble now that he could not leave his bed. The staff took him food every day and cleaned his room. One night one of the ground staff, Balu, came to Christine and said, 'Goat Baba has diarrhoea. Red blood has come.'

She went down to Goat Baba's room. He was lying on the bed moaning with his arms flailing. He struggled for breath. His body had shrunk so that it was just a skeleton covered with accidental flesh. You could see the shape of his skull.

They called the doctor who owned the private hospital that had treated Goat Baba before. He advised them to send the old man to his hospital.

'But he's going to die,' Christine said. 'What good can it do sending him to hospital?'

'Madam,' he answered. 'If you infuse money I can infuse life. He is dehydrated, and we will give fluids, and antibiotics for the diarrhoea.'

'But you can't give him back his life, you can only prolong his discomfort for a few days.'

'You in the West leave your old people,' he said. 'But here in India we have the extended family and we try to the last moment to save the life.'

'Well, Goat Baba was left long ago by his Indian family,' Christine replied, 'and it was Westerners who cared for him.'

The doctor did not answer.

Christine discussed what to do with the other staff members. The consensus was that they should do what the doctor said. Still beset by doubt, Christine asked them to bring the ambulance, sweep the back clean and place a mattress inside.

In the hospital Goat Baba lay with tubes in his nose attached to a cylinder of oxygen and with drips in his arms.

Once again the staff members took it in shifts to sit beside him. At ten o'clock in the evening, two days after Goat Baba had been admitted to hospital, Sunil came to the cottage and told Christine and Jeremy that Goat Baba had torn the drips from his arms. The doctors wanted to insert a new drip into his ankle.

Christine had been doubtful all along that they were doing the right thing. It seemed to her unnecessary and cruel to intervene further when he would surely die in a few hours anyway.

She and Jeremy drove to the hospital. Three male nurses were stitching with thick catgut a deep hole they had cut above Goat Baba's ankle. Goat Baba was moaning and trying to kick. Although there was a bottle of local anaesthetic on the sheet, it seemed as though the site had not been anaesthetised properly. Christine suspected they had used the normal practice of just pouring some of the drug onto the site to be operated, and then pouring a bit more into the open wound.

'Are you the doctor in charge?' Jeremy demanded of a young man with a supercilious expression who stood behind a laminex counter.

He did not answer.

'Do you speak English?' Jeremy asked.

'Yes,' he said.

'Are you the doctor in charge?' Jeremy repeated, and again he affected not to understand.

Sunil told the doctor that Goat Baba was going to die in a few hours and they should not be putting a needle into his leg.

'You are to stop this treatment at once,' Christine said. 'It's inhumane and cruel and we wouldn't do it to a dog.'

'Madam,' the doctor answered, 'it is my duty to do everything until the moment that the patient dies. If you want me to stop treatment, then you take the patient now.'

'You're not letting him die with dignity. You're denying his last, most precious right, his right to die in peace,' she said.

If they were to take him back to the shelter he would probably have died as he bounced along the road in the back of the animal ambulance. It was obvious that the self-righteous doctor with his lack of compassion had won.

'I'm too angry to stay any longer,' Christine said. Knowing that if she did not leave she would make a scene, she returned to the shelter with Jeremy. The others stayed behind. At five thirty in the morning one of them came to the door, and said that Goat Baba had died.

Of the original patients from Mishy's time only Sambu was left.

CHAPTER 21

With the assistance of a lawyer in Jaipur, Christine and Jeremy had prepared all the forms they required to register the new Darjeeling Trust. One day in October 1993 they had gone into the city where they trudged from office to office signing pieces of paper, or sometimes not signing and instead being directed with a sorrowful waggle of the head to still more offices. At the end of a long day, to their great surprise it was done.

In November Christine went back to Darjeeling alone, this time by train, to see Dr Yonzone, who had informed her that he had some possible sites in Kalimpong for her to look at.

Dr Yonzone greeted her with his usual peal of laughter and clapping of hands, and showed her to her accommodation. The flat where she and Jeremy had previously stayed was occupied by some of Dr Yonzone's relatives, so Christine moved into another set of rooms underneath the house. There was a small bedroom just big enough for a three-quarter bed. It was necessary to stand the bed on plastic bags because the water soaked up from the floorboards into the wooden legs and then into the mattress and sheets. The damp was not restricted to the bed. Christine was fascinated to see mushrooms and a strange, spreading brown fungus thriving on the walls. The kitchen was a small room with a few wooden benches. There was a cemented corner in the floor, with a hole in it for a drain where one squatted to do the washing up.

While there was rather too much water where it was not wanted, there was an acute shortage of water for household use. The coming of the water was an important occasion. It happened only every two or three days, and when it did Christine had to act straightaway, whether she was in her nightgown or deep in meditation or whatever. The first member of the household to hear the hose gurgling and spluttering would seize it and fill a collection of small galvanised drums, the storage tank having collapsed the previous year owing to poor workmanship.

Mr and Mrs Yonzone always graciously offered Christine first use of the hose. There was no time for polite refusal as no one knew for how long the water would flow. The main hose was quickly attached to a secondary hose, which was then plunged into the drum outside Christine's door. As the water level rose there was always a time of great indecision – should she return the water-bearing, productive hose to the Yonzones or should she hang on to it until her tank was full to the brim, thus avoiding a second change should their tank fill, while hers still had space for more? Like life itself, there was no correct answer.

Sometimes the hose would give a final gurgle and cease to produce while it was still in Christine's tank. Then she had the embarrassing task of returning the now-dry hose to the eagerly waiting Mrs Yonzone. Her host was always gracious in her disappointment, brushing aside Christine's profound apologies, explaining she had a bit extra somewhere else. Over time she had realised the virtue of having hidden stores, kept in secret places indoors, which she resorted to only in emergencies.

Because of the water shortage it was a luxury to flush the toilet. The cistern was placed near the ceiling, which was at least four metres high, although the room itself was only about a metre wide. Thus the bathroom was like a long, sanctified corridor, with the toilet right at the end, rather like an elaborate shrine. The toilet itself was a beautiful porcelain piece on an elevated cement platform, discharging through the wall directly into a *nulla* outside.

Despite the discomfort Christine was happy to be staying in Darjeeling alone. Although she missed Jeremy she relished the chance to meditate in silence every day. Several times she squeezed into an overloaded Jeep and travelled to Kalimpong to look at land. On one of these trips she met Mr Donald Karthak, a small, gentle, nervous man, with eyes that looked in two directions at once, so she could never be sure which eye was looking at her.

'I have some land to sell, sister,' he said, 'because you are doing something good. I'm a pastor at the church, and I want to help you start this organisation.'

To reach Mr Karthak's land one had to walk for two or three kilometres along narrow paths between groves of bamboo, patches of forest, and small hamlets of mud and bamboo huts. Rushing creeks tumbled down the hills. Some of the water had been diverted into a network of split bamboo channels to irrigate the fields where corn grew thick and golden in the sun.

Mr Karthak's land looked out over a valley through which

ran a river; and beyond the valley forested hills led the eye to distant snow-capped mountains in Bhutan. If you looked more to the west there were other mountains, which were in Tibet. As soon as she saw it Christine knew this place was perfect.

She sat with Mr Karthak in his house. His wife brought boiled eggs and steaming tea and curry. While they ate, hens foraged underfoot. Mr Karthak told her he would sell her two and a half acres of land for 2.2 lakh (a lakh is 100,000 rupees). Christine eagerly agreed.

Leaving Dr Yonzone to begin the legal process, Christine returned to Jaipur. In April the following year, 1994, she and Jeremy, with Sita again a passenger on the back seat, set off to drive to Darjeeling once more. The journey was easier this time as they knew how to navigate through the towns, and the best places to stop.

They were driving along a narrow potholed road on the way to Allahabad among fields sown with green crops and small villages of mud houses, when Jeremy, losing concentration for a second, went too close to a pony-cart carrying a family to town. The Gypsy collided with a protruding hub cap, smashing in their front bumper bar and knocking the wheel off the cart.

They had frequently been told that people murdered drivers who caused accidents, and indeed a mob was already racing up the road towards them.

'Please drive on,' Christine begged.

Jeremy refused. The wheel was making a terrible noise where it rubbed against the bumper bar and he didn't know if he could proceed. It would be worse to try to go, he reasoned, and then to be chased and caught.

To Christine's dismay he pulled on the handbrake, opened the door, and walked round to the bonnet, where he stood examining the wheel. A little further down the road the family, looking equally forlorn, were examining their cart with its missing wheel. Fortunately nobody was injured, and the pony seemed unconcerned, even relieved at being able to rest.

The crowd quickly surrounded them. A young man stepped forward and demanded 500 rupees.

Christine said to Jeremy, 'Let's give him the money quickly and go.' But something about the scene aroused Jeremy's dormant lawyer's instincts. He could not give the money to this man, he argued, in case he was not the owner. He began to ask a number of questions in English, which of course the man did not understand. The crowd seemed to be growing more restive.

'Just give him the money,' Christine cried in exasperation.

Eventually Jeremy conceded that that might be a good idea, but then he could not find where he had concealed the money. He fumbled under the front seat and under the pile of water bottles and wet sheets on the back seat. Eventually, after what seemed an age, he stood up and presented 500 rupees to the young man.

Far from pacifying the crowd, this only seemed to make them more volatile. A heated discussion began with much waving of arms and raised voices.

'Please can we go now?' Christine said. Jeremy started the engine, and as they drove away slowly the young man ran after the car, shouting. Reluctantly and somewhat fearfully, they stopped. He handed through the window two hundred rupees!

The strange noises from the wheel continued for the next eleven kilometres until they came to a town. There, for the equivalent of A$2, they had the bumper bar straightened and were able to continue on their way. Five days later, exhausted and suffering from diarrhoea, they arrived in Darjeeling and moved into Dr Yonzone's damp lower rooms.

When Christine saw the land at Kalimpong again she gazed upon it with something close to rapture. 'Do you like it?' she asked, turning shiny-eyed to Jeremy.

'It's good,' he said. 'But I'm worried about the fact that there's no road. Shouldn't we buy land with a road?'

'Any land on a road is too expensive for our budget,' Christine said.

'A road will be coming soon,' Mr Karthak added.

'And what about water?'

'There's water,' Mr Karthak said, waving vaguely to a bamboo pipe from which a permanent dribble of water ran into a large tank outside his house.

'And what about the road?' Jeremy asked. 'When would they be building it?'

'Soon,' Mr Karthak replied.

As matters progressed, Mr Karthak became vague. A valuer, after examining the land, declared that it was only worth 1.2 lakh. Mr Karthak agreed to drop the price to that amount, but then seemed reluctant to proceed further.

Was he upset at the lower price? they asked the valuer.

No, not at all. He was happy with the price, the valuer assured them. But still Mr Karthak looked downcast.

They arranged to have the land surveyed. After making an appointment to meet Mr Karthak and the surveyor a few days later, Jeremy and Christine returned to Darjeeling, not at all sure that they really had an agreement. At the proposed time they arrived to find Mr Karthak looking worried. He had thought he had over two acres of land, but the survey had revealed it was only about an acre. As he only had such a small amount he might not be able to sell them any land.

When they visited the surveyor, Mr Loden, he explained that the land was in fact 1.5 acres. It seemed that when Mr Karthak had been a child his relatives had put some of his land in their names, so strictly speaking it did not belong to him, although he was living on the land and his house was built on it. It was all becoming terribly complicated; it looked as though their search would have to begin all over again.

For several days Jeremy and Christine's lives became a cycle of constant travel, as they looked at site after site, but none of them was as good as the one they really wanted. Eventually Mr Loden said he would show them a piece of land that belonged to one of Mr Karthak's relatives.

Christine was by now thoroughly disillusioned with the whole idea. She thought that if this last piece of land was unsuitable she would return the money to the donors and give up the idea of a shelter in Kalimpong. At five o'clock, just as it was getting dark, they saw the land. it was completely unsuitable, having a development area next door and an illegal settlement above. It was also a bad shape and did not face in the right direction.

'This is no good,' Christine said.

Mr Loden nodded as though this was just what he had expected. He paused, then said, 'Mr Karthak says that if you did not like this land, he could sell you one acre of his own land.'

It was dusk. They squatted on the path with the lights of

Kalimpong glittering on a dark ridge in the distance. Although only one acre was now available, Christine and Jeremy agreed that they should have one last attempt at reaching an agreement.

They went back to Mr Karthak's house. Night had now fallen, and they would have to walk back along the narrow pathways to the road without lights. This time they were determined to come to the point. Mr Loden told Mr Karthak he would have to be absolutely straightforward with them. Christine suggested they should return to their original agreement of one lakh per acre. Mr Karthak immediately agreed. They then realised that despite his protestations he had not been happy with the lower price that Mr Loden had negotiated. Also, land was the lifeblood of the village, and to sell land that had been in the family for generations was an extremely difficult thing to do. Mr Karthak had been torn in two by his wish to help build an animal shelter and the desire to hold on to the land for his family. Even though the income from using the land as paddy was minimal, and required a huge amount of effort, ploughing with bullocks and sowing the bunches of rice shoots by hand, it was a difficult step for him to sell.

The deal was done, but there would be many further complications and delays before the trust became the owner of Mr Karthak's land, Mr Karthak became a trustee, and they found an architect to design the shelter and staff to run it. This branch of Help in Suffering would be called the Kalimpong Animal Shelter.

In 1995 Christine received a letter from a Lithuanian veterinarian which stated that she had received instructions in a dream that she should come and work for Help in Suffering in India.

It says much about Christine's open-mindedness that she did not dismiss this surprising job application out of hand. In fact, she embraced it. Aldona Skeraityte was blonde and middle-aged – a mystic, a solo mountain climber, strong, capable, and more than a little strange. She did not seem in the least perturbed when Christine explained in a letter that the shelter was only just being established, conditions were primitive and she would be living alone in a room in the mountains.

While Jeremy had remained in Jaipur, Christine had been spending long periods of time in Darjeeling overseeing the development of the new shelter. After being constantly ill in Dr Yonzone's damp little basement she had moved into a much nicer flat over the top of Pilgrim's old restaurant. Her new landlord was Mr Lama, a Tibetan friend of Dr Yonzone. Because he supported what she was doing he gave her the flat at a very reasonable rent.

Jeremy flew to Darjeeling to meet the new recruit. On the day Aldona was due to arrive they took a Jeep down the mountain to Siliguri airport. They were disturbed to discover that Aldona could speak barely a word of English. 'She must have had someone else writing the letters for her,' muses Christine. 'I couldn't explain anything; I couldn't tell her what we were doing; she had no idea what was going on and she had never been to India before. It was really a hotbed for misunderstanding and miscommunication, and there was plenty.'

In Kalimpong they had rented a little mountain hut for Aldona, which belonged to their architect, Ashok Pradhan. It consisted of a large dining room with an attached kitchen, and a bedroom with a bathroom attached. There was a separate room that she could use as a dispensary. Aldona stayed there for three months while they designed and built a small cottage on the new land. When she moved in, there was still no road and it was a twenty-minute walk to transport. The electricity had not yet been connected and there was no heat. Aldona spent several months living in these conditions without being fazed in the least. With her mountaineering background she was used to discomfort.

Christine soon discovered that Aldona was an independent spirit who didn't like to be given guidance. She had some distinctly unusual ideas about veterinary practice, some of which did not seem exactly what the shelter should be doing. For example, she spent hours washing people's dogs for them with a mixture of some sort of poison for the eradication of fleas. Christine surmised that she was probably lonely and it provided her with an opportunity to talk to families. Aldona made extensive use of homeopathic medicine and, as well as that, she appeared to have the power of healing. Once she came across a dog on a path which had been bitten by a snake. The dog had turned blue and was dying and its owners were distraught with grief. Aldona had with her a stone which she'd picked up because she thought it had healing potential.

'Make this hot,' she said.

They made it hot in a fire; she put it on the snake bite and the dog recovered.

For all her eccentricities Aldona was a compassionate and caring vet. She would happily walk for hours through the steep Himalayan paths to treat a sick animal, and never refused a call even if late at night. An English volunteer was astonished when Aldona asked him to walk for two hours to administer a couple of drops of a homeopathic medicine to a sick cow!

The spot where the shelter was to be built was named Salimbong – Salim being a type of extinct bird. The overall area was called Bong Busty. When they were about to begin building, Christine received a visit from representatives of the *punchayat* – or village council – telling her that she would only be allowed to employ local people. There was an implicit threat that if she did not comply there would be trouble.

Christine told them that she could not do as they wished. For a start, Aldona came from outside, and if the villagers wanted them there she would have to hire the best people she could find without restrictions. She told them that she would be happy to hire locals for the construction work.

The villagers were far from satisfied. The *punchayats* run the affairs of the village. They have a lot of independent power, as has been proven by test cases in the courts. They are run along democratic lines, but like all such bodies they are open to influence. Fortunately the head of the building firm, Mahindra and Co., which had been hired to construct the shelter, was a leading member of the *punchayat*. He was able to speak on the shelter's behalf. After that the building went off without further trouble, and today the *punchayat* is a staunch supporter.

In the summer of 1997 Christine was paying a visit to a Tibetan friend Norden and his family in Kalimpong to discuss a donation he was going to make to help build the new dispensary. Norden owned a Tibetan mastiff – a huge dog whose ancestors used to travel with Tibetan merchants into Kalimpong on selling trips. The merchants would spread their wares out in the marketplace and if anyone tried to steal something the dogs would attack. Mastiffs are not suitable as pets – they are trained for one thing only. While they spoke, Norden kept the dog on a chain, which he held in his hand.

They finished their conversation. Then, as Christine stood

up, the dog, without warning, broke free of the chain and leapt at her, seizing her throat and lower face in its massive jaws. She remembers thinking as the hot, wet mouth and teeth sank into her chin and neck, 'I don't want a scarred face.' After that her mind went blank. Later, she was told that she bent down and waited motionless while Norden called the dog, which gradually let go of its hold on her face. If the dog had shaken his head while he held Christine in his mouth, her neck could have been broken, and the massive tears further extended and deepened.

'I remember saying, "Perhaps I should wash myself," as the blood ran down my neck and onto my shirt. I didn't know what else I could do. I remember Norden and his sister standing around not knowing what to do, and looking horrified.

'There was a lot of blood. I walked to the bathroom, and when I lifted my face from the basin and looked into the mirror above, I saw that my neck had a long, deep incision which ran from the jaw under the chin, close to the jugular vein, finishing under the ear. There were bleeding slashes on my chin, my lip had been torn, and parts of it seemed to be hanging from my face. I was scheduled to speak at a conference in London in six weeks' time and I wondered how I could still manage to meet this commitment.'

Norden called Aldona at the shelter then drove Christine to a private hospital on the edge of town. In the waiting room patients stared in amazement at her torn face dripping blood. The doctor, coming hastily from his surgery wiping his hands on a cloth, stared at her face for a few moments. Then, shaking his head, he said, 'I cannot operate.'

Christine had thought he might say this as dog bites usually become infected. They need to be kept open, for if they are stitched the infection collects inside.

'I don't want to have a scarred face,' she told him. 'Please stitch it.'

The doctor looked again at the hanging lip, the wide, bleeding gash down the side of the neck, the torn chin.

'I will stitch it,' he said. 'Come.'

She lay on a metal table and he poured bleach into the wounds. The bleach ran onto her blouse and stained the collar. Then he injected some local anaesthetic, but because the wounds covered her whole face he could not inject it in many places, so she felt him stitching.

There were too many stitches to count. He cut a flap of hanging skin from the inner lip and threw it into the waste bin. She did not know if he had removed something vital. Then he wrapped her whole face in gauze and white plaster, gave her tetanus and anti-rabies shots and antibiotic tablets.

Norden invited her to stay in his guest house while she recovered. That evening a maid came with tea and food which she could not eat. 'Dog should be killed,' she said, raising her sleeve to show long pink scars on her forearm. 'Look what it did to me when I was giving it food.'

Christine lay awake all night listening to the mastiff grunting and growling as it patrolled the grounds. In the morning Aldona came. She was shocked at what she saw. The doctor had stitched the wound with the thickest twine she had ever seen. She had learned enough English by now to exclaim, 'My gosh,' that's going to leave huge scars all over your chin.'

As Christine had feared, the wound was already showing signs of becoming infected. Aldona removed the plaster and bandages and pus began seeping out. She steamed leaves of the castor-oil plant and put them over the wounds. After a day they turned black and crisp.

'See, all out, all out,' she said.

The doctor had prescribed the incorrect antibiotic. Aldona replaced it. Later that day Christine called a meeting of trustees to tell them what had happened. Only after it was over did she begin to feel fear. 'I had seen what happened to dogs in the shelter that had been bitten by other dogs. Sometimes the whole skin sloughs off. The infections are hard to cure. I thought I was going to be horribly scarred forever.'

After two days in Norden's guest house Aldona drove Christine down to Siliguri to catch a plane back to Delhi. Jeremy was there to meet her and take her to the home of some Indian friends. She was by now emotionally very fragile. 'I became full of shock. I couldn't even go outside without a feeling of panic, and I couldn't sleep at all even though I was exhausted. I had the terrors that my whole face was going to fall off. Instead of being grateful that I hadn't died I was thinking all the time wasn't it terrible what had happened. The gratefulness came later.'

After a few more days of rest and further medical treatment, Jeremy drove her home to Jaipur. When Sunil saw her he burst into tears. In the cottage she looked in the mirror and saw pus oozing from the wounds. 'I thought my whole face would turn gangrenous.'

Despite Christine's worst fears the antibiotics did their job. Six weeks after the accident she was well enough to address the conference in London, which had been organised by Compassion in World Farming. Then she flew home to Australia.

When the wounds had all healed a part of Christine's mouth was turning inward. The doctor in Kalimpong had accidentally stitched a bit of her lip onto something inside. A cosmetic surgeon in Sydney was able to repair the damage, and more surgery at a later date restored her face further. Today she is able to speak normally, and the scars from that horrific attack are barely visible.

Reflecting on the attack nearly a decade later, Christine puts it down, like everything else in her life, to fate. She cites a curious incident which had taken place three years before when an Indian friend read her palm. Such things are taken very seriously in India. Many highly educated people would not dream of making an important decision without first consulting a palmist or an astrologer.

'What did you see?' Christine had asked.

'Oh, nothing really.'

'But you did. It was something bad, so you don't want to tell me.'

Her friend just smiled, so she told him that she was not worried about reading palms and he could tell her anything.

'Your life-line ends before it should. Your life will finish early.'

'When?' she asked.

'About now.'

Christine had laughed, but her friend did not laugh at all.

Recounting this incident she now says, 'I'm sure I was meant to die at that time. I'd had my fortune told twice and both times predicted a terrible accident. I believe I've been given a chance to return to life to finish the things I have to finish doing for the animals.'

CHAPTER 22

The central fact of Hinduism is cow protection. Cow protection to me is one of the most wonderful phenomena in human evolution. It takes the human being beyond his species. The cow to me means the entire sub-human world. Man through the cow is enjoined to realise his identity with all that lives . . . The motive that actuates cow protection is not purely selfish, though selfish consideration undoubtedly enters into it. If it were purely selfish the cow would be killed as in other countries after it had ceased to give full use.

Gandhi

Nothing about Christine's work in India was more frustrating than the question of sacred cows. She came up against the problem early on when a cow was brought into the shelter with a broken femur after being hit by a motor vehicle. The humane thing to do was to put the creature out of her misery straight away, but when Christine suggested this to Daya he shook his head. To euthanase a cow would be to invite trouble from the trustees, the law and possibly even one of the militant cow-protection groups who had been known to murder people they suspected of slaughtering a sacred beast. The best they could do was to keep the cow sedated and wait. It took many days for it to die.

Hindus worship the cow as mother, as a provider of labour, milk and as representative of all animal life. The killing of cows violates not only their religious beliefs but is also outlawed in Article 48 of the Indian constitution.

When a cow stops giving milk or becomes too old to have calves it is usually turned out onto the street, where it forages among the rubbish piles for sustenance. Unlike a horse, which is very choosy about what it eats, a cow simply slurps up every-thing with its tongue, including plastic bags, pieces of scrap metal and all manner of rubbish. This all ends up in the first of the cow's four stomachs – the rumen – where food is supposed to be broken down before passing on through the intestines. Plastic bags and other solid objects churn around and around like clothes in a washing machine until they become compacted into a solid mass. Surgical removal is not possible. The cow cannot eat properly. Starving and weak, it is doomed to die a painful death. In post mortems of cows the veterinarians at Help in Suffering have found as much as forty kilos of compressed plastic along with other heavy objects in one animal.

Most of the cows that the shelter rescues have been in road accidents or, with a belly full of plastic bags, they may have been lying in the road dehydrating for days. It made Christine deeply frustrated and not a little bitter every time she had to watch a cow die in pain. 'Here was the sacred, beloved icon of

Hinduism being turned out onto the street after they'd finished their milking days because no one wanted to kill their mother . . . Well, if they don't want to kill their mother, which is quite understandable and I fully support, then they have to provide some place for their mother so she can live satisfactorily until her days come to an end. That's what we do with horses and dogs. if you share your family life with a cow for ten years because she lives in the courtyard outside the kitchen then it's quite understandable that you don't want to kill her the day she stops giving milk. That's good. But when an animal is suffering terribly the kindest thing you can do for it is kill it.'

Even in her frustration she understands and can appreciate the beauty of the Hindu beliefs. 'There is this tradition of *ahimsa*, which translates as "harmlessness". It doesn't literally mean that but that's near enough. They think it's a good thing to look after animals because it's part of the Hindu tradition to respect all life. In western countries we say it's all right to kill animals as long as they don't suffer – cruelty is the issue in the west; but in India the issue is not so much cruelty: everything suffers – the humans suffer, the animals suffer, it's part of living to suffer – but the issue is the taking of life.

'Some of the very orthodox Hindus don't want any animal killed because they believe that's interfering with their karma . . . but how do you say it's the karma of this animal to suffer for ten days until it dies a natural death? Mightn't it have been the good karma of the animal that we've come along and said, "Right, let's give it a merciful, painless death?"'

Even though they were restricted in what they could do, the shelter would never refuse a call to a sick cow. An English volunteer, Jack Reece, was called out one day to attend to a cow that had collapsed on a rubbish heap. It was *Posh Burrah*,

231

when once a year the temples feed the poor. The cow was located near a big temple, and when the ambulance arrived the access was blocked by rows of long carpets upon which sat hundreds of people. Teams of people walked along the rows ladling out dahl and vegetables and rice onto plates.

As there were four sittings scheduled there was no way they were going to be able to get to the cow for many hours. Then someone told Jack that there was a back way. They walked down an alley about three metres wide, which slowly reduced to two, then a metre and a half. Finally they came upon the cow, collapsed on a sea of plastic bags, vegetable waste and rubbish that had been thrown in the alley between the houses. By the light of a candle Jack examined it and concluded that it was a typical plastic-bag cow – with its stomach full of rubbish it was starving and beyond help. Nevertheless, if he could get it to the shelter he would be able to make its last hours more comfortable.

They borrowed a vegetable cart with four rickety pram wheels. With a couple of dozen people helping, they managed with great difficulty to heave the cow on board. At one stage they had to put some timber over the open sewer which flowed beside the alley so that the wheels could pass. Eventually they emerged into the square where the ambulance was parked and transferred the cow to the vehicle. Thus it was able to spend its last hours under proper veterinary care and free of pain.

Jack Reece was a valuable recruit. Having spent three and a half years in a large animal practice in Devon, England, he knew a lot about horses and cows. After seeing an advertisement for volunteers in a veterinary journal, he had come to

India initially for six months, and liked it so much he extended his stay to a year.

He returned home in February to a typical English winter. 'You don't realise how awful the winter is until you've lived somewhere else,' Jack recalls. 'I lasted six weeks and came back for another year.'

That second year extended to fifteen months. When he returned to England once more he found that his time at Help in Suffering had spoiled conventional veterinary practice for him. 'At home you need the bedside manner. Some practices think it's the most important thing. But it's a show. Here we're not just looking after a bunch of pampered pets, we're making a difference to lives. The shelter makes a difference to the lives of a lot of people.'

After that second stint at Help in Suffering Jack was soon back yet again. He has a great affection for his Indian colleagues at the shelter – the drivers and compounders (veterinary assistants) and his fellow vets. Most of them come from the untouchable class. 'Most higher-class Hindus wouldn't touch dead bodies or clean up faeces or catch dogs or do all sorts of other things. In the government veterinary hospitals there's a hierarchy; here we do everything. There are three compounders here – two are illiterate, and one's just taught himself to read and write – if I had a dog to spay I'd have one of them do it rather than some of the government vets I've seen. My relationship with the staff is one of the reasons I keep coming back. I've got sixteen Indian brothers and sisters here. They're lovely.'

Jack also enjoys the challenge of working without all the technological aids that are available in the west. One of his most satisfying cases involved a little Jersey calf that was hit by a minibus. She had a hole in her chest that was so big that you could look in and see her lung. The lungs normally stick to the chest wall under negative pressure. Because of the wound one lung had collapsed. In order to get it working again they needed to close the wound.

In England Jack would have sent the calf to a veterinary hospital. The chances of operating successfully were slim, nevertheless he decided to try. Assisted by a couple of the compounders of whom he was so proud, he laid her on her side. This had the effect of making her breathing more difficult as her one good lung was now being squashed under her own weight.

Ideally they would have had a ventilator, but here the patient had to breathe on her own. They administered anaesthetic and strapped bits of rib to other bits of rib. Then, while one person cupped a hand over the hole to restore the pressure in the chest, another prepared a suture. Lift the hand away, make a stitch and close the wound with the hand again; lift the hand away, stich and repeat . . .

Jack recalls, 'When we'd finished I thought, If she recovers from the anaesthetic she'll die of infection. I went down every morning expecting to see her, if not dead, then dying. We kept her full of antibiotics – lots of them. After about ten days she was still alive, and I thought, this is amazing, it shouldn't happen. We continued the antibiotics for two or three weeks, always worrying that she'd break down. Eventually there was perfect healing except for one small sinus which occasionally discharged a bit, and she licked it clean.'

They named the little Jersey Thora, after the thoracic surgery she had undergone, and gave her to one of the staff. After a while he left to take up a job in his village, so he passed her on to the woman who ran a little shop around the corner from the shelter. While she had her, Thora had two calves and, every time she was milked, she gave about ten litres, which is exceptional for an Indian cow.

Four years after her operation Thora became ill. She was struggling with her breathing and had a raging temperature. Jack suspected that something had gone wrong with the repair. 'We treated her aggressively, but you get this feeling, and she died outside the corner shop. We post-mortemed her. Couldn't actually pinpoint what the problem was but her chest was not normal.'

Possibly, if they had been in England and sent Thora to a veterinary hospital the outcome would have been different. However, with their admittedly primitive facilities they had given her four extra years of life and provided her owner with a valuable resource.

Over the years Christine has formed a great affection for her unconventional Englishman. They have their little spats now and then – Jack sometimes thinks that Christine is too soft-hearted – but they are united in their disdain for material things and their deep commitment to all living creatures. Jack professes not to become emotionally involved with his patients, nevertheless, there have been a few animals who have stolen his heart. One was a disreputable street dog named Buffer whose beat was the Jaipur railway station. One day someone rang up and said there was an injured dog on Platform Seven. The ambulance staff went out and returned with a dog that had been run over by a train – one front leg was almost completely severed.

'It was literally hanging on by a thread,' Jack remembers. 'The bone had been cut, it really was just dangling in the breeze, and there was this big open wound where you could see both ends of the bone. Balu fetched me to see him in the dispensary. It was a male dog, about one year old and, as I went up to him, he looked at me with warm eyes – they were friendly eyes – and he wagged his tail, in spite of the fact that his leg was hanging off. I sort of looked at him and he kept on wagging his tail, and I said to Balu, "Will these people have him back?" Balu said, "Yes, the chap who runs the office on Platform Seven said he'd have him back." So I said, "Right, you've saved his life, Balu. I was going to put him down, but we'll amputate his leg and fix him up provided there's someone who'll give him a bit of TLC.'"

It was a long rehabilitation for Buffer. They vaccinated him and when he was well enough they castrated him. But when they returned him to the railway station the people there refused to accept him, so they took him back to the shelter. For several months Buffer slept on the doormat to the dispensary, which he now regarded as home after having been in the kennels for so long. Then one day he just decided he'd come and go, which he's been doing ever since. He wanders up to the *chai* store, then he might drop by the butcher's shop hoping for a handout, then on to a nearby shantytown. But he always comes back to the shelter. He knows all the staff, and if he sees any of them out in the street he wags his tail in greeting. If he hadn't been brought up in the street he obviously would have made a very nice pet.

In contrast to Jack's supposedly unemotional approach, Christine unreservedly loves each and every animal she sees.

236

BLACK DOG IN MANALI

In this orchard village
of apples and marigolds,
the temple bell sounds
from far mountains
and under my feet
at the stained table
the black dog lies.

I give her one caress
and she, having searched a lifetime,
at last finding her God,
gazing with intent eyes
at every dispensed glance,
moves her tail,
forever hopeful of eternal love.

Black dog do not come
for what can I give?
I am leaving in an aircraft.
Do not love me.
Do not surrender.
See how the other street dogs,
tails tucked, run in fear.

You come to the hotel door,
lie in wait for my future exit,
trusting the bond will last forever.
But the gardeners, on order,
lift their brooms,

and you, whimpering, confused,
run crying up the road.

Invariably, when Christine goes into Jaipur on an errand the
journey is interrupted by frequent stops. The staff have become
used to her calling them to rescue some dog or horse or camel
or cat or donkey which she has found in need of care. Most of
them are treated then returned to where they were found, but
there are a few that for one reason or another end up staying.

The shelter is rather like a small zoo. At the time of writing
there are some calves whose mothers have been killed by cars
or who were so full of plastic bags they were unable to give
milk; there are a couple of horses, two or three donkeys and a
buffalo. In one cage live three squirrels who fell out of a tree
when they were babies – they are now too domesticated to go
back into the wild. There are a couple of tough-looking street
cats and two monkeys who cannot be released into the wild. In
another cage is a sparrow with a hurt wing recuperating in a
nest made of cotton wool in a flowerpot. Another contains
kites, mynah birds and some peacocks, who are all recovering
from injuries of one sort or another.

The birds fare particularly badly during the annual kite-
flying festival. The skies of Jaipur are peppered with kites.
Their owners glue ground glass to their strings and try to cut off
their rivals. If a bird flies into the string it practically severs
its wing. During the festival the shelter organises teams of
rescuers with boxes on the back of motor scooters to bring in
the victims for treatment.

The real characters are a collection of street dogs who, for
various reasons, have ended up making the place home. Jimmi
is a female, despite her name. She's a would-be thoroughbred

who went wrong. Her owner was trying to breed German Shepherds, but the bitch got out and mated with a street dog,
producing two puppies. The owner brought them to the shelter
to rehome. They found a new owner for Jimmi's brother,
Marshall, but there was something about Jimmi that made
Christine want to keep her. Jimmi absolutely adores Christine,
and she will faithfully follow her everywhere she goes. That's
the German Shepherd genes in her; the street-dog part makes
her fall upon with fury any other dog who comes near.

Tar Baby was a puppy when she was rescued after falling
into hot tar being used in road building. When she was brought
in all of her outer skin had peeled off so that she looked like
a little pink mouse. Kathy Nolan nursed her in her room for
weeks until she healed and her hair grew back. She's a small,
graceful dog with pretty eyes and long white and tan hair.
She's very gentle with humans but will kill any cat that crosses
her path.

Charisma was dumped at the gate one day. Christine sus-
pects she came from the same source as Jimmi, as she looks
very similar but smaller. She's a faithful, friendly dog who
was very endearing as a pup, which is why she came to be
called Charisma. They decided to keep her because no one
came along to claim her, and she was so friendly.

Robin is probably a mixture of Spitz and some sort of nondescript brown dog. She was brought in with a crushed leg after
having been run over. The shelter staff told her owner that they
would have to amputate the leg if she was to survive. The
owner agreed, but when he saw her with only three legs he
didn't want her any more. Robin was cared for by a volunteer,
Brian Rogers. When he went home Christine inherited her.
She's old and frail now, and rather shy, so it's hard to believe

that in her younger days she used to beat up Jimmi, standing over her and growling so ferociously that Jimmi would whimper in fear. Now that she's old Jimmi has had her revenge a couple of times and nearly killed her, so Christine keeps Robin in the fenced-off cottage garden out of harm's way.

Rocky has a Labrador's body and personality but his legs are disproportionately short. Furthermore, the front ones are genetically deformed. Incapable of surviving on the street, he would have been a prime candidate for euthanasia. But he's still around. Why? 'Because he's cute,' says Christine.

Marshall, another cripple, lives with Balu. Marshall considers it his job to protect the shelter from strangers. He has sunk his teeth into several people. Every time he misbehaves Christine says he has to be put to sleep. Marshall then mysteriously disappears. After a month or so when everyone has forgotten his misdeeds he reappears. Balu denies having anything to do with it.

Toby has adopted the area just outside Christine's garden gate as his territory. He's a stocky little street dog, brown and white with red eyes from some childhood disease.

Black Lucy is a small black Labrador who could not be rehomed because of her partial blindness. She was surrendered because she had terrible ear problems. She was shaking and scratching in pain, but Sunil treated her and eventually the ears cleared up. She hangs around the kitchen a lot and plays with Manju's daughter Ranjana. Yes, Manju finally had a daughter, whom she asked Christine to name; and there is a son, too, Raval. After so much heartbreak with her other pregnancies they are especially loved.

There are another half-dozen or so dogs who come and go. One or two, after being treated for injury, were released then found their way back from twenty or more kilometres away. They took them back only to find a few days later they had turned up again. After they'd gone to so much effort Christine found it impossible to send them away again.

Why did they not just euthanase apparently hopeless cases like Robin or Tar Baby? Christine says no other topic causes more disputes among the staff than whether or not to kill animals. 'We tried to make rules, but how can you make rules? It has to be an individual decision about every dog, and some dogs just stay; I don't know why, it just happens that way.'

CHAPTER 23

Travelling into Jaipur one day from the shelter Christine was outraged to see two people sitting on a cart beating a thin, starved-looking horse with a whip. She shouted to Daya to stop the car. As they pulled up, the horse, in a panicked attempt to escape his tormentors, reared up and ran the cart into a ditch. Even then, rather than try to talk to him and coax him out, they kept beating and beating.

Christine ran over in a fury. 'I'm not going to let this happen,' she cried. 'I'm going to buy this horse. I'm not giving it back to these people.'

The horse's owner had different ideas. He didn't understand what this demented white woman was making a fuss about, and had no intention of selling her his horse. Christine recalls, 'An argument began which went on and on for what seemed like hours until finally this man told us we could buy his horse. It was irrational and stupid, but anyway we bought it and we brought him back here.'

They named the horse Badal, which means 'cloud' in Hindi. He was a Mawari horse – a Rajasthani breed with long, curly ears and slightly curved, flared nostrils. Marawi horses have a proud history. They came with the Rajputs into Rajasthan many centuries ago. They have a special gait that is neither a trot nor a walk, which they can keep up without pause across kilometre after kilometre of desert. By nature they are more like a dog than a horse: they often become devoted to one person and they can learn to do all sorts of tricks. The most famous Mawari horse, Chetak, is memorialised by a statue in Udaipur, the only fortress state never conquered by the Moghuls. Legend has it that when the Moghul army invaded, the king rode out on his beloved horse Chetak to do battle. Though the battle was won, the mortally wounded horse carried his king back to safety before he died under a tree.

Badal hardly looked like a thoroughbred when they got him home. His coat was ragged and he had numerous sores and scabs from beatings. With good care he was soon transformed. His coat became sleek and shiny, his ribs were no longer visible and he was full of energy. He was a bay with four white socks – a lucky sign according to Indians who know horses. His single flaw was that one eye was brown and the other blue.

After his wounds had healed Christine threw a soft Rajasthani cloth saddle over him and, with some trepidation, mounted. Badal carried her obediently as far as the gate, then refused to go further. There was a long tussle of wills until he decided to co-operate.

Every day Daya and Christine would take him to a nearby open space and 'lunge' him, placing a long halter around his neck and having him run around in a circle first one way then the other. At first Badal kicked and reared, but he soon learned to do as he was told. His neck muscles and balance improved and he carried himself as a proud Mawari horse should.

Christine knew she could not keep him tied up most of the time at the shelter, so she offered him to an Indian friend in Udaipur who ran a riding school. He said he would love to have him. They found a horse float and driver. Badal and Balu travelled together in the float on the fifteen-hour journey to Udaipur.

When they arrived the riding-school owner took one look at Badal and declared he couldn't possibly have him as he had a chalk eye, and it would be bad luck for the stables. So, without even allowing the horse to leave the float or feeding him, he sent them off on the long journey back to Jaipur.

Christine was at a loss. Then she remembered an unusual Englishman she had met in Manali. Mark Braham was in his seventies. He had lived for many years in India studying yoga and riding all over the Himalayas on his own, carrying hardly any supplies or equipment, and camping at night. He was a mystic and a loner, but he loved horses and knew how to care for them. The last time they had met, Mark had bemoaned the fact that he could not find a decent horse.

Christine knew that Badal would enjoy life with Mark much more than living at Help in Suffering. She wrote to him, and a short time later in the searing heat of the Rajasthani summer Mark set off with Badal, riding northwards across the plains then up through the winding mountain roads to the Himalayas.

They rode in the cool of the mornings and rested up in the worst heat of the day. By the time they arrived in the high country Mark and Badal had developed a deep affection for one another. For six months they roamed the mountains together.

Badal learned things that a Rajasthani horse does not normally know. For instance, he had never seen a creek before. The first time he had to cross one he was afraid. However, he soon became as sure-footed on the steep, narrow tracks as any mountain pony.

Then Mark had to return to England for a while, so Badal came back to stay at the shelter.

In 1999 the shelter had begun a collaborative program with the London-based Brooke Hospital for Animals. The organisation had been started by an Englishwoman, Dorothy Brooke. In 1930 she had travelled to Cairo, where she was shocked to see the condition of the horses that the British left behind after the First World War ended. They were pulling heavy loads and were starving and ill-treated. On her return to England she wrote to newspapers pointing out what a shameful thing this was to do to the horses that had gone to war for Britain. The public responded by flooding her with money, which she used to found the Brooke Hospital for Animals. She worked originally in Cairo and Luxor, but now the hospital looked after equines in many developing countries.

The shelter's Brooke team was headed by a recent graduate, Ashok Tanwar. Ashok had been highly-placed in the entrance exam for government service, but, like Sunil, he had elected to forsake the security of a government job to do more satisfying work with animals. Ashok was an extremely competent vet. He had a playful nature which made him see the humour in any situation, and he got on well with everyone.

Mark Braham returned from Britain, and about a year after their first trek he once again took Badal into the Himalayas.

Mark had long been concerned about the condition of the trekking ponies that were used in the summer months to carry Indian and foreign tourists. He had seen that there was often not enough food or water for them, they were not properly shod and so were often lame, and they suffered terribly from saddle sores from poorly designed harnesses. When Mark heard about the equine program he suggested that together they do something to help these suffering animals.

Mark proposed that he would organise a camp with Ashok as the vet. They would shoe the horses, vaccinate and worm them, and try to teach their owners about proper saddles, harnesses and nutrition.

Christine agreed that it was a good idea, but said it would have to be done every year if it was to be effective, as education was more important than just dabbing at the wounds.

With that agreement Mark set about organising things. It was like an army manoeuvre. He arranged for a huge tent to be made, obtained hundreds of shoes for the horses, and when all was ready the HIS team travelled to Manali in Himachal Pradesh. While they were on their way they heard that Badal had fallen ill. The people who had been looking after him had been unable to get him any feed, so they had given him some cow pellets to eat. That, and perhaps the effect of the altitude, had made him colicky. When Christine, Ashok and the rest of the team arrived Badal was still alive. Ashok did what he could but he was unable to save him. It was a sad end for a beautiful and spirited creature. Christine had felt a special bond with the little Mawari stallion.

Mark and Ashok, with a team of local helpers, worked for more than a week trying to educate the horse owners. In the end they came to realise that it was a near-impossible task. The owners just didn't have the food or the facilities to look after their animals properly, and they were obstinate about forsaking short-term profits for the horses' long-term health. After the tourist season finished someone saw the shoes they had provided for sale in the market.

There were no more Himalayan horse camps. Mark Braham became ill shortly afterwards and died of leukemia. The trekking ponies are still working and still suffering. While it was disappointing, the exercise taught Christine a valuable lesson. 'There's so much to do but you have to do a few things properly – you can't spread yourself too thin, nothing works then.'

The Brooke Hospital team has more than enough to occupy them in Rajasthan. They estimate that there are 25,000 horses and donkeys in and around Jaipur which need veterinary care. The team is made up of five people – the vet Ashok, a compounder/saddler, a compounder/farrier, a driver and the manager.

A typical day's work: they leave the shelter at dawn and drive for about half an hour to the Lal Kothi vegetable market in Jaipur, where about 250 horses work transporting vegetables. They set up in an open space near one of the entrances. While they wait for patients someone orders *chai* from a nearby stall. A small boy arrives with the *chai* in small, slightly grubby glasses in a rusty wire carrier. While they drink they watch the creaking wooden carts loaded high with produce making their way into the market. Their clients will not come to them until they have unloaded.

After fifteen minutes the first person arrives with a typically wiry little chestnut mare pulling an ancient, wobbly-wheeled cart. Ashok knows this horse, as he knows all the horses he treats. She first came to him about two months ago with an abscess on her back leg. It had been treated with local medicine made of coconut oil and herbs, which had made it worse. After regular treatment with proper medicine it's slowly getting better. The injury would heal faster if the owner could rest his horse, but he cannot do that as he depends upon it to feed his family. Instead he is using it only enough to pay for its feed – or so he says. Ashok applies some ointment and makes a note in the book in which he keeps a record of every animal.

Ashok makes up many of the medicines he uses from ingredients he buys in bulk: zinc oxide for harness wounds, nasal balm for nasal discharge and coughing, and others that would be expensive to buy from drug suppliers. By so doing he saves the shelter 40,000 rupees per year.

Most of the carts have been unloaded by now and the clients begin to arrive in greater numbers. Another skinny little horse needs de-worming. The bridle is chafing, so the saddler, Arjun, makes some repairs. Arjun was trained at a saddlery in Delhi. Squatting in the dust with a few rudimentary tools he expertly repairs and sometimes makes entirely new harnesses while the owners wait. Medical treatment is free but they charge a small amount for a harness so that the owners will feel they have a stake in their equipment. If they need a new saddle HIS will give them a 60 per cent subsidy, which they can then pay back.

Arjun has a slight, wiry frame, with an angular handsome face, long black hair and a straggly moustache. He is a Bhil, a traditional tribe who live in Pokhran in the northwest of India. Christine met him in the year 2000 when she was on a retreat in Mount Abu. He was working at a hotel owned by the

Thakoor of Pokhran – the Indian equivalent of an aristocratic lord. Arjun had not been paid for a month, so Christine engaged him as a cook during her stay. She was so impressed by his intelligence and initiative that she offered him a job. A few days after she had returned to Jaipur he turned up, and he's been there ever since.

Arjun is an orphan. He left school in sixth grade to work as an offsider on a truck that did long-haul trips all over India. He has been married for three years. His wife stays in a small hamlet of a dozen huts in Pokhara, about three kilometres from the nearest road, without running water or electricity. He goes home to see her and his child twice a year. Arjun is good at everything he does, and is eager to take on responsibility.

A boy arrives sitting cross-legged on his empty cart. Arif is sixteen. His father lost his hand in a trucking accident and can no longer work. Two of Arif's brothers own horses, and between them they are supporting a family of ten and helping send the oldest brother to university. Rakhee, the Brooke program's manager, is trying to get the brother a scholarship. The pony needs worming and treatment for some harness sores.

Another little pony arrives with harness sores on its back, legs and chest. One eye is weeping. The driver is just a child – twelve years old, he tells Ashok. The horse belongs to his father, but he is too sick to work so the son has had to leave school. Ashok tells him that it is time to retire the horse. The boy shakes his head with an old man's certainty. That is not possible. The whole family depends on this little pony. So they treat the sores, and make a new harness, which will help.

A bent old man wearing a *dhoti*, with a grubby turban wound around his head, pulls up with his cart. His face is whiskered and deeply wrinkled. His horse looks as old in horse years as he is. It has abrasions on both front legs from a fall, and its ankles are swollen due to bad shoes. This is another of Ashok's long-term patients. The horse should really be euthanased but the old man has to support his family so they give it pain-killers every day, dress its sores and make sure it has a good, soft harness.

Many of the horses Ashok sees are lame from being badly shod. There are seventeen farriers in Jaipur, but none of them really knew what they were doing until the Brooke program started. Help in Suffering hired an ex-Indian army farrier to teach them the correct methods, and donated proper tools. The young ones were willing to learn, but some of the old ones refuse to change.

Another boy brings in his horse for a checkup following a procedure a couple of days ago. The horse had an obstructed oesophagus, which Ashok cured by putting a tube through its nose and into its stomach and 'wiggling it around'. It has had injections to reduce swelling and for pain, and some anti-biotics. The horse is still not eating well so Ashok puts a drip into its neck containing dextrose, a carbohydrate which the body does not need to break down, so that it turns directly into energy. Ashok says the horse is doing well and will be fine.

Now a man comes with a tall, extremely thin mare. The owner says that in the past week she has lost her appetite. Ashok takes her temperature by inserting a thermometer into the rectum, then he feels her body and asks more questions of the owner. He announces that he will take a blood sample. 'I think this horse has babesiosis, but I'll check to be sure.'

Babesiosis comes from the tick-borne Babesia parasite. Before the Brooke team had begun work in Jaipur its presence in the equines had not been identified. The streets were full of pathetically thin, weak horses that were being whipped and beaten to force them to work. Babesia cause the destruction of the red blood cells. Oxygen cannot be carried properly round the body and distributed to the various organs, and the immune system of the animal fails to function, appetite is lost and the health of the horse rapidly declines. The Brooke team discovered that with the use of injectable Imazol the parasite could be killed and the horse would slowly regain its health.

'I'll give Imazol now,' Ashok says, 'because I'm fairly sure this is babesiosis, and it's important to catch it early.' He explains to the owner that he will return next week with the result of the blood test: if it confirms the horse has babesiosis, he will give a second shot of Imazol. He deftly injects the horse with vitamin B complex and also an antibiotic to deal with secondary infections.

The sick parade continues until lunchtime – horses with toothache, horses with loss of appetite, the sick, the sore and the lame. Each cart is checked and if need be one of the compounders quickly nails on a couple of reflectors, for accidents are frequent at night. The reflectors are free.

After lunch the team takes the van with all its equipment to Purani Busty, which roughly translates as 'old living area'. It is a suburb of small, cement and stone flat-roofed dwellings, built wall to wall, with narrow unpaved roads between. They set up close to a small park. Over 150 donkeys work in this area, mostly carrying building materials of stone, brick and rubble in saddlebags as they have done for centuries.

Ashok examines his first patient. The owner tells him that the donkey is lame. Ashok addresses him in Rajasthani, calling him 'uncle' respectfully, and using the polite form of 'you'.

Without being asked, Arjun produces a folded cotton bag from the van in which a number of hoof tools are neatly arranged in pouches. He selects a sharp picking knife with a wooden handle and begins to cut away dead hoof. The donkey tries to rear and kick, but its owner holds it firmly. It is only the size of a calf, with fluffy grey hair and long black ears.

After the necrotic tissue has been cut from the tiny hoof, Ashok takes the hoof squeezers, shaped like a large pair of tongs. As he gently presses, a jet of yellow pus bursts from the hoof. The donkey probably injured itself grazing on a rubbish dump where wire and glass are a constant hazard.

The next donkey has a string of green, semi-hardened mucous swinging from its nostrils. 'Strangles,' pronounces Ashok. He begins to clean the nostrils with wads of cotton wool. Then he feels under the neck. 'The glands can become so swollen that the donkey will choke,' he explains.

'Will he be all right?' asks the anxious owner.

'He will be all right.'

Ashok says, 'When we first came the donkeys were so poor you could not believe. There was so much bone, and so much sores from their bad harness. They used plastic string under the tail and under the girth. They were so thin and hungry. Now look, they are very healthy.'

And so it goes. Ashok moves from animal to animal, feeling and pressing. The compounders administer medicine and repair harnesses, and the owners leave without saying thanks, for that is their way. Since the Brooke program began they have treated 60,000 horses and donkeys in Jaipur.

Christine has an uncanny ability to find staff who are as dedicated as she is. The manager of the Brooke Hospital team is Rakhee Sharma. She is a handsome figure in her flowing Rajasthani salwar kameez; you can see the compassion in her eyes. Rakhee's life has been as hard as many of those she helps. Her father died of a brain tumour when she was five. She had an eighteen-month-old sister at the time. Unable to look after both children, her mother sent Rakhee to an orphanage, where she stayed until she was seventeen. Then she moved into a one-room flat with her mother and sister, and began going to college. She loved animals and spent all of her spare time helping out at Help in Suffering. Five years ago they offered to train her and give her a job.

A lot of the success of the equine program has been due to Rakhee. Many of the animal owners are traditional people. At first they were deeply suspicious of outsiders wanting to interfere. The breakthrough came with the salt-sellers who visit Jaipur every summer. Their hard-working little donkeys suffered terribly from harness injuries. Although they were emaciated and infested with worms, the owners believed if they treated them they would go blind.

Rakhee realised that the women of the camps had power and influence. She spent long hours talking with them, and through them eventually persuaded the men that there was a better way to treat their animals. One day ten salt-sellers visited the shelter seeking help. The word soon spread that these outsiders knew what they were doing.

Despite her education and her relatively grand status, Rakhee always speaks courteously to the poor horse and donkey owners. They in turn address her respectfully as 'elder sister'. Rakhee is 31 years old. With her wages saved from Help in Suffering she has bought a little house for her mother and her sister and herself. She has paid for her sister to train in a beauty salon, and is currently searching for a husband for her. Once her sister is married she will then be able to think about marriage herself. This may not be easy, as her husband will have to be prepared to care for her mother; Indian wives usually live with their mother-in-law.

There had been so much to do when they first came to India that it was eighteen months before Christine and Jeremy had returned to Australia for a short holiday. Having no home of their own they spent their six-week holiday staying with Christine's mother, Jeremy's parents, with Miles and his wife Joyce, and with Anne on the property in Coonamble.

Although by Australian standards none of their hosts lived ostentatiously Christine was overwhelmed by the plenty she saw all about her. The refrigerators crammed with food, the wine with dinner, even the *Sydney Morning Herald*, which came over the gate every morning, seemed wanton luxuries after India.

At Coonamble she went riding one morning with one of her nieces, Vanessa. It was a good season and the rape grew as high as the horses' chests. Christine's horse, Boss Girl, had a white, arched neck, her coat was glossy with good health and she pranced through the fields with a proud step. How different this mare was, she mused, to the horses and ponies in Jaipur who laboured under the hot sun, thin, tired and crippled, whipped and goaded as they dragged their overloaded carts.

The cattle were glossy and fat. They could drink from the bore when they were thirsty and rest under the trees when they were hot. They did not labour under the yoke and they were never hungry or exhausted. It was true that one day men and dogs would come to round them up, and they would die degrading deaths, but until that day they lived in contentment.

She tried to understand why the world was so unjust; why

some lived surrounded by love and wealth while others only knew grief and hunger. The poverty and injustice with which she was so familiar sometimes seemed beyond human intervention, yet she knew she had to keep going back to India so that in one small part of the planet things would become better.

Since Jeremy had left Australia his father, Geoffrey, had continued to express his disapproval by not once writing. When they met in Sydney things between them were civil, but as the time came for them to leave again it became clear that his father was upset. 'Maybe he felt he was losing a son for the last years of his life,' suggests Jeremy.

Jeremy was upset, too. In the old days, even if they did not see one another much, they used to speak regularly on the telephone. They had enjoyed a warm father–son relationship. When Jeremy arrived back in Jaipur he wondered what he could do to mend things. Neither he nor his father had ever been much good at writing letters. Instead, he hit upon the idea of recording a tape. 'On the tape I explained why I'd left . . . I told him I loved him, and that I felt this was something I had to do. I sent it off, and a little while later Mum wrote and said my father had listened to it. He understood my motives and I had his blessing. He didn't feel that he could write but we'd talk about it the next time we went home.'

A year later, in May 1995, Jeremy's father suffered a heart attack while watching a game of football. Jeremy was in Darjeeling when he received word that his father was in hospital in a coma. It took almost a week to get home and, by then, Geoffrey had died. Jeremy was glad that they had made their peace in time.

CHAPTER 24

The ABC program was going well. An average of twenty dogs a week were being spayed, vaccinated and released back onto the street after full recovery. By 1995, eighteen months after it had begun, they estimated that all the dogs in the three pilot suburbs, plus a fourth which they added, had been treated.

The major question was whether the dog population in that area had reduced or stabilised. They had counted dogs in Malviyanagar, Durgapura and Mansarowar three times – before beginning the operations, just after completing the work, and again two to three months later. To their relief they found that the final count in each area showed the population had definitely stabilised.

They were discovering a lot about street dogs that they hadn't known. By identifying them through their ear tattoos they found that some had travelled sixteen kilometres or more from their original area. Others seemed to remain in one place for their lifetime, most likely because of a good food source. For instance, if a street dog lived outside a residence and was fed regularly and cared for, it would hardly wander at all.

Already they were seeing changes in dog demographics. Whereas before they used to see wandering or lost puppies all the time, now there were very few. There was a definite reduction in the feral dog population that lived behind the shelter along the river. In the past, twenty or 30 large wild dogs used to live there, their numbers kept high by street dogs from Mansarowar and Durgapura joining the pack. After the street-dog population lost its breeding capacity there were no new pups available to boost the pack. There had been another big pack of dogs in Durgapura that used to kill stray calves at night, much to the dismay of the local people. After the pilot program they had either died or moved on.

Although there were no statistics yet, it seemed to Christine that there were less rabid dogs in their area. They had often sighted rabid dogs roaming the fields, or even coming out of the *nulla* into the shelter to attack their own dogs; now they hardly saw them at all.

Their success evidently impressed the Animal Welfare Board of India, for one day its chairman, Lieutenant General Chatterjee, visited the shelter with a proposal.

General Chatterjee was a tall man with an imposing military bearing. He and the ABC staff sat on seats in the shade of the neem trees sipping *chai* that Manju had made. 'Jaipur's a high-profile city,' said General Chatterjee. 'A successful program is needed to establish once and for all the efficacy of ABC methods. Couldn't you increase the throughput of dogs and cover the whole of Jaipur?'

'It'd be a big job,' said Christine. 'But we could try.'

Christine estimated that there were fifteen thousand dogs in Jaipur, of which half would be male, leaving them with 7,500 to be spayed. If they could spay 50 per week it would amount to 2,600 dogs per year; thus they would cover the whole city within two or three years. (In fact this calculation was completely wrong. As the population of Jaipur continued to grow, so did the dog population. In reality there are probably more than 40 thousand street dogs living in Jaipur.)

Janine Vogler said she would find the extra funding. Jeremy designed twenty new kennels, bringing the total to 40, and supervised their building. Every day the dog-catching vehicle and staff went out to catch dogs at the increased rate. As time went on the people of Jaipur stopped stoning the dogs and abusing them because they knew they had been vaccinated against rabies. Travelling through the city Christine kept seeing dogs that she thought of as her dogs. She could identify them because of the v-shaped nick in the ear. It seemed to her that the dogs, tolerated now – even welcomed – lent a richness to Jaipur that could not be equalled in the empty, sterile cities of the west, where animals were never seen.

Some other Indian cities were conducting ABC programs, too. Four people from WSPA came on a tour of the country to show the latest catching methods in the UK. They were convinced that the sack used at HIS was inhumane. They proposed to demonstrate a long pole with a light chain lasso at the end that you slipped over the dog's head then pulled taut. At A$220 it was a lot more expensive than a sack.

First the British team showed a video of the pole in action.

The operator approached a small dog on the street, which wagged its tail and obligingly held still as the catcher slipped the noose over its neck.

Jack told them that Jaipur dogs were not like well-behaved British dogs. They were semi-wild creatures, and it was highly unlikely that the pole would work.

The visitors insisted on going ahead with their demonstration. The team had caught ten street dogs for them. They turned the first one out into the yard; the pole operator approached and, after a lot of trouble, managed to get the lasso over its head. The dog screamed with terror and tore at the lasso, breaking some teeth and bruising its neck in the process.

It was hardly an impressive beginning, but the visitors were not yet swayed. They called for another dog. It ran from the kennel, deftly avoided the lasso then sank its teeth into the operator's leg. After that they gave up.

Says Christine, 'The whole thing was a complete farce. We realised that you just have to quietly go on your way, as you've discovered is best, with appropriate technology.'

While things were improving in Jaipur, many other Indian cities continued to treat their street dogs with appalling cruelty. At a conference in Delhi Christine heard from the President of the Society for the Protection of Cruelty to Animals, Pradeep Kumar Nath, about a program which had been running for many years in Visakaputnam in Andhra Pradesh. Street dogs were regularly being rounded up and electrocuted under inhumane conditions. Christine was so horrified by photographs Pradeep showed her that she determined to go to Visakaputnam to investigate.

The dogs were lassoed with a wire noose, suffering terrible injuries in the process. As they were caught they were thrown into a cage on the back of a truck. It took about three days to fill the cage. During that time the first dogs to be caught were left without food or water. Eventually when the cage was full with dogs piled three deep on top of each other they turned a hose on them. When they were saturated they clamped electric wires to the cage and turned on the current.

What followed was a scene from hell. As they thrashed about in agony, dogs were howling and screaming and vomiting and bleeding from the anus. After five minutes they turned the current off. The dogs that were dead were pushed out of the way so that those who were only half dead could be placed near the wire. Then the current was turned on and the whole hideous process was repeated. When it was over they drove them off and buried them, including some who were still alive.

'It was the most ghastly thing I've ever seen,' says Christine. 'The whole thing was pointless. They'd been doing it for years and the dog population stayed exactly the same. It made not the slightest difference to rabies or the population.'

She was determined to do something about it. Pradeep told her that mere lobbying would not change anything, they would have to go to the courts. Christine suggested they enlist the help of Dr D. R. Mehta, the Chairman of the Security Industries Board. She knew Dr Mehta well. He had visited the shelter several times and had given generous donations. He was the founder of Jaipur Foot, an organisation which provided artificial limbs to people from all over India absolutely free of charge. Dr Mehta, a Jain, invited Christine to stay at his family flat in Mumbai, and organised a meeting of some of his influential Jain friends. After they had heard her descriptions and seen the photographs they each guaranteed a large sum of money. Dr Mehta instructed a barrister to take a challenge to the courts as soon as possible.

For once things moved quickly, perhaps due to the status of those involved. A judge heard the case straight away and concluded that since the Jain people had guaranteed the money and the SPCA had the expertise to run an ABC program, the electrocutions should stop forthwith.

Pradeep has since trained staff who have been running an ABC program with great success. They no longer electrocute dogs in Visakaputnam.

As the time drew near for their Scottish volunteer Ngaire to return home, Daya came to Christine one day and announced that he was also leaving to live in Scotland with her. They had recently married in Bangalore with Mishy acting as a witness, and had a new baby, so it was hardly a surprise. Christine felt immensely sad that Daya was leaving. They had worked so long together and been through so much that it was like losing a member of her family. For all Daya's abilities he had no formal qualifications. She worried that he would be unable to use the skills he had learned at Help in Suffering in his new country. Nevertheless, love and the comforts of the west were powerful temptations. She wished him well. When the day of his departure came all the staff went to the airport. They wept when he waved goodbye; and Daya also wept, and was gone.

It was soon time to farewell another stalwart. Mishy, 90 years old, wrote to Christine from Bangalore saying that she could no longer look after her two dogs, Bonny and Freckles. She asked if Christine would take care of them. The unwritten message was that Mishy was dying. In Bangalore she had started another animal shelter, Compassion Unlimited Plus Action – CUPA – with the help of an Indian friend, Suparna Ganguly. Suparna had been a young girl when she had met Mishy while working as a volunteer in her first shelter in New Delhi. Now, more than three decades later, when Mishy was too frail to look after herself any longer, Suparna was nursing her. Christine wrote back saying she would be honoured to look after the two dogs. Then, secure in the knowledge that her beloved pets would be cared for, Mishy, the eccentric and eternally selfless founder of Help in Suffering, passed away. Suparna wrote with the sad news. She said Mishy had predicted the date of her death a long time ago. She was out by just a few hours, having died early in the morning a day later.

CHAPTER 25

Christine is immensely proud of the specialised teams that have evolved at Help in Suffering. On a typical day, just after dawn the camel team – veterinarian Devi Shankar Rajoria, driver Omprakesh, and compounder Rajendra – head out of Jaipur to the small town of Chomu, forty kilometres to the north. Whenever they see a camel cart they slow down and look it over. If need be they pull in ahead: Rajendra grabs two reflectors, a hammer and some nails and hurries back down the road. There is a short conversation with the owner, who is sometimes suspicious that this is some government busybody who wants to interfere. But once he realises that there's no trouble and he doesn't need to pay anything, he wags his head in affirmation. Rajendra quickly nails on the reflectors and they continue on their way.

In Chomu the camel drivers gather in an open field with carts carrying towering loads of fodder. Some have come 50 or

60 kilometres to this market, where they will wait sometimes for two or three days before making a sale. There are perhaps 50 camels here, and Devi knows them all.

A common ailment is an infection from the wooden nose peg to which the reins are attached. A man comes to Devi leading a handsome palomino camel with elaborate geometrical designs shaved into its fur. The spot where the peg goes through its nose is caked with dried pus. Devi cleans it with antiseptic until he can see clean, pink flesh, then applies iodine ointment. He hands out suprazole worm tablets and tells the owner how to administer them.

Devi has lectured the camel owners endlessly about these nose pegs. They are only really necessary when the camels are in rut, but it's hard to persuade the owners to use a less cruel method of harness. His focus is on getting them to use a better-designed peg that does not rub so severely against the inside of the nostril. He also tells them that the thread should be thin, so that if the animal tosses its head the harness will break rather than the flesh of the nostril. His persistence is slowly paying off as he is seeing fewer wounds from nose pegs.

Devi holds back the lecture on this occasion. He and his two assistants stand with the drivers and chat, listening respectfully to their talk of families, weather, the cost of feed. They are thin village men, dressed in turbans and *kurtas* and *dhotis* wrapped like trousers, engaged in an activity that has not changed in generations. They move at their own pace. If you are to be accepted you need to adapt to their ways.

Eventually one of the men asks Devi almost off-handedly if he'd take a look at his beast. It has a discharge from one eye and, in an attempt to cure it, the owner has put mud on the eyebrow. The camel stands quietly as Devi administers eye-drops and gives it an anti-inflammatory injection.

Devi likes camels. They are difficult to work with but with time he has learned how to deal with them. An old textbook says that 999 out of 1,000 camels are placid and easy to handle. The remaining one bears terrible grudges, and will try to bite your head off and sit on you until you die. Such attacks, it says, are always fatal. Perhaps this is why the drivers all wear something on their head. Over the years Devi has been kicked once or twice but he has not yet been bitten.

The next beast he encounters looks like it might be that one in a thousand. Its owner tells Devi that it hasn't been eating. When Devi tries to look down its throat it gurgles angrily and rears up. The owner puts the fingers of one hand in its nostrils and with the other grabs the lower lip. While the beast lurches and shuffles, Devi examines it.

His diagnosis – vitamin B deficiency. Before administering an injection of vitamin B complex they tie its front leg back on itself so that the animal is immobilised.

Another patient arrives – this one with diarrhoea and a swollen knee joint where another camel has bitten it. The diarrhoea is probably from a change of diet. Devi prescribes vitamin B complex to make the gut work properly, injects an anti-inflammatory and applies medicine to the knee.

When they are in rut and fighting one another, camels will sometimes bite the lower mandible of their rival, breaking it. Devi has had to repair about fifteen such injuries. After sedating the camel he drills holes and inserts wire, which he then twists to hold the broken jaw together. Before the HIS camel program the owners treated these injuries with traditional methods. Invariably the wounds became infected, the infection spread to the bone and the animals died a slow, painful death.

Devi often used to see camels with sunken burns running down their necks. The camel drivers thought they could cure colds by branding them. Some camels had wounds on the knees or ankles where their owners had been trying to heal injuries with the same method. Instead, the wounds had become infected and were crawling with maggots, which had eaten deep into the flesh. Devi distributed illustrated leaflets that explained to the owners that it was not in their interest to treat their animals this way; and they listened, for no one had ever bothered to come before to the places where they congregated and tried to help them. If an animal has to stay at the shelter for rehabilitation they will loan the owner another camel so he can keep working. If they have to put one down they will compensate the owner according to his means.

Over four or five hours they treat about 30 camels: some for only minor things such as de-worming, but others have drips put into them, and one, protesting loudly, has half a bucket of medicine poured down its throat. It is all done quietly and efficiently. The camel owners trust them completely.

Omprakesh is a keen songwriter. On the way home in the Jeep he treats his colleagues to a performance of his latest composition. Roughly translated it goes like this:

Men are selfish,
they only think of themselves,
they should think of their environment
and all the animals, instead.

Like practically everyone who works at the shelter, Omprakesh is an untouchable. The use of the term is now politically incorrect. These days they are called 'dalits', or 'sweepers'. It is illegal to discriminate against anyone on grounds of caste, but it still happens.

Although the shelter has always paid more than the average wage, providing hospital insurance and retirement funds, still many of the staff used to receive hardly enough to live on. One of the reasons for this was that they sent much of their wages back to relatives in their villages. Without exception the staff came from villages where there was no work, and survival was difficult for them. Another factor was that all of them had undergone arranged marriages when they were teenagers. This meant that they usually had at least two children to support by the time they were twenty-years-old.

Those from remote villages needed accommodation nearby, as there were no more facilities for them to live within the grounds of the shelter. Because Jaipur had a rapidly expanding population rent was very expensive. However, the most difficult problem was that almost without exception landlords would not give accommodation to sweepers, whom they said were 'dirty'. And although it was against the law to say this, and to deny accommodation just because of a person's caste, it was impossible to prove such a thing, so the landlords went unpunished.

Christine and Jeremy became more and more troubled by this injustice. With some extra funds that Janine had raised in Europe they were able to purchase a small block of land adjoining the shelter. They built a block of six flats to house the families of six of the village staff.

The neighbours, who had never complained about the barking dogs, began to complain that they would be having sweepers living opposite, and these people would give a 'bad glance' to their daughter. They ignored these objections.

When building began only six staff needed flats; however, by the time the six flats were completed there were at least twice that number in need. It fell to Christine to decide, in consultation with Nirmal and Jack, which of the staff should be allocated the rooms. Before she decided she wanted to see the places where they lived with their families.

Suresh, his wife and his two toddlers rented a small room about two metres by two metres, with a corrugated-iron roof and a cement floor. There was no space even for a cooler or a fan; in any case he could not afford to run such luxuries. Electricity cost about 500 rupees a month, the rent cost 500 rupees a month, and Suresh's salary was about 2,500, with which he had to feed himself, his wife and his two babies.

In the block where Suresh lived there were four such rooms, built of a rough single layer of brick, placed in a small plot with nothing but dust outside, and a drain full of stinking grey water. There were no sealed roads in this area, no sewage facilities, no phone connections. Yet each one of these shanty rooms was spotlessly clean, and the few simple kitchen utensils on a shelf on the wall, and a bed, were the only furnishings. There was a shared toilet for the four families, and a shared tap from which they all filled their buckets. All their cooking was done outside in a dusty compound in the heat of the sun, which hovered between forty to forty-five degrees Celsius for several months of the year.

Because it was so hard for sweepers to find accommodation, they were grossly overcharged when they did manage to locate a room – even though such rooms were pitiful slums. Ramnivas lived in a room at the bottom of an unpaved, undrained slope of earth, in a gully that was previously used as a rubbish dump. It flooded every time it rained. He had no toilet, and had to go without any privacy to a nearby empty block of land. One night he was bitten on the finger by a rat, which had come in through holes in the flooring. Once when it rained during the monsoon the water rose to the level of his bed, and all his books were ruined. As he was putting himself through university in his spare time this caused him considerable difficulty.

After much discussion, Nirmal, Jack and Christine decided which six staff members and their families would be given the large rooms with attached bathrooms and kitchens that they had built. When she announced who were to receive new rooms, free of charge, all of the staff clapped. Those who were not yet allocated rooms did not complain. Psychologists could probably analyse endlessly why people who have hardly anything can be perpetually happy. 'The answer,' Christine believes, 'is that in the shelter love abounds. We have a motto that caste is left at the gate. Our vets eat with the staff and work with the staff and drink from the same glasses as the staff and cut open dead animals to find out why they've died. Our managers thank our staff for their bravery, and consult them and hold meetings and let them make decisions and respect their views and opinions. In return, Babu and Balu and Rajendra and Shiv and Arjun and Mukesh and Suresh and Udichand and Dulichand and Manju and Raju and Driverji and Shri Nath and Felliram and Ramswaroop and Ramnivas and the others teach us their customs and invite us to their villages, to funerals and feasts and marriages, and we are honoured to share life with them.'

It was very satisfying for Christine to see the staff in their new rooms, which were large and cool, each with its own tiled bathroom and kitchen. Suresh's baby would not be attacked by rats any more, and neither would his wife need to wait at the tap to fill a bucket. Christine immediately decided to appeal for more money to the fundraising committee that she had started some years back in Sydney. They told her that there was enough – four lakhs, or about US$10,000 – to build more rooms for the rest of the staff. They bought another plot with money from Animaux-Secours, and began to build four more flats, so that all of the staff could live as was their right.

CHAPTER 26

By 2001 Jack and Sunil thought that they must have made a difference to the incidence of rabies in Jaipur, but as there were no reliable government statistics available they had no means of really knowing how successful they were.

Most rabies cases, they knew, were sent to the infectious diseases unit at the government hospital. Sunil spent many days at the hospital painstakingly sifting through piles of dusty ledgers containing handwritten records of the 70 or so cases of rabies that had been reported each year. He began by going back eleven years, checking patients' addresses to see whether they came from the Jaipur area or from outside. Wading through list after list he discounted patients who were not from the ABC area. In order to get some confirmation he went to some of the addresses that were given and knocked on the doors to check that the information was correct.

It was not an exactly scientific method. There was no legal

requirement to report cases of rabies, nor for rabies cases to go to an infectious diseases hospital. Nevertheless, Sunil felt confident that it gave a reasonably accurate picture.

When he came to Christine with his results she could see that he was excited. 'It took much time,' he said, 'but now I have figures. See.' He held out a piece of paper.

Christine read it. 'You've gone back eleven years.'

'Yes, this gives a true picture. You will see for every year in Jaipur, 30, 40 people died of rabies. But in the last eighteen months, no person has died of rabies.'

'Sunil, this is incredible. It shows at last that our program is working.'

There could be no doubt that the program they had begun so hesitantly seven years previously had proved a spectacular success. As a result, the municipality of Jaipur has recently built a new facility for a vastly expanded ABC program, and they have contracted Help in Suffering to run it. HIS has helped to establish ABC programs in Kota, Kathmandu, Ahmedabad, Vishakapatnam, Ajmer, Delhi, Jodhpur and Silvasa.

The ABC programs and the day-to-day rescue and rehoming work is funded with money raised in Europe, the UK, the USA, Australia, and by the Indian government. The bulk of this money comes from Animaux-Secours through the tireless efforts of Janine Vogler, who campaigns relentlessly in Europe through newsletters and personal appeals. She has the great gift of inspiring people. Janine says it is integral to her efforts that people know Christine and Jeremy will be administering the funds.

Various other programs are individually financed. Money for the camel project comes from the Marchig Trust (Switzerland), the Carpenter Trust (UK), HIS UK and Animaux-Secours. HIS treats well over 2,000 camels per year in the field and at the Jaipur compound.

Money for the elephant project comes from *elephant family UK*. HIS has brought about tremendous improvements in the working conditions of the elephants of Jaipur.

The equine project is supported by Brooke Hospital for Animals (UK). HIS treats over 7,000 horses and donkeys per year. In addition they conduct more than 200 awareness sessions in the field, attended by about 1,000 owners. More than 1,500 harnesses made of wire or plastic string are replaced or repaired.

In 1999, after four years in Kalimpong, Aldona was ready to return home. Not that she ever said she wanted to leave – she was too loyal for that. Christine, sensing that she was lonely and ready for a change, told her she should feel free to go if she wanted to, and Aldona gladly accepted her offer. She had been a wonderful asset to the shelter and they would miss her.

Aldona's departure heralded a time of uncertainty at Kalimpong. Christine was unable to find an Indian vet to take over. For the next three years a succession of volunteers came and went. By now it was more attractive for them to come to India than in the early days. HIS was able to arrange for overseas sponsors to help them with air fares and expense allowances. Some were successful, while others turned out to be more trouble than they were worth. Every time a new one took over he or she instituted a different system, so that the staff never knew where they were. There were also difficulties with a manager they had hired. He was a Brahmin, and there were many tasks that he considered beneath him. He fell out with some of the volunteers and he was not especially liked by the staff.

During this difficult time Christine became wise in the ways of volunteers. Some had taken up veterinary science because they genuinely loved animals. Disillusioned by western practice, but still full of passion, these young idealists did very good work. There were others, like Jack and Aldona, who came because they preferred an almost monastic life in India to their own countries. But there were a few who Christine remembers for causing no end of trouble. 'They've gone drinking in the town and walked back through the hills at night singing and drunk, or the women won't wear the appropriate clothes. One insisted on driving and smashed up the vehicle. One had some psychological problem; the minute I met her I could tell. Others have just been very young and wanted an adventure. Now we don't accept the ones who sound as though they want an adventure.'

All of these problems vanished with the arrival in 2001 of Naveen Pandey. Naveen's father was a teacher in Chittaranjan near Kolkata. The family owned a small farm at Bodhgaya where Naveen had spent every holiday surrounded by cows and horses, bullocks and buffaloes. From childhood he had always wanted to be a vet. He had been top of his class all through school, and when he studied veterinary science at Hyderabad University he had continued to come first each year. Upon graduation he had been awarded three university gold medals – one for having the highest grade points, another for genetics, and the third for animal nutrition.

The year Naveen had graduated 110,000 people applied for 303 government positions. Naturally he was one of those who were accepted. But instead of taking that easy route he had set up his own practice near his home, making house calls on a bicycle. He became aware of Help in Suffering when he saw a government report on the Internet about the amount of funding they gave each year. He wrote to them outlining his qualifications, asking them to tell him more about what they did. The next thing he knew Christine was on the telephone offering him a job. 'No one knew where Kalimpong was exactly. My grandfather thought it would be a small village with a lot of snow and no people – a very isolated place. He told me to think twice before going. But my brother, who's in the air force, said, "Go and see what they're doing. If you like it stay, and if you don't like it come back, no one can stop you."'

Naveen caught the bus from New Delhi to Jaipur. At the shelter he was shown to his room. He was resting on his bed when Christine knocked on the door and introduced herself. 'I'd been expecting a very strong European woman, but she was so soft. She asked if I would like to rest first or see the shelter. I said I'd see the shelter.'

Two of the vets were treating a camel which had a fractured jaw. It was the first time Naveen had seen a camel. They asked him if he would like to assist, and he eagerly agreed. During the following days, Naveen, like many of his countrymen before him, found Christine's tolerance and willingness to consult others quite beguiling. In three weeks' time she and Jeremy were due to make one of their regular visits to Kalimpong. When they went Naveen was with them.

Naveen has proven to be a skilled surgeon, a gifted diagnostician, and an able administrator, who gets on well with the other staff members. When he arrived there was no phone at the shelter, so if they needed to make a call it entailed a long walk to town. There was no electricity either, they used a generator when operations were taking place. Even when the power was put on it was unreliable. The staff often needed to empty all the anti-rabies vaccinations into ice boxes and carry them to friends' refrigerators in town.

An ABC program had been running for three years. The road to the shelter had still not been built. The staff would take the dogs in the ambulance as far as they could go, then carry them in their arms or lead them the last three kilometres.

At first they had tried to catch the dogs with a sack as they did in Jaipur. But they soon found that Kalimpong dogs were more docile than the street dogs of Jaipur. One theory was that they lived in closer proximity to humans, and many were descended from domesticated breeds such as Spitz, Doberman, Dachshund and Spaniel, which the British had left behind when they departed the hill stations. The method now is to coax them with a piece of biscuit until they are close enough, then simply pick them up.

They have now spayed 85 per cent of the female dogs in the area, which is twenty per cent above the level considered necessary to stabilise the population. As rabies is not a notifiable disease in Kalimpong no official records are kept. Unofficially, Naveen has learned from friends at the hospitals that ten people had died of rabies in Kalimpong in the year 2000. Because of the sustained effort of the ABC program there were no deaths from 2001 to 2004. In 2005 two people died from rabies after being bitten by their own pets – not by street dogs. It seems clear that the program has made a great impact but, because of these two cases, Naveen is cautious about claiming to have completely controlled rabies. It will probably take a few more years before they can say that.

A large part of the Kalimpong shelter's work is with farm animals – pigs, chickens, cows and goats. They conduct regular outreach programs to remote villages. Christine, Naveen and five other staff set out in two four-wheel-drive vehicles soon after dawn. They follow a narrow winding road down the mountain with a sheer drop on one side, at the bottom of which rushes a pale green torrent. When they reach the river they pause at a grubby little stall for breakfast of *chai* and *momos* cooked by a smiling young woman with Tibetan features. Then they cross the bridge and commence a long, slow climb over a narrow road, which is more like a dried riverbed. Up and up they bounce and swerve for an hour or more, through squalid villages perched on the side of steep, terraced hills, until they come to the town of Sinji. As they pass through the narrow streets, people stop and stare. On the other side they pull up at the school, where they are welcomed by the principal.

On the cricket pitch they set up an open-air operating theatre. The autoclave is a pressure cooker heated over a fire. The table has been commandeered from one of the classrooms. Two bricks are placed under each leg to bring it up to the correct height. A stool is provided for Naveen, but it is a bit low, so someone runs to fetch a couple of cushions. The drip stand is a bamboo stick.

The word has gone out a few days before. People start to drift in with their dogs to be vaccinated and spayed. There are about a dozen dogs, and a small boy has a cat in a sack which he dumps carelessly onto the ground.

While the medical team sets up Christine wanders off to take photographs. She snaps several shots of a handsome rooster, then some goats, some chickens and one or two dogs. While she clicks away she talks to them gently. You can see how she loves them, but one wonders what she will do with these pictures of what are, after all, fairly nondescript animals. She even photographs a lizard – seven shots just to make sure. She comes back smiling, happy as always to be with animals.

Naveen is scrubbed, gloved and gowned. He is a slim young man, round-faced, always neatly dressed. His movements are precise; he worries about every detail before proceeding. The first dog has been anaesthetised and its abdomen shaved. It is placed on the table and the villagers gather in a circle to watch silently as Naveen makes his incision. When he has finished, one of the compounders gently lays the dog on the grass with a couple of hot-water bottles.

Over the next few hours they spay fourteen dogs and vaccinate them against rabies. When they wake up their owners carry them home to recover. The team will be in the area for a week so, in the following days, they will check each one to make sure there are no complications.

The villagers are happy to walk two or three hours to get their dogs treated. They know rabies all too well in this area. It is common for two or three children to die each year from the disease.

When the dogs have been done, the team has several farms to visit. There are no roads. They reach the farms by walking the stony little paths that wind up and down the hills. In the following days they will tramp for hours from door to door, vaccinating and treating farm animals.

The farmers sometimes ask them to castrate a pig. The traditional method has been to crush the testicles between two pieces of wood. Quite apart from the terrible pain the animals suffered, complications and infections used to be common. The farmers have learned that when the HIS vet does it the pig will suffer no ill effects.

The cattle suffer from a range of illnesses, often due to poor diet or badly designed facilities. Their owners are generally too poor to even feed and clothe themselves properly, so the shelter does not charge for vaccinations or veterinary treatment.

Back at the shelter they find that the work has been piling up. Christine has administrative matters to attend to, while Naveen has a long list of cases waiting. Knowing he has a big day ahead of him, he goes to bed early. At five o'clock the next morning one of the staff knocks on Naveen's door and tells him that a cow nearby is having difficulty delivering a calf. It is a cold, rainy day. Naveen hauls himself from his warm bed and drives for an hour or so. Then they stop and walk for another hour until they reach the farm. When Naveen sees the cow he surmises that it has been mated with a bull that was too big – a problem he sees a lot.

The calf's leg is turned around and stuck behind the pelvic opening. Naveen first has to push the calf back inside and correct the abnormal position, taking care not to inflict too much pain on the cow. After 45 minutes he is sweating despite the cold. It's more difficult than he had anticipated and he thinks he will have to call for more staff and instruments to perform a caesarean. Still, he perseveres a little longer and eventually a healthy little red calf emerges into the world.

The next day he is called to another obstructed labour. He puts his hand inside and feels the calf's heartbeat. He can get it out but he needs an injection of oxytocin, which helps the uterine muscles contract. Having none in his bag, he asks the farmer to wait while he goes into town to buy some. Half an hour later he returns, only to find that the farmer has tied a rope to the calf's leg and forcibly dragged it out of the mother, killing it in the process. Naveen is saddened, as he is sure he could have delivered a healthy calf. Ignorance is no less a problem here than it is in Jaipur.

Every time Christine visits Kalimpong Naveen has some new and curious case to report. One day a woman came to the Kalimpong shelter in great distress, carrying a cat with a needle in its stomach. She told Naveen that she had been doing some sewing while at the same time the cat was eating its dinner on the table. A piece of meat fell onto a needle and the cat swallowed both together. She had driven all the way from Darjeeling to Kalimpong to see him. Although it was 7.30 at night Naveen took the cat straight away into town in the hope that one of the private hospitals with X-ray facilities would still be open.

They had all finished work for the day so Naveen spent the night in town with the cat. First thing in the morning he went to the hospital and asked them to perform an X-ray. The staff looked mystified.

'Just charge the same as you would for a human,' said Naveen.

'But we don't know how to X-ray a cat.'

'Never mind. Imagine it's a person, and do it.'

With some reluctance they X-rayed the cat. There was no sign of a needle inside.

'Please do it again,' insisted Naveen. 'Only this time do it laterally.'

This time they could clearly see a needle in the cat's abdomen.

Naveen at first thought that he would have to open the abdomen – an operation he had never done before. After thinking about it some more he came up with an elegant and far simpler solution. 'I opened the skin and put my fingers in that little cavity and got hold of the abdomen and felt the needle with both fingers. Then I just pushed it through the stomach wall. It was so easy. I got out a threaded needle with the thread intact and it left just a tiny little hole.

As with the shelter in Jaipur there are a few dogs in Kalimpong who have just stayed on after treatment. One, Mango, likes to sit on the verandah outside Naveen's front door. She gets very possessive if another dog dares to approach. Mango is never allowed inside, but Naveen has relaxed his standards once or twice where puppies have been concerned.

Once, a little boy came with a sick pup in his arms after walking for three hours from his village. Very young pups will often die if they are kept in the kennels – the same thing happens in the Jaipur shelter as well. Distemper and parvovirus can survive in soil or dust for years. Even if the kennels are constantly disinfected the virus seems to thrive. This time Naveen broke his rule and allowed the pup into his house. He fed the pup every day until after five or six days it was well enough to leave. Apart from the usual messes puppies make it had eaten Naveen's mobile-phone charger, which cost him 380 rupees to replace.

Another time a woman and her daughter came in with a pup in the last stages of parvovirus infection. By the time it arrived it was completely dehydrated, and Naveen knew he had no hope of saving it. Sure enough the pup died about an hour later.

'The lady started crying, and her daughter too,' Naveen recalls. 'They said whenever they keep a pup it dies, and they thought they would never be able to have a dog. I told them it was simply that their dogs were not vaccinated against parvo and distemper. I promised that I would get them a pup.'

Naveen knew a man who had asked to have his dog spayed at the shelter. However, he was not prepared to pay for it, even though he was rich and owned a building in Mumbai. Naveen told him he would do the operation if the man gave him a pup the next time his dog had a litter. He vaccinated the pup and took it to meet its delighted new owners.

Naveen says that he wants to spend the rest of his working life in Kalimpong. He will certainly never be short of things to do. The trust has recently opened a veterinary clinic in Darjeeling, and they have bought land nearby where they plan to conduct another ABC program. These projects will be Naveen's responsibility in addition to his work in Kalimpong.

He loves his job, although for someone who was brought up in one of Southern India's biggest cities, Kalimpong can be a cold, lonely place. Naveen's father died three years ago. His mother is looking for a suitable wife for him. When they find one his happiness will be complete.

While things were at last running smoothly in Kalimpong thanks to Naveen, back in Jaipur a crisis was brewing. The shelter had employed a fundamentalist Brahmin to help Nirmal with the books. Mr Sharma refused to do anything he considered was beneath his caste, such as helping to carry medicines to the dispensary, or sharing the water jug with other members of staff. In a place where everyone pitched in cheerfully to help one another he was an aberration. When his contract expired after a year they did not renew it.

Mr Sharma teamed up with another man, Mr Gupta, who had been supplying the shelter with medicines at a higher price than he should have. When the shelter had found out and ordered their supplies elsewhere, Mr Gupta took it badly. The two persuaded a friend who owned a newspaper in Jodhpur to write a series of articles saying that HIS was killing cows. They said they had videotaped proof. Some articles were published, and the pair sent material to other newspapers and to the trustees, demanding that they take action against this evil western woman who was flaunting Hindu traditions.

Although the shelter was not guilty it would have been easy to make them appear so. As Christine pointed out, 'If you anaesthetise a cow and sedate it and give it painkiller, that's not killing a cow. Most cattle we were rescuing were so near death they died overnight anyway.'

The pair pressed the Prime Minister's office to act against the shelter. The department passed the problem on to local bureaucrats in Jaipur. No one at an official level wanted anything to do with it, but what worried Christine most was that the Shiv Sena might become involved. Shiv Sena was a political party with a strong nationalist ideology, whose more extreme followers had been known to murder people whom they thought were slaughtering cattle. There was a real possibility that the shelter could be smashed or its staff attacked.

The trustees discussed taking legal action, but in the end they decided the wisest course would be for Christine and Jeremy to leave the country for a while. Shiv Sena had recently staged a violent demonstration in South India against a fashion parade that had exposed women's bodies. There were worries that they might cause trouble for the shelter as well. As much as Christine and Jeremy hated to retreat, they concurred, taking their leave a little earlier than planned. By the time they returned the whole affair had blown over. Curiously, some nine months later the same newspaper published an article saying what wonderful work HIS was doing.

You have to wonder what sort of toll this takes on Christine. 'I get exhausted, and sometimes I don't sleep, but it doesn't really take a toll because I'm the one who gets all the benefit from this. The whole purpose of life seems to me to be to learn and to grow and to try to understand more, so both of us have been so fortunate that all this happened in an accidental way.

'I don't get stressed now because I've managed to objectify it. The thing that does worry me is that all these people who I love so much, their lives and the animals that they help, all depend on this income for which ultimately I'm the connecting point between the donors and the recipients. That's my burden, really. I worry about when I'm older, could we start a corpus fund so there'll always be enough money.

'But people will come. Mishy once said, "When Help in Suffering needs someone, God sends someone", in this case being myself; but previously she said it about Janine, who brought the money to her. I believe that if something is good and right and if you even put in your own money then money is attracted. But as soon as you could say the blessing of God or the blessing of the Rishis is withdrawn because the slightest taint of corruption enters, then that place will start to die. Hence it's really important that everyone who works for us is a good person. Of course everyone has their faults, but I think that they all are basically very good people.'

CHAPTER 27

While they were working long hours at the shelter Christine and Jeremy did not often have time where just the two of them were together. Sometimes, if they had been in town to purchase drugs or other equipment, they went to the Indian Coffee House, where they ate *idli* and drank iced coffee. If visitors came they took them to Amer fortress-palace – the ancient structure built in 1592 by Maharaja Mansingh, eleven kilometres north of the old city. For Christine these brief escapes were a precious part of their time together.

Christine's mother Suzanne visited twice and stayed at the shelter. Cameron also came before he was married. He told Christine that he had never really understood her work before. Now that he had seen it he said he admired what she and his father were doing. With Cameron everything was settled, and Christine was content. Miles, however, did not come, partly because he had a wife and two children, but also because he did not want to. He had still not forgiven his mother for moving away.

Amer fortress-palace was the obvious destination to take visitors. The vast stone walls and balustrades were built on a cliff above a lake. Once the surrounding hills had been forested, but now only sparse patches of thorny bush showed through. Ruined walls ran like rope dropped randomly over a contoured map, while scattered here and there were crumbling forts and ancient *havelis*. When you walked in the old stone passages of the palace, still coated with plaster and murals, you could imagine the veiled, silken women with sliding eyes, hidden behind carved fretwork, and the cooks in ancient kitchens, and maharajas and princes sitting cross-legged on carpets, and the assembly of elephants decorated with tassels and mirrors and embroidery as they carried the rulers in processions on ivory and gold *howdahs*.

At Amer there was still a congregation of elephants. They assembled each day at the bottom of the hill in a large enclosure. Tourists paid their money and climbed onto the *howdah* by means of an ancient stone mounting platform. Then the elephants laboured slowly uphill along the winding pathway bordered by stone parapets. They shuffled along, slow and dreaming and closed, as though they wished to be somewhere else. If you looked closely you could see that they had abscesses from the harness; some had opaque eyes, perhaps because of bad feeding or too much sun; some had cracked toenails from walking on the hot tar; and some were thin and gaunt because they had not been fed enough. Many of the elephants had scarred heads, or even open, bleeding wounds where the *ankush* (a steel rod with a hook and a sharpened point at one end) had been sunken into their skull to enforce obedience.

Christine could not understand how the tourists could ride the elephants, laughing and joking, and not be mindful of the sadness of the noble creatures who carried them. She wanted to help them but there was no one at the shelter who knew much about elephant veterinary science, and, besides, the *mahouts* and elephant owners lived in their own closed Muslim community. They had their own traditions, which dated back centuries. They did not trust the government, and they did not trust outsiders. The shelter was helping the cattle and dogs and cats and birds and monkeys and camels and all the equines, but in Christine's mind it would not be complete until it helped the elephants as well.

One of the people Ashok had got to know through his work with the Brooke team was the owner of a wedding horse. The man had seen the horse, a mare, at the horse fair, and despite being very poor he had somehow raised 6,000 rupees to buy her because, he told Ashok, he loved her face. The mare was a magnificent animal. At first it was easy to mistake her for a stallion, because her neck was thick and arched, and her body was as big as a draught horse, yet her bones and limbs were fine.

She had not always been like this. When the owner bought her she had been so rundown that he brought her to Ashok, who had diagnosed babesiosis. With proper treatment, slowly the thin, wracked figure had turned into a sleek, powerful steed. By hiring her out for weddings her owner had become a rich man. The horse was now worth 70,000 rupees.

With his newfound success the owner had bought some elephants. He was so pleased with the work of the Brooke team that he asked Ashok to take a look at one, which had an abscess on its back. Ashok told the man that as he was employed by

Brooke he could not help, but he could ask one of the other vets to give free treatment.

Christine was thrilled when she heard. She went with Jack and Sunil into the old walled city, down narrow, cobbled lanes with houses where the doors opened directly onto the street. In an open courtyard three elephants stood. One of them towered above the others. Its name was Mustana.

He stood with all four ankles chained to bolts sunk in the cement. Urine and faeces swilled around his feet. There was no food before him and no water. He rocked gently back and forth, lifting first one foot and then another. While Christine watched a little boy ran up to him, touched his trunk and climbed onto it, then the great elephant lifted him onto his shoulders, where the boy lay, his head resting on the massive skull.

'There's the abscess,' Sunil said, pointing to the body above the ribs, under the backbone. 'It was probably caused by rubbing from the *howdah*. It needs to be cleaned with antiseptic every day.'

'Biggest elephant in Jaipur,' the owner said in Hindi. He wore a polo shirt and had a lot of oil in his hair, so that it was black and smeared against his skull. 'Name, Mustana. Will not hurt at all. Very safe.'

'He's blind,' Sunil said.

'Why is he blind?' asked Christine.

'Probably not fed properly. Elephants need lots of green food, but here they only seem to get dry sugar-cane stalks and chapatti.'

'And I can't see any water,' said Christine.

'They need 200 to 250 litres of water a day,' Jack said, 'otherwise they get dehydrated and constipated. The faeces can compact and they can die from it. Also, their skin needs to be washed daily to prevent warts and lice.'

Jack, with his tall, thin build and fair hair, looked out of place among the small dark men who surrounded them. They peered curiously at the contents of the medicine box as Jack unpacked it. Watching the scene, it occurred to Christine that Jack had become Indian. Sometimes he tried to return to his life in England, as his parents were worried for his future, but every time he felt uncomfortable because of the affluence. He was like a monk – an aesthetic who ate little and owned nothing, and was content to merge into the anonymity of India. It was Jack who organised the staff parties, and who went out on rescues with the men at night, and who laughed with them, and in the winter sat by the fire with them. And it was Jack who had given them so much self-esteem because he was from a foreign land. Christine could never have the same rapport because she was the boss. Once Jack had told her, 'I'm glad I'm not managing trustee, because they would never treat me as an equal.' And it was true, because every time Christine walked past they jumped to their feet and smiled and, if she gave them a certificate, they touched her feet. They would not sit on the same bench as her, nor would they drink or eat until she had eaten first. It did not matter what she said to them, still they could not be equal, but they could be equal with Jack, and they were blended, fair and dark together.

The owner said to Christine, 'You touch,' and pointed to Mustana.

Gingerly she stretched out her hand and touched his thick trunk. It was a moment of such significance for her that she later wrote of it thus:

All of his majesty and dignity and silence flowed into me, so that through the touching I was him, and in him, and I looked at his eye so far above, which was blind, and small, but did not seem blind, because it was still a golden brown, and I was filled with grief and shame that he should be chained like this, in the small courtyard, on cement, in the sun, when he was meant to be pacing and stretching under the canopy, marching through grasses which brushed his knees, and bringing branches crashing, and making birds rise, and filling the whole earth with his triumph and trumpeting. But he was here in bondage, sending some secret thrilling greatness through my hand and my skin and into my being. And I thought that he accepted this bondage because of his love for the piddling weaklings who crawled around him and did not even feed him properly, because he could have ranted and broken his chains and killed whoever walked near him, but instead he stood mildly, because of the child who crawled on him, and the brothers who brought him buckets of water sometimes when they deemed it necessary but not at all when he wanted it. And I knew why elephants were sacred, and in holy books. And somehow our shelter could not have been complete if this connection had not occurred. And perhaps it was the son of the God of the Wind, perhaps it was that Being, Ganesha, who had brought our shelter to the feet of the elephants.

Jack asked the owner to make Mustana lie down so that he could reach the wound. Mustana was afraid because he knew the pain that would follow when the abscess was cleaned, so he urinated and defecated and had an erection, and swung to and fro and, finally, when they had shouted at him and pushed the hooked end of the *ankush* into his flesh, he lay down.

Giving the elephant a local anaesthetic was not an option as it would have needed so many injections with thick needles that they would have been more painful than the treatment itself. Mustana beat his trunk on the cement floor as Jack cleaned the open wound, but he did not try to stand up or hurt Jack. It was as if he realised that Jack was trying to help him.

Mustana's successful treatment became the shelter's entrée into the closed world of the elephant owners. When they heard that Mustana had been cured, they began, hesitantly at first, and still with a great deal of mistrust, to invite Help in Suffering to look at their elephants. Another step forward occurred with the arrival of another baby elephant. The mother had been purchased from Kerala, already pregnant, and had given birth in Jaipur. As with the last baby elephant the newspapers were full of the story, and the Chief Minister and various dignitaries had visited.

Sunil was worried that the owners might not be feeding the baby correctly, as had happened last time. He and Christine drove through the streets of the old city to the compound near Amer where the mother and baby were being kept. The mother stood with her front legs chained to the stone floor. One of her back legs was chained also. It was pulled backwards and stretched out behind her so that she could not stand comfortably. She could not lie down, nor could she reach the baby, who was wandering on the periphery of the enclosure, sniffing people who sat watching on wobbling plastic chairs.

The baby shambled slowly towards Christine and pushed its head against her knees. It had pinkish grey, rubbery skin, and a tiny trunk that furled and unfurled. The eyes were unseeing. It was noticing the world through its trunk and its mouth.

The mother elephant had been given a pile of branches from the peepal tree. Traditionally this was thought to be good for her. She was swaying from one foot to another and ceaselessly moving her trunk. From time to time she chewed some of the peepal leaves with an expression of reluctance and distaste. She was very thin, and her backbone protruded. She did not seem interested in anything, neither the visitors, nor the owner, nor her baby.

Sunil spoke to the owner for some time. He turned to Christine and shook his head. The owners had starved the mother elephant for several days before and after the delivery. Now they were complaining that she had very little milk.

'Were you able to tell them to feed her properly?' Christine asked.

'They said they will feed,' he said.

The baby and her mother were owned by three brothers who between them had twenty elephants. Sunil treated several of the others for abscesses and other problems before leaving.

A few days later they came back to see how the baby was faring. The mother's milk had dried up completely and the baby was no longer trying to suckle from her. It drank reconstituted cow's milk from a bottle held by the owner, then a stream of liquid brown diarrhoea squirted from beneath its tail. It shuffled listlessly on its perfect, tiny, cushioned feet with the pink toenails, sniffing one visitor and then another with the moist tip of its trunk. It looked very weak and listless. Its eyes were vacant, and it seemed lost.

At Sunil's request the owners unfastened the chains and led the mother round the room, pulling her by means of the rope round her neck and shouting at her. There was no love, no caressing, no affection. The baby ran after the mother; now and then she touched it with her trunk but still remained disinterested.

A renowned elephant vet from Burma, Dr Khyne U Mar, was soon due to stay at Help in Suffering for three months to research a blood parasite that had been noted in some of the Jaipur elephants. As soon as she arrived Christine arranged for her to visit some of the elephant owners. Dr Khyne had spent seven years managing the Burmese government's timber elephants before moving to England, where she was a consultant to the world-renowned elephant welfare organisation, *elephant family*. Perhaps her reputation had reached even the elephant owners of Jaipur, for they listened with respect when she told them that their elephants did not breed and did not come into *musth* because they were not being fed properly. She explained that elephants would only breed if they knew and liked each other, not just because humans wanted them to.

Dr Khyne took particular care to instruct the baby's owner on proper feeding. Following her visit, at last they began to feed the mother and baby properly. The next time Christine saw them they were both stronger and were putting on weight.

A few weeks later there was a festival to name the baby. The brothers erected a large tent, and invited dignitaries who were waited on by the *mahouts* and owners. The baby was called Gori, which means 'white person', because of her pale complexion.

Soon Sunil and Jack were calling upon the elephants regularly. There were about 100 working elephants in Jaipur. They carried tourists to and from the Amer palace and worked at weddings. Two government vets from Kerala had examined them and written a report saying they all had worms, most had foot lesions, 26 were dehydrated and anaemic, six had ulcerating wounds and four were blind in both eyes. They found that they were receiving an inadequate diet of stalks, they were inadequately watered and the method of restraining them was crude and cruel. The elephants often had to walk in full heat on the hot tarmac and their nails and footpads were often injured. The vets had recommended to the elephant owners' association that the animals only work in the morning and late afternoon, but often they made four or more trips up the hill to the Amer palace, including some in the midday heat. And then in the evenings they might be called upon to work at a wedding.

During one visit Sunil treated an elephant that had a gaping hole on its front leg. The owner had hired out the elephant to some people in Amer. They had chained her with a leg band that had inward-pointing spikes which pierced the skin. Then Babu Khan, the medicine man used by all the elephant owners, had suggested they pour lime powder into the wound which, of course, had made it far worse.

Sunil had been treating the elephant for some weeks, and its wound was slowly healing. During that time Christine had got to know one of the *mahouts*, Munna Khan. Munna, who was more outgoing than most *mahouts*, had told her how he had wanted to work with elephants ever since he had been a small boy watching them begging for their masters in the streets of Delhi. He had run away and come to Jaipur to fulfil his dream. But his salary was very low – 900 rupees per month – and he was always thinking about ways to improve his lot in life.

Munna was in charge of a former circus elephant. She was

small, and Christine thought she always had a sweet expression on her face. One day Christine asked Munna if it would be all right to touch her.

'You can touch. She is very friendly. Would you like to ride her?'

'Oh no, it's OK,' said Christine.

Munna took no notice. He unchained the elephant and at a few shouted commands from him she stepped forward. Christine noticed he had no *ankush*, not even a stick in his hand. He shouted a few more firm commands and the elephant lay down, her great bulk swaying awkwardly as she sank to the ground.

Munna climbed onto her and threw a padded cotton mattress over her back, then secured this with a rope wound around her girth, and another under her tail.

He then invited Christine to climb up. The elephant remained motionless while she clawed her way up the roped mattress then sat with her knees pressed tightly against the neck. On command the elephant lurched to her feet and then moved slowly out the gate and along the road. Munna walked beside them and whenever he spoke the elephant obeyed.

There were no scars on her head from the *ankush*. This was because the elephant and the *mahout* had been together for a long time and understood one another. Once Christine had seen a *mahout* wrap his arms around the trunk of his blind elephant. He placed his head in her mouth as she lifted her trunk. Then, as he moved away from her, she reached out her trunk and gently encircled his body, pulling him towards her in a loving embrace. This relationship between man and beast was as it should be. But because the *mahouts* were so poorly paid they often did not stay long enough to form a bond with one elephant, which was why so many of them were forced to use the *ankush* to make them obey, and why so many of the elephants had bleeding wounds on their heads.

It was early evening. As he led them through the full-moon streets, Munna told Christine he had three children. He suggested that if she would loan him one and a half lakh he could buy his own elephant and repay her quickly, as the earnings from an elephant were very good.

'I wish I could buy an elephant,' she said. 'But I'm not rich enough for that. Maybe you could work for us instead, helping to treat the animals.'

He seemed pleased with this suggestion.

After thirteen years Christine and Jeremy had become well-known in Jaipur. Christine's godson, on a backpacking holiday in India, arrived in the pink city by train with the intention of looking up his godmother. He knew that the Help in Suffering animal shelter was located at Durgapura, on the outskirts of the city, but he had no idea how to find it. Unusually, when he got down from the train, the station was practically deserted. The young Australian approached a group of rickshaw drivers and began trying to explain what he was looking for. 'Christine Townend . . . Help in Suffering . . .'

They looked puzzled.

'She looks after sick animals. Horses . . . donkeys . . .' He gazed skywards for inspiration. The sun beat down out of the bright sky with oven force. He could feel the sweat oozing over his body. '. . . er . . . camels?'

A crowd was forming. The young man tried again. 'An Australian lady . . . she looks after animals. Cows, monkeys, you name it. Has anyone heard of her?' He felt his face burning. The heat was making him dizzy. 'Elephants . . . she looks after elephants?' He lifted his hands, palms upwards, and raised his eyebrows. The crowd waited. Desperately he plunged on. 'And dogs. She cares for dogs, too.'

The eyes of one of the rickshaw drivers lit up. 'Ah! Dog-Wallah!'

'Yes. Dog-Wallah. That's her. She's the Dog-Wallah.'

Suddenly there was a hubbub as everyone spoke at once. Of course, Dog-Wallah. Everyone knew the Dog-Wallah. She was a wonderful lady. Was he a friend of the Dog-Wallah? A relative? Her godson! Oh my goodness, it was an honour to meet him.

'Do you know where I can find her?' This to the rickshaw driver.

'Yes, I know. I can find.'

And he did.

The Townends were friendly with many of the city's most influential citizens, some of whom had become trustees. When they went to social functions, often someone would come up and congratulate them for making Jaipur a better place.

In October 2002 they received an invitation from her highness, the Rajmata of Jaipur, to attend a garden party at her palace. The Rajmata, or Queen Mother, was the widow of the last Maharaja of Jaipur. Although the Indian government had taken away much of her wealth, she still lived in a splendid mansion set in immaculate grounds, walled off from the rest of the city, which had grown around it.

The Rajmata had once been described by *Vogue* as one of the ten most beautiful women in the world. The daughter of the Maharaja of Cooch Behar, she had been educated in

England, Switzerland and India. She mixed with princes and kings as she grew up. Her family had owned dozens of elephants and she was very knowledgeable about them.

When she was a child an elephant had been taking some children from her school for a ride. With a pile of little children on its back it had slipped into a ditch and become stuck. The teacher panicked, but the Rajmata spoke to the elephant calmly, ordering it to move this way and that until it extracted itself from the ditch.

The Rajmata was a passionate animal-lover. It was she who had loaned Mishy the land to start Help in Suffering. She told Christine, as they chatted on her immaculate lawn, that she was terribly upset at the plight of Jaipur's elephants. Her friend Mark Shand, an Englishman who had founded the welfare organisation *elephant family*, was coming to stay with her soon. She intended to ask him to try to help.

Mark arrived a short time later. When he saw the work that Help in Suffering was doing he offered to fund an elephant program if Christine would run it for him. She immediately agreed.

As always, the big problem was finding a vet. As well as being a skilled practitioner he or she would have to speak good English, be able to use a computer, and not be afraid of elephants. After a long search Christine despaired of finding anyone with the right credentials. She was bemoaning her lack of success to a visiting veterinarian from the Brooke Hospital program in Delhi.

'Why don't you talk to my brother,' he said. 'He's a vet. He lives in Kerala.'

And so it was that in July 2003 Madhulal Valliatte joined HIS. Christine then thought of Munna, the personable young *mahout* whom she had come to know and respect. Munna accepted her offer to become Madhu's compounder. After training for three months with two elephant specialists in Kerala, Drs Panniker and Cheeran, Madhu was ready to begin work.

The elephant team consists of Madhu, Munna, and the driver Ramswarup. Early in the morning they leave the shelter and drive into the twisting labyrinth of Old Jaipur. They stop the Jeep and walk up a narrow laneway that is only just big enough for an elephant to pass through, ending at a walled yard where three elephants are standing in chains.

Madhu knows the name of each of the 100 elephants he treats. He knows their temperaments, too, which is important because an unfriendly elephant can kill you as easily as swatting a fly. When Sunil had begun working with elephants he treated a big bull with an infection where its tusk entered the skin. It was suffering from an elephant-sized toothache. Only after Sunil had treated the elephant three or four times, causing it a lot of discomfort, did the *mahout* mention it had killed four people.

Madhu approaches an elephant with a swollen, painful-looking abscess under its tail. 'This one is called Leshme,' he says. 'This was caused by a rope harness. That abscess was infested with maggots.'

Madhu cleans the wound with cotton wool dipped in antiseptic. The elephant shifts its feet and shudders, and the mahout shouts now and then to keep it in place. Madhu explains he has tried to get the owner to cover the rope with bicycle tube to make it softer, but he has not done so. He has been treating Leshme for a couple of months and her wound is slowly improving. After he finishes cleaning he prescribes anti-inflammatories.

The next elephant is another female. She has an abscess on her side from lying on the concrete *than*. These *thans* are cement 'beds' concentrically hollowed so that they are lower in the middle than at the sides. The *than* has not changed in centuries, except now they are made of cement rather than stone. The purpose of the sloped *than* is ostensibly to make it easier for the elephant to stand up and lie down. In reality, when the elephant is sleeping it rubs the side of its head on the cement, causing sores that later turn into abscesses.

Munna pumps an iodine/water solution into the wound with a hand pump, then scours it with large balls of cotton wool dipped in the solution and held with forceps. He alternates the procedures several times. Each time pus runs out of the wound. Again, the elephant holds steady even though she is in obvious discomfort. She has had the abscess for three weeks, Madhu says, and it will take another month before it is completely better. Elephants heal very slowly.

He moves on to another female – Champa by name. She has a wound at the base of her ear where the *mahout* has been using the *ankush* too heavily. It is the old story of a *mahout* who does not know his elephant and therefore has to be cruel to control her.

In order to reach the wound they have to make Champa lie down. Munna speaks the commands. At first she doesn't want to obey, but then she slowly folds her front legs and sinks to the ground. Munna climbs on top of her to clean out the wound. When he has finished he dresses it with antibiotic cream.

Champa also has an abscess on her side from the harness. Madhu has told the owner he should use wide, soft straps, but he is obstinate and will not change. They have tried to get the owners to use lighter *howdahs*, but so far none of them has done so.

Madhu is a solidly built man, slow-moving and gentle – rather like an elephant himself. He smiles as he explains his work. You can tell that he loves these big animals. He talks to them softly and draws attention to their good points. He takes time to speak with the owners and the *mahouts*. They are brusque, hard men, and it is hard to tell what they think.

The team moves on to another compound. Here there is an elephant with a hole between its shoulder blades the size of a dinner plate. Moti is her name. It means 'pearl' in Hindi. Madhu pleaded with Moti's owner for eighteen months before he would allow him to treat the injury. The owner had preferred instead to use the traditional medicine man. He had filled the wound with a tarry-looking substance which was useless. Madhu told the owner that he would have to rest the elephant, but he refused, sending her out day after day to carry tourists at Amer Fort.

The wound had been caused by the constant rubbing of the *howdah*, which weighs about 70 kilos, plus four tourists on top. Moti is a very small elephant; that great weight slipping around on her back had rubbed her raw. The skin around the circumference of the wound formed a hard, wall-like surface, raised so that Madhu was able to poke his hand deeply inside. The wound's surface was bare, exposed muscle that had been rubbed for so long it had no subcutaneous fascia, so skin could not re-grow. That wound could never heal.

Christine and the team were in despair over Moti. Christine discussed the problem with Janine at Animaux-Secours. Some of the more radical members wanted to stage an international boycott of Rajasthan. Christine thought of complaining to Rajasthan Tourism, the government department that controls the elephants, but she knew if they adopted either of these strategies the owners would shut out Madhu and the years of patient diplomacy would have been wasted.

In the end a more subtle solution was found. Janine arranged for several French people to write letters of complaint to Rajasthan Tourism. At the same time the shelter's joint managing trustee, Mrs Timmie Kumar, who has great influence in Jaipur, had a quiet word with the minister and showed her photographs of Moti's wound. Worried about an international scandal, the minister ordered Moti's owner to stop her working. Now Christine hoped to find somewhere where Moti could rest with proper food and care and spend her remaining days in comfort.

After visiting one more compound the team drives to Amer. A line of tourist buses is parked nose-to-tail for half a kilometre in the street outside. At the base of the fort, elephants draped in colourful cloths wait in the walled yard to take their turn. They make a stirring sight. You would never know that under the finery there are wounds that cause them pain whenever they move.

Madhu and Munna stroll among the elephants chatting to *mahouts* and owners, now and then stopping to examine an animal, handing over some tablets. Madhu rubs one's trunk affectionately. 'This is one of my favourites,' he says. The elephant rumbles with pleasure as it recognises him.

Another one approaches and he shepherds us aside. 'This one is not so friendly.'

The murderer with the sore tusk is there too, dressed in his finery. The tourists laugh and snap pictures as they queue for the ride up the hill.

CHAPTER 28

Christine could not know every detail of the day-to-day running of the elephant program. But there is one elephant she will never forget. She was one of Madhu's favourite patients, another elephant named Champa. Because many Jaipur elephants are called Champa she was referred to in his notes as 'elephant number twelve'.

Champa was 55 years old. Madhu first got to know her a couple of months after he began working for Help in Suffering. Her owner called him in a panic saying that she had not eaten for 24 hours and was in severe pain. Madhu examined her and found she had a high pulse-rate, subnormal temperature and was severely dehydrated. He concluded that she was suffering from constipation due to being fed dried-up sugar cane and thin millet stalks instead of proper green food.

He inserted a drip through which he administered fluids, along with a gastric sedative and antispasmodic drugs. Then he and Munna began administering an enema of warm soapy water through a rubber hose. It had been eleven in the morning when they arrived. By six p.m. the first balls of faeces came out. They were exhausted but pleased to have saved Champa's life.

Two months later Champa's owner called again. The old elephant was lying on her side and was unable to get up. She had been in this position for 30 hours. Normally an elephant cannot survive lying down for more than a day, as its enormous body weight causes the lungs to collapse. Madhu knew that he had to quickly get her on her feet somehow.

A crowd of elephant owners and *mahouts* had come to watch the drama. Madhu administered a dextrose drip and asked some helpers to dig four holes a little more than a metre deep. Then all the men helped drag Champa so that her legs went into the holes. To prevent her from falling over they made a frame around her by tying logs together. As she turned into the vertical position Madhu was shocked to see that there was a big bed sore on one thigh. He feared that it was going to develop into an abscess.

For five days Champa stood in the holes while they fed her and administered medicine. When Madhu thought she was strong enough her *mahout* ordered her to pick up her legs one by one. Each time she did they shovelled a little bit of earth into the holes. Soon Champa was standing. She swayed uncertainly, but managed to remain on her feet.

As Madhu had suspected, the bed sore had become a big abscess and ruptured. They cleaned the wound and for the next few weeks came each day to treat it. Hungrily, Champa took the special food they gave her – chapatti, jaggery, lucerne, bananas and other delicacies. Upon examining her teeth they found that her molars were worn away. Perhaps this was why she was so weak, as she could not digest the rough food on which the Jaipur elephants survive.

Slowly, the brave elephant recovered. Her owner was so pleased that he offered Madhu money. Madhu refused, telling him to spend it instead on proper green food. However, Champa only got a decent diet now and then, as she had now retired from work and her owner did not consider it worthwhile to feed her properly. Also, her *mahout* was reluctant to give her the attention she needed as the owner did not pay him an adequate wage.

Through their trials together Madhu had developed a deep affection for Champa. She was a good-natured animal who seemed to have a great will to live. She always bore his ministrations with patience and dignity. She had overcome an impossible ordeal, lying on her side for 35 hours. He worried about how much longer she would survive.

He was not surprised when in December he received yet another phone call. Again Champa was unable to get up. You might have thought that by now euthanasia would be the most humane option but, as with cows, it is not culturally acceptable to euthanase an elephant. They went through the same rescue routine as before, administering medicines and digging holes for her legs. This time she was in the holes for two days before once again she was able to walk. Again she had abscesses where she had been lying.

It was hard to imagine that things could get much worse for Champa, but then her *mahout* quit on short notice. He just could not feed his family on the pittance he was paid. Fearing for Champa's future, Sunil and Madhu called for a meeting with the owner. After a lot of persuasion he agreed to find a new place for Champa with adequate feed and a new *mahout*.

As good as his word, he placed Champa with another man who owned five elephants. Here the attitude was different. There was plenty of food and water and, best of all, she had companions around her. Her injuries began healing and her new *mahout*, Imran, treated her kindly. Madhu felt a sense of relief that Champa might at last know some contentment.

For the next couple of months Champa continued to improve. Her abscesses cleared up and she put on weight. The mobile clinic visited her every day. Each time they came Champa greeted them with outstretched trunk and a friendly rumble, as if to say thank you.

In March the phone rang again. It was Imran saying that Champa was vomiting continuously. When Madhu arrived she was swaying to and fro from one foot to another. In the routine that was now familiar to both, Madhu examined his patient. The diagnosis – an obstruction of the oesophagus. Madhu gave her medicines, which he hoped would help. He resolved that if her condition had not changed by the next morning he would have to open her mouth and pass a stomach tube – an extremely difficult procedure with an elephant.

At eight the next morning Champa had shown no sign of improvement. Madhu asked the owner to arrange two big logs and some assistants for later in the day, but the operation never took place. A few hours later Champa lay down and quietly died.

Madhu and Christine took the loss hard. Champa had worked all her life, carrying tourists up to the Amer fortress-palace. She had been deprived of decent food, working long hours with nothing but harsh treatment in exchange, yet she had remained good-natured to the end. The story of Champa – elephant number twelve – was the story of all the working elephants of Jaipur.

CHAPTER 29

At about the same time that Help in Suffering had begun treating elephants, the Rajasthani government conceived a plan to dedicate a site of 50 acres where all the elephants could live together. It would get them out of the small garages and badly lit courtyards in the city where most of them lived, and it would be close to Amer so that they did not have to walk long distances – up to ten kilometres in some cases – to and from work. This so-called 'elephant village' would also have homes for the *mahouts*. It was thought the whole thing would be a tourist attraction.

When Christine heard about the plan in early 2002 she was pleased that the government was at last thinking about the elephants' welfare. Then she was dismayed to learn that they were also planning to build four hotels on the site; the elephants would be crammed into what space was left. It was obvious that the elephants would be moving from one slum to another. If the plan went ahead they would likely be doomed to live even more miserably than they did already.

Through a friend who worked in the government, Sunil arranged for him and Christine to meet the Minister for Tourism, Mrs Beena Kak. At the Secretariat they filled in forms and were issued passes before being directed down endless corridors until they came to her office. The minister had a small carpeted room with framed pictures of wildlife on the walls. She sat by herself behind a big glass-topped desk and listened carefully without interrupting as Sunil explained what HIS did.

'Then who is this lady who has been here for so long and who does all the good work that people talk about?' she asked him.

'Madam, it is none other than her,' Sunil said, pointing to Christine.

'Well, I congratulate you on your wonderful work. Your achievements are well known.'

'Thank you,' said Christine. 'It's quite a privilege to be told that by a minister. I'm one of a team of people, and they're doing so much good work.'

Sunil had prepared a submission for the minister, which she glanced at briefly.

'We're worried that the plans are a disaster,' said Christine, 'and the elephants will be kept in tiny garages, and it wouldn't be nice for the tourists to see.'

The minister told her that the architect had researched elephants. 'I've told these people that I want the elephants to be free to break the trees and to roll in the sugar cane. I told them I wanted fields of crops for them to eat. Could you draw a plan of how you would like it to be?'

'Of course,' said Christine.

Just then, Mr Yadav, the assistant director of tourism, came in. The minister explained to him that they needed a design where the elephants could be free. 'These are great souls,' she said. 'We cannot have them confined. Why do we need these hotels on the site?'

'Well, it needs to be self-funding,' Mr Yadav said. 'The government would sell the land so that it could fund the building of the elephant village.'

'Who would build this hotel?' the minister asked.

'The hotels will go to the private sector.'

'Well I don't see why we should have the hotel, because there wouldn't be enough space. I want this to be a model for all of India.'

'It is for you, madam, to tell us what you want,' Mr Yadav said.

Christine was encouraged by that exchange. It seemed that the minister had the elephants' well-being at heart. At Mrs Kak's instigation Christine and Sunil had many meetings with Mr Yadav and the architect, Pramod Jain. Although he had indeed gone to Kerala to research the needs of elephants, Mr Jain had many misconceptions about them. For instance he had been told that the concrete *than* on which they slept was state-of-the-art. What was really needed, Christine told him, was some sort of soft mat for the elephants to lie on. HIS had found a material which they thought would be suitably comfortable and also durable; they hoped to persuade one of the elephant owners to try it as an experiment. But, as always, they were up against centuries of ingrained tradition.

After several amicable meetings there came a day when Mr Jain and Mr Yadav invited HIS to see the site of the proposed elephant village. After passing Amer fort with its elephants congregating at the entrance area, they followed a narrow dirt track into the hinterland. It was flat, dry, rocky land without trees, but with some houses and small villages along the road. A river ran through it. It was good to see such a gush of running water going through a drought-stricken area, but unfortunately the water was stained dark grey and smelled of effluent.

The car stopped on a road flanked by eroded fields. On one side were some small stone walls where new plots were being developed; on the other side was a large rubbish tip.

After a long silence from Mr Jain, he put his head in his hands and exclaimed, 'Oh shit, oh shit, oh shit.'

Christine looked at him in surprise.

'This is terrible. This is unbelievable. See this rubbish dump, this is the elephant village,' he groaned.

They stared in amazement. Piles of plastic bags, intermixed with dirt and black filth, spread into the distance. Small trails of smoke rose into the sky, while pigs and dogs rummaged in the waste. Tractors pulling trailers kept depositing more rubbish in ever-growing piles.

'Can you believe,' Mr Jain said, and his eyes filled with tears. 'For thirty years I've tried to get this elephant village started. Now look what they've done. It's inco-ordination. The Jaipur Development Authority has not spoken to the Tourism Department. I cannot believe it. I looked at this place only a year ago and it was empty.'

They walked back to the car. Mr Jain's eyes were still glistening. It seemed pointless now to even talk about plans for an elephant village.

Life went on, and Christine had heard no more about an elephant village until the birthday celebrations for Gori, the baby elephant which Sunil had saved. Sunil and Christine were walking into the tent just as the new director of tourism was leaving. They stopped and spoke about the baby elephant for a few moments then, almost as an afterthought, the director said, 'You don't need to worry about the elephant village. We've cleaned up all the rubbish and we've allocated more land. There'll be 130 acres now.' While Christine was absorbing this he added, 'I don't believe in governments doing things. They're not very efficient. We'd like to build the facilities so that your shelter could run the veterinary facility at the elephant village.'

After the endless fighting and lobbying and meetings with bureaucrats, then the disappointment of losing the land, this was tremendous news, all the more startling for being imparted in such an off-hand way. The next day Christine, Jeremy, Sunil, Mark Shand and Khyne U Mar drove out to the site. The rubbish had gone. They walked to a small hill that looked over the land. Christine imagined scores of elephants grazing peacefully in lush fields, rolling in the dust, without shackles, as was their right. Mark Shand said it was a good place and his trust would like to help.

It seemed as though Christine's long campaign on behalf of the elephants had at last been successful; then in September 2005 there was an incident at Amer Fort which touched off a new crisis. It was 9.30 in the morning. Tourists were milling about waiting to board their elephants for the ride up to the fortress. The Indian leader of a group of about twenty people was urging them to fondle an elephant and take photographs, assuring them that it was perfectly safe. Suddenly this elephant lost its temper, seized a woman with its trunk and threw her several metres. Her leg was badly broken in the fall. In the confusion the tour leader fell down. The tourists looked on in horror as the furious elephant stamped him to death.

The Chief Minister immediately banned all elephant rides at Amer. Mark Shand, who was a personal friend of the CM, had arrived in Jaipur the day after the death. He was accompanied by Dr Khyne U Mar. HIS and *elephant family* proposed to the CM that a committee of experts, made up of government vets, Dr Khyne and Dr Madhu should examine and report upon every elephant working in Jaipur. They found that twenty were unfit for work. Some males were considered too dangerous, while others were blind or lame, or simply too weak. The owners, furious at seeing their livelihood curtailed, accused HIS of turning against them. For a few anxious weeks it looked as though HIS would be shut out. Eventually, through patient diplomacy, Christine and Madhu managed to regain their confidence.

As if that was not a big enough setback, later in the year Christine decided to have some soil and water tests done at the site of the elephant village, to gauge what effect the rubbish dump might have had. To her dismay, the tests revealed that the soil was highly toxic. Furthermore, the hydrological survey showed there was not enough water. There was no way the elephants could live there.

It is typical of Christine that she immediately began thinking of other ways to protect the elephants – not only in Rajasthan but in all of India. It seemed to her there were really two issues, both inextricably linked. Firstly, there was the problem of captive elephants, such as those in Jaipur, who had nowhere to go when they could no longer work. Secondly, there was the invasion of elephant habitat by the constantly expanding human population.

Christine has come up with a plan that is breathtaking in its ambition. She wants to start an 'elephant homeland', most likely in West Bengal or Assam. Before doing so she hopes to bring together the various animal-welfare groups in India who for decades have been trying to tackle these twin issues with little success. After her experience with Animals Australia she knows they would be so much more effective if they could speak with one voice. The first step would be to create an informal working group so that the various organisations could work together. While each organisation would retain its own independence, they would stay in touch through regular meetings, coming together to participate in specific campaigns.

The Indian organisations, perhaps funded by overseas sponsors, could purchase and maintain their own pieces of land, with their own name and sponsors on it. Over the decades the amount of land will increase as more international donors come forward. Eventually, perhaps the lands could be connected, thus making elephant corridors where the animals could live in their natural state unmolested by humans.

West Bengal, where the Kalimpong shelter is based, faces the worst elephant/human conflict of all the states of India. There, an average of 47 people are killed each year by elephants, due to the fact that the natural habitat of the wild elephants has been eroded by tea gardens and villages. Starving elephants are left with nowhere to roam and forage for food.

Christine realises she is no expert in elephant conservation. She has sought and received promises of support from several non-government organisations who are. They have vowed to begin by purchasing small retirement and rescue areas in various states where old or injured captive elephants could live out their last days in comfort.

Once some land acquisitions have been made, Christine envisages that the Indian organisations could, together with the Indian Government, issue a worldwide appeal for funds to purchase land for the elephant homeland, perhaps from one of the tea gardens that are no longer profitable. It could be partly funded by having tourists come to view the elephants at night. Massive fencing and trenches may be required. HIS would seek government help and invite sponsors to pay for perhaps a kilometre of fencing with their names on it. The elephants that are now forced to destroy the villagers' crops to stay alive would be encouraged into the homeland with food. Elephants who are too old or sick to work could spend their retirement there in a separate area to the wild elephants, as they need to be kept apart.

Christine says, 'I know this sounds wildly optimistic, and hopelessly imaginative, but even if we never get beyond the first stage of running an elephant rescue centre, and even if we only keep on it the twenty elephants from Jaipur which have nowhere to go, at least we have made a beginning, and we will have floated an idea which might find recognition as the problem continues to worsen.

'When you see the elephants walking in the wild, gliding through the forest and shining with health, and completely accepting human presence – as in Kaziranga National Park in Assam, because they know they are safe – you can only long to restore the disintegrating relationship, which is a total violation of the ancient human and elephant partnership.'

In the meantime the HIS/*elephant family* team continues to make small gains for the elephants of Jaipur. The government has erected a shade cloth over the courtyard at Amer, so the elephants no longer have to stand in the searing sun while they wait to work. The *ankush* has recently been replaced by bamboo sticks – a tremendous breakthrough. The tourism department has restricted the number of trips the elephants make each day at Amer to three. Those twenty weak or aggressive elephants have been forbidden to work. A light *howdah* is being developed with better cushioning to replace the old-fashioned type that caused such terrible injuries to Moti. The government has allocated two rooms at Amer for the HIS team to work from and they have erected signs asking tourists to report any incidence of cruelty that they see.

Some might say that the elephant homeland is an impossible dream. But just as Christine's other visions have come to pass, through stubbornness and absolute belief in the rightness of her cause, so, hopefully, will this – another small candle to light the darkness, adding to the others she has lit in a lifetime of dedication. And the lives of the elephants, along with the horses, and dogs, and cats, and monkeys, and birds, and donkeys, and camels, and cattle of Jaipur will be better.

CHAPTER 30

After its tentative beginnings, Animal Liberation has grown into a powerful, respected organisation with 3,500 members. There are branches in New South Wales, Victoria, Queensland, South Australia and the Australian Capital Territory. The current NSW Executive Director, Mark Pearson, says that Christine's philosophy is still the guiding force behind the organisation. 'She taught us that it's each individual animal that matters, not a flock or a herd, but the individual. Some people who become involved in Animal Liberation come with baggage and use the movement to pursue their own personal agendas. With Christine there's no other agenda than the animal's interest.'

Pearson recalls Christine likening their campaigning to the slow drip, drip, drip of water wearing away stone. It can seem as if you will never get anywhere, then, sometimes when you least expect it, there will be a breakthrough.

In April 2003 Pearson was inadvertently sent an e-mail inviting him to a CSIRO research field day into mulesing. He promptly accepted. Their mulesing pictures were all quite old and possibly no longer accurate as the procedure used to be even more radical than it is now. On the appointed day he turned up at the site at Urunga in New South Wales with a digital video camera. 'I just started filming. They didn't know who I was at first, then someone from the Department of Agriculture turned up and recognised me, and the tone changed.'

By the time Pearson had been outed he had managed to film some graphic sequences of lambs being mulesed. The footage was sent to animal-rights organisations around the world. Ingrid Newkirk from the American lobby group PETA was so shocked she decided to start a campaign. PETA is the largest animal-rights group in the world. Initially they appealed to the Australian wool industry and government. When those overtures were rebuffed they decided to mount an international campaign targeting retailers of Australian wool. As a result, some large fashion houses, including Abercrombie & Fitch and J. Crew in the US, and the British-based New Look and George, have refused to use Australian wool until mulesing has been banned.

For decades farmers had been saying there was no alternative to mulesing. Faced with an economic boycott, industry and government have now agreed to fast-track research so that mulesing will be outlawed by 2010. In the meantime farmers will have to use a spray-on anaesthetic that lessens the pain of the operation by 85 per cent. This has been a great victory, although Animal Liberation is still working towards a ban earlier than 2010.

There has been progress, too, with battery chicken farming. Supermarkets now have to say on the label where their eggs come from and, as a result, people are buying less battery-laid eggs. Legislation has forced the producers to provide bigger cages. Pearson thinks that the next government review in 2008 could legislate to provide so-called furnished cages, as are widely used in Europe, with a perch, space for a nest box and a dust bath. The expense of building them, he surmises, might lead the producers to opt for barn production. They would then be able to campaign for the barns to have opening sides so that the birds can have a little bit of sunshine and natural light.

In 1997 Animal Liberation managed to have the tethering of pigs outlawed. The catalyst came when workers at an abattoir noticed that on sows from a New South Wales piggery the flesh of their necks had grown around the chain. Now they are campaigning to get them out of stalls altogether and into something more like a natural environment.

There have been some gains in the fight to stop the live sheep trade. The industry is no longer self-regulated. Every ship has to have a veterinarian on board, and the animals have a little more space than they did when Christine began campaigning. There is still terrible suffering and loss of life. At the time of writing Animal Liberation received a legal brief which they believe opens the way for the prosecution of exporters in Western Australia on the grounds that they are transporting animals 'in a manner likely to cause suffering'.

Says Pearson, 'If they get up and win, that's the end of the live sheep trade, because WA does 80 per cent.'

Christine would say that she has had nothing to do with any of it. This is not just knee-jerk modesty, it is something she believes; it is rooted in her spiritual understanding of the way lives work. 'I never really decided anything. It's all been like that, except of course one has the free will to not follow what

one's programmed, born, to do. Everyone has something different that they can give back, and you can choose either to give
it back or not to give it back. If you do accept your situation
then everything comes to you and life is rich.'

Lately, as they enter their seventh decades, she and Jeremy
have found the Rajasthani summers harder to bear. They now
spend the hottest months at their home in the Blue Mountains
west of Sydney. They are in touch with Help in Suffering via
e-mail every day.

One of the key trustees is Mrs Timmie Kumar. Timmie originally came from Agra, where she had founded a small animal
shelter. When she moved to Jaipur five years ago she visited the
shelter and immediately hit it off with Jeremy and Christine.
Timmie is small and bubbly and full of energy – rather like
Christine's sister Anne. In fact, Christine thinks of her almost
as a sister, so well do they work together.

Timmie's husband Apurv manages the Clark Amer hotel in
Jaipur, one of five 5-star hotels his family owns in India. It is a
popular meeting place for Jaipur's leading citizens and, because
of her connections, Timmie only has to pick up the phone to
have the ear of ministers or leading bureaucrats.

It has always been Christine's wish for local people eventually to run Help in Suffering. Recently Timmie agreed to
become joint managing trustee of the Jaipur shelter. This has
freed Christine from the gruelling ten- and twelve-hour days
that have been her lot, and will allow her to concentrate more
on such things as long-term policy. During those times she
spends in Australia she is confident that with Timmie, and key
Indian personnel such as Nirmal, Sunil and Naveen, Help in
Suffering is in good hands.

Since she was a little girl Christine has loved to paint. For the first time in her life she has the time seriously to pursue that calling. An exhibition of her work, arranged by Timmie in Jaipur to raise money for Help in Suffering, sold out within two hours. She is planning further exhibitions in Australia.

After so many trials her marriage with Jeremy is strong – stronger than it has ever been. Perhaps she should have the last word on that.

> I looked at him reading on the bed, and we had been together for forty years, and we knew everything about each other, but still we stayed together, and we had argued, and not argued, and loved, and not loved, and we had been apart, and estranged, and then not estranged. And I wanted to grow old with him, not for any reason which I could isolate except that I loved him. But it was not movie love, or anything swooning or grabbing and kissing love, because we were quite opposite. And because we were opposite the missed parts fitted the holes of the other so you could put it together. And I had been 21 when I married him, but now I was in my early sixties and most of my life he had always been there, and I was with him, so it was not love, but more than love, it was a continuous mutual secret adoration. As the years had passed it had become more revered and more secret, and we pretended it was not there, and even argued, but we knew it was there and could not ever be destroyed and was forever growing more intense. And it was the animals which had parted us from time to time, but the animals had also brought us together again, and we were just like all humans who could not live fully without their presence.

ACKNOWLEDGEMENTS

At first I was wary of writing Christine Townend's biography. She and Jeremy have been friends of mine for 30 years. Digging into someone's life can be an intrusive process; I feared that if I was to do my job properly it might threaten our friendship. However, from the beginning Christine assured me that I shouldn't worry. She invited me to ask whatever questions I wanted, talk to whom I liked, and write the story just as I saw it. After some vacillating I decided to go ahead. Even after more than three decades as a journalist and author I still get excited by a good story – and I knew what a good story this was.

As well as making herself available for many hours of tape-recorded conversations in India and Australia, Christine gave me an unpublished manuscript that she had written, with the generous offer to use it as I wished. This was a priceless resource. Many reported conversations and descriptions of events have been taken from this source.

There is often trouble when the subject of a biography reads the manuscript. It must be a strange experience to see oneself through someone else's eyes. I am sure no one comes away from it entirely satisfied. For your unconditional co-operation and understanding, Chris, I thank you.

Thanks too to Jeremy Townend and Jack Reece, who read the manuscript with painstaking care and corrected errors of fact. Kristin Parsons offered insights from her close friendship with Christine. Also helpful were Christine's godson, Stewart Parsons, Ann and Neil Kennedy, Gillian Coote, Mark Pearson, Miles and Cameron Townend, Suzanne Woolcott, Elva Julien, Timmie Kumar, John Singh and his sister Jane Singh, R. J. Lobo, Dr T. Ramchandani, Neelam MacDonald, Donald Karthak, and all of the wonderful staff at Help in Suffering in Jaipur and Kalimpong, who patiently endured my endless questions.

As ever, thanks to my wife Anna, who took many of the photographs and offered valuable advice; to Tom Gilliatt, a truly creative publisher; and to my wise and wonderful agent, Deb Callaghan.

HELP IN SUFFERING ADDRESSES

INDIA

Help in Suffering
Maharani Farm, Durgapura
Jaipur
Rajasthan-302018
www.his-india.com
E-mail: hisjpr@datainfosys.net

UNITED KINGDOM

Help in Suffering (UK)
Charity no. 1081579
C/o Mrs June Harney
49 Baring Road
Beaconsfield, Bucks, HP9 2NF

AUSTRALIA

Help in Suffering (NSW)
PO Box 210
Nana Glen NSW 2450

EUROPE

Mrs Janine Vogler
Amis Suisses du Refuge de l'Espoir
Banque Union de Banque Suisses
Compte no. 434 132 29X